ENV BOOKS SERIES

NUTRACEUTICALS AND PHARMACEUTICALS FROM MEDICINAL PLANTS

Editors

Dr. Pawan Kumar 'Bharti'

Society for Environment, Health Awareness of Nutrition & Toxicology (SEHAT)
B-225/5D, Top Floor, Subhash Gali
Road No. 7, Block B, Ashok Nagar
Shahdara, Delhi - 110 093
(India)

Dr. M.M. Abid Ali Khan

Sr. Associate Professor of Botany
Shia P.G., College (Lucknow University)
Lucknow (UP), (India)

&

Dr. Ashok K. Rathoure

GM-Consultancy
Eco Group of Companies, New Civil Road
Surat (Gujarat) (India)

DPH

DISCOVERY PUBLISHING HOUSE PVT. LTD.
INDIA

Published by:
Namit Wasan
DISCOVERY PUBLISHING HOUSE PVT. LTD.
4383/4B, Ansari Road, Darya Ganj
New Delhi-110 002 (India)
Phone : +91-11-23279245, 43596064-65
Fax : +91-11-23253475
E-mail : discoverypublishinghouse@gmail.com
namitwasan9@gmail.com
sales@discoverypublishinggroup.com
web : www.discoverypublishinggroup.com

***First Edition:* 2018**

ISBN: 978-93-86841-55-1

Nutraceuticals and Pharmaceuticals from Medicinal Plants

Printed at:
Infinity Imaging Systems
Delhi

ENV Books Series, India

Calls descriptive and error free chapters for upcoming volumes of books on various environmental issues. Send your manuscripts to envbooks@gmail.com

Founding Editor (Editor-in-Chief)

Dr. Pawan Kumar 'Bharti'
Society for Environment, Health, Awareness of Nutrition & Toxicology (SEHAT-India)
1775, Sohanganj, Near Clock Tower, Delhi-7, (India)
E-mail:*gurupawanbharti@rediffmail.com*

Other Important Titles by Editor-in-Chief:

1. **Advances in Biotechnology and Ecological Sciences**
   Bharti, P.K., Chauhan, A. and Ray, J. (eds.)
   (ISBN: 978-93-5056-358-8).
2. **Advances in Agriculture and Ecology**
   Bharti, P.K.; Chauhan, A. and Ezeaku Peter Ikemefuna (eds.)
   (ISBN: 978-93-5056-362-5).
3. **Agriculture and Environmental Biotechnology**
   Bharti, P.K. and Chauhan, A. (eds.)
   (ISBN: 978-93-5056-479-0).
4. **Agriculture Crops and Food Security**
   Bharti, P.K., and Chauhan, A. (eds.)
   (ISBN: 978-93-5056-881-1)
5. **Agriculture Development and Sustainable Environment**
   Ray, J. and Bharti, P.K. (eds.)
   (ISBN: 978-93-5056-759-3).
6. **Agriculture Ecology and Environment**
   Bharti, P.K. and Olubukola O. Babalola (eds.)
   (ISBN: 978-93-5056-480-6).
7. **Agriculture Ecology, Sustainable Development and Agribusiness Management**
   Mehta Piyush; Sharma Pankaj; and 'Bharti' P.K. (eds.)
   (ISBN: 978-93-5056-851-4).
8. **Agriculture, Environment and Nano-science**
   Bharti, Pawan K. (ed.)
   (ISBN: 978-93-5056-760-5).
9. **Agriculture Production and Climate Change**
   Khalid, Monowar Alam; Bharti, P.K. and Chauhan, Alka (eds.)
   (ISBN: 978-93-86841-54-4).

10. **Agricultural Practices and Crop Disease Control**
Chauhan Alka and Sharma Anubhuti (eds.)
(ISBN: 978-93-5056-859-0).

11. **Agro-biodiversity:** ***Conservation and Sustainable Development***
Sharma, Pankaj; Singh, Narayan; and Bharti, P.K. (eds.)
(ISBN: 978-93-505-782-1).

12. **Agro-forestry and Climate Change**
Bharti, Pawan K. and Singh, Narayan (eds.)
(ISBN: 978-93-5056-514-8).

13. **Agro-forestry and Sustainable Agriculture**
Sharma, Pankaj; Bharti, P.K. (eds.)
(ISBN: 978-93-5056-786-9).

14. **Air Pollution and Ecosystem Health**
Swami Abhishek and Bharti, P.K. (eds.)
(ISBN: 978-93-5056-877-4).

15. **Aquaculture and Fisheries Environment**
Gupta, S.K. and Pawan K. Bharti (eds.)
(ISBN: 978-93-5056-408-0).

16. **Aquatic Biodiversity and Pollution**
Bharti, P.K.; Chauhan, A. and Kaoud, H.A.H. (eds.)
(ISBN: 978-93-5056-359-5).

17. **Aquatic Ecology and Biotechnology**
Bharti, P.K. and Zaki, M.S.A. (eds.)
(ISBN: 978-93-5056-451-6).

18. **Aquatic Environment and Toxicology**
Bharti, Pawan K. (ed.)
(ISBN: 978-93-5056-236-9).

19. **Biodiversity, Biotechnology and Environmental Conservation**
Bharti, P.K. and Bhandari, G. (eds.)
(ISBN: 978-93-5056-750-0).

20. **Biodiversity, Biotechnology & Pollution Control**
Bharti, P.K., and Chauhan, A. (eds.)
(ISBN: 978-93-5056-887-3)

21. **Biodiversity of Aquatic Ecosystem:** ***Significance, Threat and Conservation***
Bharti, P.K. and Kaoud, H.A.H. (eds.)
(ISBN: 978-93-5056-297-0).

22. **Biological Diversity and Ecology**
Arya, M.K.; Bharti, P.K. and Ritesh Joshi (eds.)
(ISBN: 978-93-5056-785-2).

23. **Bioremediation and Microbial Biotechnology**
Gupta, Sandeep; and Bharti, P.K. (eds.)
(ISBN: 978-93-5056-783-8).

24. **Biotechnological Approaches and Water Ecosystem**
Zaki, M.S.A.; and Bharti, P.K. (eds.)
(ISBN: 978-93-5056-779-1).
25. **Biotechnology, Agro-ecology and Environment**
Chauhan, Avnish and Bharti, P.K. (eds.)
(ISBN: 978-93-5056-757-9).
26. **Biotechnology and Environmental Management**
Arya Arun; Maheswari Raaz K., & Bharti, P.K (eds.)
(ISBN: 978-93-5056-862-0).
27. **Clean Technologies and Environmental Protection**
Chauhan, A.; Sharma, S. and Bharti, P.K. (eds.)
(ISBN: 978-93-5056-731-9).
28. **Climate Change and Agriculture**
Bharti, P.K. and Chauhan, Avnish (eds.)
(ISBN: 978-93-5056-148-5).
29. **Climate Change and Biodiversity**
Bharti, P.K. and Chauhan, Avnish (eds.)
(ISBN: 978-93-5056-360-1).
30. **Climate Change, Disaster Management and Environment**
Chauhan, Alka; Bharti, P.K. (eds.)
(ISBN: 978-93-5056-784-5).
31. **Conservation and Cultivation of Medicinal Plants**
Bharti, P.K. and Singh Narayan (eds.)
(ISBN: 978-93-5056-740-1).
32. **Crop Irrigation and Farming System**
Chauhan, Alka and P.K. Bharti (eds.)
(ISBN: 978-93-86841-40-7).
33. **Crop Productivity and Plant Disease Management**
Chauhan, Alka; Bharti, P.K. and Sadana, Deepti (eds.)
(ISBN: 978-93-5056-791-3).
34. **Ecotourism, Environmental Problems & Sustainable Development**
Singh, Soubam Premchandra; Rathoure, Ashok Kr., and Bharti, P.K. (eds.)
(ISBN: 978-93-86841-57-5).
35. **Eco-toxicology and Eco-technology**
Bharti, P.K. and Zaki, M. (eds.)
(ISBN: 978-93-5056-313-7).
36. **Energy Technologies for Clean Environment**
Bharti, Chhavi Kumar and Bharti, P.K. (Eds.)
(ISBN: 978-93-86841-22-3).
37. **Environmental Biotechnology and Application**
Bharti, P.K. and Chauhan, Avnish (eds.)
(ISBN: 978-93-5056-262-8).

38. **Environmental Conservation and Biotechnology**
Chauhan, A. and P.K. Bharti (eds.)
(ISBN: 978-93-5056-512-4).

39. **Environmental Economics and Sustainability**
José G. Vargas-Hernández; Khalid Alam Monowar and Bharti, P.K. (eds.)
(ISBN: 978-93-86841-37-7).

40. **Environmental Health and Problems**
Bharti, P.K. and Gajananda, Kh. (eds.)
(ISBN: 978-93-5056-263-5).

41. **Environmental Pollution and Biodiversity**
Bharti, P.K.; Chauhan, Avnish and Kumar, P. (eds.)
(ISBN: 978-93-5056-149-2).

42. **E-waste and Environmental Issues**
Bhalla, R., and Bharti, P.K. (eds.)
(ISBN: 978-93-5056-886-6)

43. **Experiments on Enhancement of Agricultural Yield**
Chauhan, Alka and P.K. Bharti (eds.)
(ISBN: 978-93-86841-50-6).

44. **Farming Techniques and Crop Production**
Chauhan Alka; Sharma Anubhuti; Ray Jaswant and 'Bharti' P.K. (eds.)
(ISBN: 978-93-5056-855-2).

45. **Faunal Biodiversity and Biotechnology**
Sethi, V. Kumar; Bharti, P.K. (eds.)
(ISBN: 978-93-86841-44-5).

46. **Fisheries and Toxicology**
Zaki, M.S.A.; Bharti, P.K. and Chauhan, A. (eds.)
(ISBN: 978-93-5056-452-3).

47. **Fish Habitat and Aquaculture**
Bharti, P.K.; Gupta Kr. Sanjay (eds.)
(ISBN: 978-93-5056-744-9).

48. **Forest and Biodiversity Conservation**
Chauhan Alka; Bharti, P.K. (eds.)
(ISBN: 978-93-5056-873-6).

49. **Food Processing, Management and Nanotechnology**
Chauhan, Avnish; Bharti, P.K. (eds.)
(ISBN: 978-93-5056-796-8).

50. **Food Technology and Research Advancement**
Chauhan, Avnish; Bharti, P.K. (eds.)
(ISBN: 978-93-86841-49-0).

51. **Freshwater Ecosystem and Xenobiotics**
Bharti, P.K.; Zaki, M. and Chauhan, A. (eds.)
(ISBN: 978-93-5056-299-4).

52. **Geospatial Technology and Ecosystem Assessment**
'Bharti' Chhavi Kumar; Chauhan, Alka & Bharti, P.K. (eds.)
(ISBN: 978-93-86841-36-0).

53. **Geospatial Technology and Water Management**
Chauhan, Alka; Bharti, P.K. (eds.)
(ISBN: 978-93-5056-885-9).

54. **Heavy Metals and Metalloids in Biosphere:** ***Impacts & Assessment***
Chauhan, Avnish, Gupta, Sandeep; and Bharti, P.K. (eds.)
(ISBN: 978-93-5056-860-6).

55. **Land Reclamation, Soil Quality and Agriculture**
Bharti, P.K., and Chauhan, A. (ed.)
(ISBN: 978-93-5056-882-8).

56. **Limnology and Aquatic Science**
Sharma, S., and Bharti, P.K. (eds.)
(ISBN: 978-93-5056-735-7).

57. **Medicinal and Nutritional Values of Plants**
Chauhan, Alka; Bharti, P.K. (eds.)
(ISBN: 978-93-5056-883-5).

58. **Medicinal Plants:** ***Distribution, Utilization and Significance***
Sharma, P.; Bharti, P.K. and Narayan Singh (eds.)
(ISBN: 978-93-5056-734-0).

59. **Microbial Applications and Environment**
Bharti, Pawan K. (ed.)
(ISBN: 978-93-5056-515-5).

60. **Microbial Ecology and Habitat**
Bharti, Pawan K. (ed.)
(ISBN: 978-93-5056-514-8).

61. **Microbial Environment and Bioremediation**
Chauhan Alka; K. Rathoure Ashok; and K Maheshwari Raaz (eds.)
(ISBN: 978-93-5056-856-9).

62. **Microbiological and Pharmacological Aspects of Biodiversity**
Sharma, P., Sharma, N.G.; Sharma, P., and Bharti, P.K. (ed.)
(ISBN: 978-93-5056-878-1).

63. **Natural Ecosystem and Climate Change**
Bharti, P.K., and Kh. Gajananda (ed.)
(ISBN: 978-93-5056-745-6).

64. **Organic Farming and Bio-fertilizers**
Sethi, Vinaya Kumar; and Bharti, P.K. (eds.)
(ISBN: 978-93-86841-23-0).

65. **Pest Management and Agro-Techniques**
Biswas, Asim; Bharti, P.K., Chauhan, Avnish (eds.)
(ISBN: 978-93-5056-794-4).

66. **Plant Biotechnology and Industrial Applications**
Chauhan, A., and Bharti, P.K. (ed.)
(ISBN: 978-93-5056-884-2).

67. **Plant Disease Management:** ***Control & Elimination Strategies***
Chauhan, A., and Bharti, P.K. (ed.)
(ISBN: 978-93-86841-41-4).

68. **Prakriti me Aushadhi (*in Hindi*)**
Singh, J.R.; Bharti, P.K. and Bharti, B.
(ISBN: 978-93-5056-200-0).

69. **Production of Fruits and Vegetables:** *Technologies and Challenges*
Chauhan, Avnish; Bharti, P.K. and Chauhan, Alka (ed.)
(ISBN: 978-93-86841-25-4).

70. **Seed Technology, Plant Growth and Cropping System**
Tyagi, P.K. and Bharti, P.K. (eds.)
(ISBN: 978-93-5056-738-8).

71. **Seed Treatment, Plant Health and Agro-technology**
Chauhan, A. and Bharti, P.K. (eds.)
(ISBN: 978-93-5056-810-1).

72. **Soil Characteristics and Agro-ecology**
Avnish Chauhan and Bharti, P.K. (eds.)
(ISBN: 978-93-5056-758-6).

73. **Soil Contamination and Conservation**
Ezeaku, P.I. and Bharti, P.K. (eds.)
(ISBN: 978-93-5056-737-1).

74. **Soil Quality and Contamination**
Bharti, P.K. and Chauhan, Avnish (eds.)
(ISBN: 978-93-5056-361-8).

75. **Sustainable Aquaculture Management**
Gupta, S.K.; Bharti, P.K (eds.)
(ISBN: 978-93-5056-797-5).

76. **Waste Disposal and Management**
Bharti, P.K.; Tabassum, B. and Bajaj, P. (eds.)
(ISBN: 978-93-5056-729-6).

77. **Waste Generation and Utilization**
Bajaj Priya; Tabassum, B., and Bharti, P.K. (eds.)
(ISBN: 978-93-5056-792-0).

78. **Waste Management and Environmental Health**
Tabassum, B., Bajaj Priya, and Bharti, P.K. (eds.)
(ISBN: 978-93-5056-777-7).

79. **Water Resources:** ***Mapping Monitoring and Management***
Tyagi, P.K., Chauhan, Avnish and Bharti, P.K. (eds.)
(ISBN: 978-93-5056-861-3).
80. **Water Resources and Agriculture**
Bharti, P.K. and Ezeaku Peter Ikemefuna (eds.)
(ISBN: 978-93-5056-481-3).
81. **Waste Resources Management:** ***Monitoring and Assessment***
Gupta, Sandeep and Bharti, P.K. (eds.)
(ISBN: 978-93-5056-799-9).

Preface

Nutraceuticals, in contrast to pharmaceuticals, are substances, which usually have not patent protection. Both pharmaceutical and nutraceutical compounds might be used to cure or prevent diseases, but only pharmaceutical compounds have governmental sanction.

A dietary supplement is considered as a product that bears or contains one or more of the following dietary ingredients: A mineral, a vitamin, an amino acid, a medical herb or other botanical, a dietary substance for use by man to supplement the diet by increasing the total daily intake, or a concentrate, metabolite, constituent, extract, or combinations of these ingredients. Nutraceuticals are of these nutritional supplements which are used for health purposes other than nutrition. Some popular nutraceuticals include ginseng, *Echinacea*, green tea, glucosamine, omega-3, lutein, folic acid, and cod liver oil. Majority of the nutraceuticals possess multiple therapeutic properties.

Nowadays, nutraceuticals have received high interests due to their potential nutritional and safety profile, other than therapeutic capability. Pharmaceutical and nutritional companies are aware of the changing trends which are due to the advantages of these compounds. Most of the nutraceuticals possess multiple therapeutic benefits.

The present book devoted towards a better understanding of the plant derived nutraceuticals based on their pharmaceutical and therapeutic indications. The book updates the subject matter of medicinal properties of plants, nutraceuticals originated from plants, plant derived pharmaceuticals and health related effects of plants.

Thanks are due to publisher and contributors from various institutions and universities.

The book will be helpful for the researchers, academia working in the field of medicinal properties of plants, nutraceuticals originated from plants, plant derived pharmaceuticals and health related effects of plants.

Editors
(envbooks@gmail.com)

Contents

Nutraceuticals and Pharmaceuticals from Medicinal Plants
Edited by: Dr. Pawan Kumar 'Bharti'; Dr. M.M. Abid Ali Khan; Dr. Ashok K. Rathoure
ISBN: 978-93-86841-55-1
Edition: 2018
Published by: Discovery Publishing House Pvt. Ltd., New Delhi (India)

1 Introduction

Over the past few years, an increasing number of dietary supplements have become available in supermarkets and health food shops and they are also available for purchase in pharmacies. The term "nutraceutical" is used to describe these medicinally or nutritionally functional foods. Nutraceuticals, which have also been called medical foods, designer foods, phytochemicals, functional foods and nutritional supplements, include such everyday products as "bio" yoghurts and fortified breakfast cereals, as well as vitamins, herbal remedies and even genetically modified foods and supplements. Many different terms and definitions are used in different countries, which can result in confusion.

The term "nutraceutical" was coined in 1989 by Stephen De Felice, founder and chairman of the Foundation for Innovation in Medicine, an American organization which encourages medical health research. He defined a nutraceutical as a "food, or parts of a food, that provide medical or health benefits, including the prevention and treatment of disease". In Canada, a functional food has been defined as being "similar in appearance to conventional foods ... consumed as part of a usual diet" whereas a nutraceutical is "a product produced from foods but sold in pills, powders, (potions) and other medicinal forms not generally associated with food".

In Britain, the Ministry of Agriculture, Fisheries and Food has developed a definition of a functional food as "a food that has a component incorporated into it to give it a specific medical or physiological benefit, other than purely nutritional benefit". Hence, both in Canada and in Britain, a functional food is essentially a food, but a nutraceutical is an isolated or concentrated form. In America, "medical foods" and "dietary supplements" are regulatory terms (see below), however "nutraceuticals", "functional foods", and other such terms are determined by consultants and marketers, based on consumer trends. Many of these new products that are being promoted to treat various disease states, find their origins in the plant kingdom. This is an obvious choice as many plants produce secondary compounds such as alkaloids to protect themselves from infection and these constituents may be useful in the treatment of human infection. There is also a long history of plant use in many cultures which can be used to identify plants with activity in the treatment of disease.

IMPLICATIONS FOR PHARMACY

Speculation on who the winners of the nutraceutical venture will be is becoming a popular topic in papers discussing the pharmaceutical industry. Because new medicines are harder to find and more expensive and risky to develop than ever before, many companies, for example, Du Pont, Abbott Laboratories and Warner Lambert, which have produced conventional pharmaceuticals in the past are now merging to survive, or are turning to nutraceuticals. This offers them a chance of a very large market. Datamonitor, a website that follows market trends, estimates the nutraceutical market at $17bn, and Dr Felice himself, speaking at a conference in 1998, put the figure at $250bn in America alone. Although these estimates vary widely, the nutraceuticals market is undoubtably very large and growing. As companies increase in size, more jobs may be created for industrial pharmacists, but the real impact of nutraceuticals on pharmacy will be in the community.

It has been suggested that a move from dietary supplements, sold in health food shops and most pharmacies, to nutraceuticals aimed at the prescription market could occur. This would not necessarily be in manufacturers' best interest, as it would limit the size of the market. However, many indications under research are for serious disease states which do not require self-medication. At present, consumers may try dietary supplements for many indications believing them to be safer than synthetic substances, and this presumption of safety is erroneous. In either case, whether prescribed by a doctor or self-selected, the logical place for the supply of these supplements is the pharmacy where pharmacists are able to offer professional advice. The challenge is therefore to be up to date with research developments so that both conventional practitioners as well as members of the public are able to receive accurate information. Future articles in this short series will be reviewing the scientific and medical claims relating to nutraceuticals which do not fall into the better known and well-researched categories such as vitamins, amino acids and herbal remedies. Most products reviewed are naturally occurring biochemicals which are effectively being used to supplement endogenous levels of these constituents that occur naturally in human metabolism, whether single component products such as glucosamine, or more complex products such as proanthocyanidin.

NUTRACEUTIC

Nutraceutic is a term derived from "nutrition" and "pharmaceutics." The term is applied to products that are isolated from herbal products, dietary supplements (nutrients), specific diets, and processed foods such as cereals, soups, and beverages that other than nutrition are also used as medicine.

In the US, the term "nutraceutical" products are regulated as drugs, food ingredients and dietary supplements. The term is not defined the same in different countries, but is usually defined as a product isolated from foods that is generally sold in medicinal forms not usually associated with food. A nutraceutical product may be defined as a substance, which has physiological benefit or provides protection against chronic diseases. Nutraceuticals may be used to improve health, delay the aging process, prevent chronic diseases, increase life expectancy, or support the structure or function of the body.

Nutraceuticals, in contrast to pharmaceuticals, are substances, which usually have not patent protection. Both pharmaceutical and nutraceutical compounds might be used to cure or prevent diseases, but only pharmaceutical compounds have governmental sanction.

A dietary supplement is considered as a product that bears or contains one or more of the following dietary ingredients: A mineral, a vitamin, an amino acid, a medical herb or other botanical, a dietary substance for use by man to supplement the diet by increasing the total daily intake, or a concentrate, metabolite, constituent, extract, or combinations of these ingredients. Nutraceuticals are of these nutritional supplements which are used for health purposes other than nutrition. Some popular nutraceuticals include ginseng, *Echinacea*, green tea, glucosamine, omega-3, lutein, folic acid, and cod liver oil. Majority of the nutraceuticals possess multiple therapeutic properties.

Nowadays, nutraceuticals have received considerable interest due to potential nutritional, safety and therapeutic effects. A market research recently proposed that the worldwide nutraceuticals market is expanding and would reach US $250 billion by 2018.

Nowadays, nutraceuticals have received high interests due to their potential nutritional and safety profile, other than therapeutic capability. Pharmaceutical and nutritional companies are aware of the changing trends which are due to the advantages of these compounds. Most of the nutraceuticals possess multiple therapeutic benefits. The present book devoted towards a better understanding of the plant derived nutraceuticals based on their pharmaceutical and therapeutic indications.

It should be noted that there might be a lot of confusion related to the terminology of nutraceuticals such as phytochemicals, pharmafoods, medical foods, functional foods, dietary supplements, designer foods, etc., There is thin dividing line in their interchangeable usage by different people on different occasions. Pharmaceuticals are mostly considered as medications which are used mainly to treat diseases, however nutraceuticals are the substances which are mostly considered to prevent diseases. This distinction between pharmaceuticals and nutraceuticals is very erroneous and superficial. Pharmaceuticals and nutraceuticals both can cure and prevent disease(s) however, only pharmaceuticals have governmental sanction. Pharmaceuticals are compounds which usually possess patent protection due to expensive testing. However, nutraceuticals do not need these testing documents.

Medical foods or medicinal foods are a specific category of therapeutic agents that are considered for the nutritional management of a specific disease. For example, medicinal foods are designed to manage inflammatory conditions, cancer, hyperhomocysteinemia, pancreatic exocrine insufficiency and other diseases. They also play a substantial protection against numerous age-related or chronic diseases. Herbal medicines that are used as a nutrient are considered in this category.

Nutraceuticals found in many fruits and vegetables are responsible for health benefits. Due to these health benefits of nutraceuticals, they might regularly be taken to cure or reduce the risk factors such as high cholesterol, high blood pressure and diabetes. Some of the most popular nutraceutical products marketed today are botanicals such as ginseng, ginkgo biloba, St. John's wort and Echinacea.

The list of nutraceuticals being studied is changing continually and reflects ongoing market developments, research, and consumer interest. With rapidly increasing interest in the nutraceutical consumption, substantial researches are absolutely necessary to warrant the nutraceuticals usage safe and effective.

The mechanistic actions of nutraceuticals are not fully clear. However, they might be involved a wide variety of biological processes, including activation of signal transduction pathways, antioxidant defenses, gene expression, cell proliferation, differentiation and preservation of mitochondrial integrity.

Nutraceuticals might be defined as substances that have physiological benefits or provide protection against chronic diseases. Nutraceuticals may be used to improve health, delay the aging process, prevent chronic diseases, increase life expectancy, or support the structure or function of the body. Nowadays, nutraceuticals have received considerable interest due to potential nutritional, safety and therapeutic effects. Recent studies have shown promising results for these compounds in various complications. In the present review much effort has been devoted to provide their diseases modifying indications related to oxidative stress including allergy, Alzheimer, cardiovascular, cancer, diabetes, eye, immune, inflammatory and Parkinson's diseases as well as obesity.

REFERENCES

Jack DB. Keep Taking the Tomatoes - The Exciting World of Nutraceuticals. Mol Med Today 1995:118-21.

Brower B. Nutraceuticals: Poised for a Healthy Slice of the Market. Nat Biotechnol 1998; 16:728-33.

Mannion M. Nutraceutical Revolution Continues at Foundation for Innovation in Medicine Conference. Am J Nat Med 1998;5:30-3.

Mazza G. Functional Foods. Pennsylvania, US: Technomic Publishing Company Inc, 1998.

Cockbill CA. Food Law and Functional Foods. Br Food J 1994; 96:3-4.

Aarts TA. How long will the "Medical Food" window of opportunity remain open? J Nutr Function Med Foods 1998, 1:45-57.

Senior K. Pharmaceuticals from plants: promise and progress. Mol Med Today 1996:60-4.

Pandey Neha, Ram Prasad Meena, Sanjay Kumar Rai and Shashi Pandey-Rai (2011): Medicinal Plants Derived Nutraceuticals: A Re-Emerging Health Aid. *International Journal of Pharma and Bio Sciences*. 2(4): 419-441.

Kalra EK. Nutraceutical – Definition and introduction. AAPS Pharm Sci. 2003;5:E25. [PMC free article] [PubMed]

Zhao J. Bentham Science Publishers; 2007. [Last accessed on 2012 Mar 24]. Nutraceuticals, Nutritional Therapy, Phytonutrients, and Phytotherapy for Improvement of Human Health: A Perspective on Plant Biotechnology Application. Available from: http://www.benthamscience.com/biot/samples/biot1-1/Zhao.pdf . [PubMed]

Chauhan B, Kumar G, Kalam N, Ansari SH. Current Concepts and Prospects of Herbal Nutraceutical: A Review. J Adv Pharm Technol Res. 2013;4:4–8. [PMC Free Article] [PubMed]

Zeisel SH. Regulation of "nutraceuticals" Science. 1999;285:1853–5. [PubMed]

Hardy G. Nutraceuticals and Functional Foods: Introduction and Meaning. Nutrition. 2000;16:688–9. [PubMed]

Webhelp:

http://www.pharmaceutical-journal.com/1-what-is-a-nutraceutical/20002095.article

https://www.ncbi.nlm.nih.gov/pmc/articles/PMC4336979/

Nutraceuticals and Pharmaceuticals from Medicinal Plants
Edited by: Dr. Pawan Kumar 'Bharti'; Dr. M.M. Abid Ali Khan; Dr. Ashok K. Rathoure
ISBN: 978-93-86841-55-1
Edition: 2018
Published by: Discovery Publishing House Pvt. Ltd., New Delhi (India)

2

Role of Nutraceuticals on Human Health and Nutrition

[1]G. Ranganna, T. Thomson, S. Firoz Hussain, M. Siva and M.M. Nagaraju

ABSTRACT

Due to change in life habits and food habits, age related diseases like diabetes, high blood pressure, high cholesterol and cardiovascular diseases *etc* are increasing. Now a days, people have reduced the intake of fruits and vegetables rich in antioxidants in their diet. Accordingly, people are becoming prone to above mentioned diseases and becoming old (ageing) at an early age. About 2500 years ago, Hippocrates, the father of modern medicine, conceptualized the relation between the use of appropriate foods for health and their therapeutic benefits. He promulgated that "let food be your medicine and medicine be your food". The pharmaceutical drugs may give relief for a short term period but associated with side effects on long term basis. In this connection, nutraceuticals play a major role in the treatment and prevention of diseases apart from providing health benefits. Nutraceutical is a food or part of a food that provides medical or health benefits, including the prevention and treatment of a disease. Nutraceutical is also known as functional food, designer food, dietary supplements, medical foods, nutritional supplements and farmaceuticals. The usage of nutraceuticals may have lesser/fewer/no side effects as they prepared from natural foods.

Keywords: Nutraceuticals, Human Health, Nutrition, Fruits, Veetables

INTRODUCTION

The term Nutraceutical is a combination of two terms *i.e.* Nutrition and Pharmaceutical. It was first coined by Dr. Stephen De Felice, in 1989. He defined Nutraceutical as the food or part of a food that provides medical or health benefits, by the prevention and treatment of a disease. Nutraceuticals are also known as functional foods, medical foods, nutritional supplements, designer foods, farmaceuticals and dietary supplements. Nutraceuticals are medicinal foods that enhance health, modulate immunity and thereby prevent and cure

1 College of Horticulture, Dr. YSR Horticultural University, Venkataramannaguem-534101, West Godavari, Andhra Pradesh, India

specific diseases. They have received considerable interest because of their presumed safety and potential nutritional and therapeutic effects. About 2500 years ago, Hippocrates, the father of modern medicine, conceptualized the relation between the use of appropriate foods for health and their therapeutic benefits. He promulgated that "let food be your medicine and medicine be your food". Due to the widely grown health concerns and side effects of allopathic system of medicine among the people, people are now concentrating on the natural foods (fruits and vegetables) rich in nutraceuticals i.e. phytochemicals such as anthocyanins, flavonoids and antioxidants along with vitamins and minerals that play a vital role in prevention and control of diseases like diabetes, cancer, obesity and chronic obstructive pulmonary diseases etc.

Why Nutraceuticals

- In general, people have got awareness that nutritional supplements are now part of their daily life.
- Increased life expectancy, globally has led to an increase in the incidence of lifestyle (age related) diseases such as diabetes, high blood pressure, cholesterol and obesity etc. As a result there has been a significant increase in the deaths due to lifestyle diseases worldwide.
- Consumers are worldwide looking to follow healthy lifestyles to obtain optimum nutrition to keep these diseases at bay, leading to an increase in consumption of nutraceuticals by health conscious consumers.
- The need for nutraceuticals can be broadly attributed to increased life expectancy, consumer awareness and health concerns and the high cost of health care worldwide.
- Prevention is better than cure. Instead of getting involved in expensive medications with possible side effects, it is always better to change the life style and prevent from the disease by taking the supplements well in time.
- Academic institutions & laboratories conducting large-scale protocol controlled studies to validate the benefits of nutritional supplements.
- Standardization of therapeutic dosages & forms besides establishment of appropriate indications, enabling doctors to make better use of nutritional supplements.
- Availability of well-documented & published clinical data authenticating efficacy & safety of nutritional supplements

Nutraceutical Market – Global and India

The global market for nutraceutical products was reached by $ 142.1 billion in 2011 and is expected to reach $ 250.2 billion by 2018, with a CAGR (compound annual growth rate) of 6.3%. Of this USA and Europe formed the largest markets accounting to 36 percent and 25 percent respectively. In 2010, the global market for nutraceuticals experienced a surge in growth, especially post the recession.

The high cost of health care and the after effects of recession especially in the developed world drove consumers towards the nutraceuticals in a bid to remain healthy and to avoid treatmental costs.

US Market	EUROPEAN Market	Indian Market
In 2010, the US nutraceutical market stood at US $ 50.4 Billion and was far by the largest nutraceutical market in the world.	The total European Nutraceutical Industry was valued about US $ 35 Billion in 2010.	In 2010, the Indian Nutraceutical industry was estimated at US $ 2 Billion, roughly 1.5 percent of the global nutraceutical industry.
US Consumers are extremely health conscious and demand specific ingredients in the nutraceutical products they consume, resulting in a need for customization of nutraceuticals for each target group.	Europeans main focus was on nutraceutical industry for innovation and development of new product results in an increase in the amount spend on R and D sector from 0.24 percent during 2004 to 0.8 to 1 percent in 2010.	The existence of alternative medicine and the Indian consumer's belief could provide a platform for the nutraceutical industry to capitalize on.
Currently, companies in the US are looking to diversify their products and are leaning more and more towards natural nutraceutical ingredients in their product offering, mainly due to an increase in consumer demand for all-natural, non-modified functional ingredients.	Companies in Europe believed that product and ingredient innovation is the way to forward the nutraceutical industry. Germany, Netherlands and Sweden have emerged as the key nutraceutical innovation hubs in Europe, while Great Britain and Spain have emerged as key test markets for new products.	There is a need to spread the awareness about the nutraceutical products by the manufacturers among the Indian masses.

The largest market for nutraceuticals is US, followed by Europe and Japan. The global market for Nutraceuticals is projected to reach US$250 billion by 2018 largely to develop a disease free lifestyle. Growth is also seen in emerging countries like BRIC nations (Brazil, Russia, India, and China), Mexico, Poland, and South East Asian countries including Taiwan, Thailand, Philippines, Vietnam, Malaysia, Singapore, North and South Korea. Globally, U.S and Japan are the most developed markets for nutraceuticals, due to wider consumer acceptability in these regions. India, China and Brazil are developing nations which show huge potential for the nutraceuticals market. Germany and Israel have emerged as the key innovation hubs for the nutraceutical industry. In Israel, the industry is driven by the development of ingredient companies such as Solbar Industries, LycoRed Natural Ingredients, Adumim Food Ingredients, Enzymotec, Algatechnologies and Frutarom etc. The nutraceutical market in Israel is currently experiencing a period of rapid growth at 7 to 8 percent per year, a bulk of revenue from nutraceutical ingredients in Israel is through exports, especially to the EU, Eastern Europe and the US.

Nutraceutical Trends in India

Even though the lowest per capita GDP in the BRICS regions, India is poised to overtake China as the most populous country (also with the largest number of undernourished children in the world) and represents an extremely favourable market for the growth of nutraceuticals. Approximately, 42% of Indian children under the age of 5 were suffering from malnutrition, nearly 300 million people are in an expanding middle class. The middle class level, with an increased disposable income has become aware of the importance of diet and nutrition for a long term good health. Only an "appropriate blend of micro/macro nutrients in our diet can help us break through the health deficit" feels Rajiv Chopra, President, DSM nutritional products, India.

Some key emerging trends in the Indian Nutraceutical space are as follows:

- Focus on wellness and preventive care.
- Increased awareness and health consciousness.
- Growth currently driven by the functional food and beverages segment.
- A large diabetic population.

Role of Research and Development in Nutraceuticals

- To test safety, purity and potency of products.
- To develop more effective and efficient means of producing ingredients for use in products.
- To develop testing methods for ensuring and verifying the consistency of the dosage of ingredients included in the company's products.
- To develop the new products either by combining existing ingredients used in nutritional supplements or identifying new ingredients that can be used in nutritional supplements.

Functional Foods

They are the processed foods containing ingredients that assist in specific bodily functions apart from being nutritious. The functional food can also be called as a nutraceutical when it helps in the prevention or treatment of a disease or disorders.

Dietary Supplements

A dietary supplement is a product that contains derived nutrients from food products that are concentrated in liquid or capsule form. According to Dietary

Supplement Health and Education Act, 1994 (DSHEA), A dietary supplement can be defined as a product which is taken by mouth that contains a "dietary ingredient" which is intended to supplement the diet. A dietary supplement may be available in various forms such as tablets, capsules, softgels, gelcaps, liquids or powders.

The dietary ingredients in the dietary supplements include:

- Vitamins
- Minerals
- Herbs
- Other botanicals
- Amino acids
- Enzymes, organ tissues, glandular and Metabolites

Farmaceuticals

The term farmaceutical is a melding of two words Farm and Pharmaceutical. These are medically valuable compounds produced from Agricultural crops.

Antioxidants

- Resveratrol from red grape.
- Flavonoids in citrus, tea and wine.
- Anthocyanins from pomegranate, strawberries etc.

1. Reducing hypercholesterolemia: Soluble dietary fiber products such as *Psyllium* seed husk.

2. Cancer prevention: Sulforaphane present in broccoli.

3. Improved Arterial health: Isoflavonoids in soyabean and clover.

Pharmaceuticals vs Nutraceuticals

Table 2.1

Pharmaceuticals	Nutraceuticals
Pharmaceuticals are designed specifically under the physician's supervision for medical use.	Nutraceuticals do not need medical supervision.
It requires the approval of Food and Drug Administration for its release in to market.	It does not require the approval of Food and Drug Administration for its release in to market.
Pharmaceuticals need prescription from a certified doctor for purchase.	Nutraceuticals are sold without restrictions in drug and health food stores.
These are associated with side effects.	They have lesser/fewer/no side effects.

Other Advantages of Nutraceuticals

- May increase the health value of our diet.
- May help us to live longer.
- May help us to avoid particular medical conditions.
- May have a physiological benefit from doing something for oneself.
- May be perceived to be more "natural" than traditional medicine and less likely to produce unpleasant side effects.
- Delay the ageing process.

Disadvantages of Nutraceuticals

- They are not subjected to testing and regulations as required in the pharmaceuticals.
- Bioavailability of nutrients is less.
- Companies creating unregulated products to create a wide margin on profit.

Disadvantages of Pharmaceuticals

Death

From deadly cancer to fatal heart attacks, some prescription drugs have been known to cause either slow or immediate death. Sometimes prescription drugs such as penicillin stimulate allergic reactions that cause anything from itching to an anaphylactic response, which can lead to death. In other cases, a drug can cause a deadly heart attack or stroke, which has been seen in patients who take the type 2 diabetes drugs Avandia or Actos. Other drugs may cause patients to do things they wouldn't ordinarily consider, including suicide. Drugs such as Accutane and some antidepressants have been linked to suicidal thoughts or actions.

Physical Debilitation

Many drugs can be physically and emotionally debilitating, including causing total or partial paralysis or severe pain. This includes headaches, stomach aches, joint and muscle pain and decreased control over bodily functions. Sometimes these side effects are caused by the drug's numbing effect on the area of the brain responsible for pain perception. Lipitor, a commonly prescribed cholesterol medication, is linked to unexpected muscle pain and loss of muscle coordination.

Stroke

Described as the rapid loss of brain function due to a blood flow disturbance, strokes have been linked to several kinds of prescription drugs. In some cases, the drugs cause blood clots to form. When these clots move through the body, they can block the blood flow to the brain. Some antipsychotic drugs, including drugs used in Alzheimer's treatment such as Risperdal, are linked to strokes. Other drugs, including the painkiller Vioxx, are also linked to stroke.

Heart Condition

Problems related to the heart, including heart attacks, congestive heart failure, lifelong heart damage and cardiomyopathy, have been linked to many prescription drugs. Sometimes, the drugs cause an increase in water-weight gain, which causes heart failure or a heart attack. Such is the case with Avandia and its sister drug, Actos. Other drugs, including the painkiller Celebrex, have been proven to be so risky that doctors refuse to prescribe them for long-term use.

Cancer

Probably one of the most shocking and overwhelming side effects of prescription drugs is cancer. Perhaps that's because most people spend their lives avoiding known carcinogens, such as cigarette smoking. When patients learn that their prescription drugs can be carcinogenic, they feel angry and misled. One of the most shocking medication-cancer connections came when Tamoxifen, a drug used to treat breast cancer, was found to increase the risk of uterine cancer. In addition, Actos, a drug that is supposed to alleviate diabetes symptoms, is linked to an 80 percent increased risk of bladder cancer in those taking the drug two years or longer.

Common Side Effects

Possibly the most common side effects of any prescription drug are gastrointestinal issues, including nausea, constipation and diarrhea, because most drugs go through the digestive system to be absorbed. Other common aftereffects include drowsiness, pain and skin reactions.

Dizziness

While dizziness may not seem like a serious side effect, it can have grave consequences. For elderly patients or those already unsteady on their feet, random dizziness can cause a fall that could lead to broken bones. For the elderly, especially those who are already battling other medical problems, a broken hip can take a deadly toll. Because dizziness is a common side effect of most prescription drugs, patients should be acutely aware of any vertigo-like feelings.

Nausea

While nausea and vomiting aren't considered deadly side effects, they can cause a cascade of medical problems, especially in the elderly or those already weakened by a disease. The resulting dehydration, internal bleeding and esophageal rupture can result in death. Chemotherapy drugs, which are aimed at treating cancer, are known to cause severe nausea and vomiting.

Area of Concern

- The cost of the nutraceutical product should be maintained to its lowest limit, so that poor people can full fill their needs.
- There will be Specific laws, for the nutraceuticals, food supplements, regarding the quality of nutrients used and also for the packaging of Nutraceuticals.
- There should be a guideline for the adulterants, so that the nutritive value should be maintained.
- Researchers designing Nutraceuticals in such a way that it will give a complementary treatment with the death causing diseases like cancer and AIDS.
- Estimating the quality, purity and safety standards.

Classification of Nutraceuticals

1. Traditional nutraceuticals:

a. Chemical constituents:

(*i*) Nutrients

(*ii*) Herbals

(*iii*) Phytochemicals

(*iv*) Anti oxidants

Nutrients: Substances with established nutritional functions, such as vitamins, minerals, amino acids and fatty acids come under the category of nutrients.

Table 2.2: List of Nutrients and their Benefits

Nutrient	Benefits
Vitamin A	Antioxidant, essential for growth and development and in the treatment of certain skin disorders. Prevent night blindness.
Vitamin E	Antioxidant, helps form blood cells, muscles, lung and nerve tissue, boosts the immune system.
Vitamin K	Essential for blood clotting
Vitamin C	Antioxidant, for healthy bones, gums, teeth and skin, in wound healing, prevent common cold and attenuate its symptoms.
Vitamin B1	Helps to convert food in to energy, essential in neurologic functions.
Vitamin B2	Helps in energy production and other chemical processes in the body, helps to maintain healthy eyes, skin and nerve function.
Vitamin B3	Helps to convert food in to energy and to maintain proper brain function.

Herbals: Nutraceuticals holds a great promise to improve health and prevent chronic diseases by means of herbals.

Table 2.3: Herbals Used and their Therapeutic Properties

Herbals (Botanical source)	Therapeutic properties
Aloe vera gel	Dilates capillaries, anti-inflammatory, wound healing properties.
Garlic (*Allium sativum*)	Anti bacterial, Anti fungal, Anti thrombotic, Anti inflammatory
Liquorice (*Glycyrhiza glabra*)	Expectorant, treatment of peptic ulcer
Ginger (*Zingiber officinale*)	Carminative, anti helmintic
Peppermint (*Mentha piperata*)	Cures cold and flu
Lavender (*Lavendula angustifolia*)	Helpful in curing depression, hypertension, stress, cold, cough and asthma
Cranberry (*Vaccinium erythrocarpum*)	Contain proanthocyanidins and are found to control cancer and ulcers.

Phytochemicals

"Phyto" is a Greek word that means plant and phytochemicals are usually related to plant pigments. The fruits are generally brightly coloured- yellow, orange red, green, blue and purple due to the presence of phytochemicals. Phytochemical is a natural bioactive substance found in plant foods, act as a natural defense system. The phytochemicals impart food colour, flavour and natural disease resistance where it works with nutrients and dietary fiber to protect against disease. The phytochemicals found in fruits, may slow the aging process, reduce cell damage, stimulate immune system and reduce the risk of many diseases, including cancer, heart disease, stroke, high blood pressure, cataracts, osteoporosis and urinary tract infection.

Table 2.4: Various Phytochemicals Available in Different Fruits

Fruit	Various phytochemicals
Avocado	Caffeic acid, chlorogenic acid, coumaric acid, cycloartenol, dopamine, phytosterols.
Durian	Dimethyl trithiolane, methyl butanoate
Guava	Ellagic acid, limonene, leucocyanidin, phytin
Jackfruit	Flavanones, dihydromorin, cycloartenone, heterophylol
Jamun	Myrcene, geranyl butyrate, terpineol, terpinyl valerate
Lime	Citronellal, limonene, naringin, phellandrene
Litchi	Cyanidin, malvidin, quercetin, acetonylgeranin
Mango	Mangiferin, gallic acid, mangiferic acid, phytin, xanthophylls
Passionfruit	Alkaloids, flavonoids, xanthophylls
Pineapple	Ananasic acid, ellagic acid, phytosterols, serotonin, vanillin
Rambutan	Damascenone
Carambola	Cryptochrome, Damascenone, phytofluene

Table 2.5: Classes of Phytochemicals and their Role in Natural Defense System

Classes of phytochemicals	Availability in fruits and role in natural defense system
Carotenoids	They are the pigments responsible for the colours of many red, green, yellow and orange fruits and vegetables. It is a large family of phytochemicals, which include α-carotene, β-carotene, lutein, lycopene, cryptoxanthin and zeaxanthin.
Flavonoids	They are also called as bioflavonoids, act as antioxidants. Some of the flavonoids which protect the health system are Resveratrol, anthocyanins, quercetin, hesperidin, kaempferol.
Phenolic compounds	They may reduce the risk of heart disease and certain types of cancer. Ellagic acid is a phenolic compound that may reduce the risk of certain types of cancer and decrease cholesterol levels.
Sulphoraphane	It is also known as isothiocyanates. It may reduce the risk of colon cancer.
Limonene	It is also known as mono-terpenes. It is found in the rinds and edible white membrane of citrus fruits. Limonene may help to protect the lungs and reduce the risk of certain types of cancer.
Indoles	They may reduce certain types of cancer.
Allium compounds	They may reduce the risk of certain types of cancer and lower cholesterol and blood pressure.

Table 2.6: Constituents, Sources and Benefits of Phytochemicals to Human Health

Constituent	Compound	Source	Effects on human health
Proanthocyanins	Tannins, cyanidin, malvidin, delphinidin	Grape, pomegranate	Cancer, heart disease, diabetes.
Anthocyanidins	Pelargonidin, peonidin, petunidin	Pomegranate and Strawberry	Cataracts, blood pressure, allergies.
Flavanones	Hesperetin, naringenin	Citrus fruits	Cancer
Flavones	Luteolin, Apigenin	Guava	Cancer, allergies, heart disease
α-carotene		Mango, papaya, kiwi fruit	Tumor growth
β-carotene		Mango, persimmon	Cancer
Monoterpenes	Limonene	Citrus fruits	Cancer

Antioxidants

Antioxidants are substances that prevent harmful molecules (free radicals) from damaging the body's DNA and act as protective agents for the more complex and functional parts of a nutritional complex. It includes specific vitamins, minerals and enzymes that protect cells against damage from oxidation. The four antioxidants many experts consider to be the most important are "ACES" are Vitamin A, Vitamin C, Vitamin E and the mineral Selenium.

Table 2.7: Antioxidants and their Roles in the Natural Defense System

Antioxidants in fruits	Role in natural defense system
β-carotene	It is the bright orange pigment that imparts colours to fruits and vegetables. Foods that contain β-carotene will be converted into vitamin A by human liver.
Vitamin C	It is sometimes called as "super antioxidant" as it is the most powerful antioxidant found in the body. It is potent enough to stop the oxidants that start free-radical chain reactions. Vitamin C plays a critical role in reducing the risk of cancer.
Vitamin E	It safeguards all the cells in the body from free radical damage.

Table 2.8: Constituents, Sources and Benefits of Antioxidants to Human Health

Constituent	Source	Effects on human wellness
Vitamin C (Ascorbic acid)	Aonla, citrus, guava, pineapple, kiwi	Prevents scurvy, helps in wound healing, healthy immune system, cardiovascular diseases.
Vitamin A (β-carotene)	Mango, papaya, orange, nectarine, pineapple, persimmon	Prevents night blindness, chronic fatigue, psoriasis, heart disease, cataracts.
Vitamin K	Cashew and other fruits	Synthesis of pro-coagulant factors, prevents osteoporosis
Vitamin E	Cashew and other fruits	Prevents heart disease, LDL-oxidation, diabetes

Prebiotics

Prebiotics are non-digestible food ingredients that stimulate the growth and/or activity of bacteria in the digestive system which are beneficial to the health of the body. They were first identified and named by Marcel Roberfroid in 1995. They are considered a functional food. Typically, Prebiotics are carbohydrates (such as oligosaccharides) but the definition does not preclude non-carbohydrates. The most prevalent forms of Prebiotics are nutritionally classed as soluble fiber.

"A prebiotic is a selectively fermented ingredient that allows specific changes, both in the composition and/or activity in the gastrointestinal microflora that confers benefits upon host well-being and health."

Properties

1. Prebiotics should have the following properties.
2. Capable of passing to large intestine without being digested and absorbed in the upper part of gastrointestinal tract.

3. Capable of being digested in the large intestine by beneficial bacteria such as *Bifidobacterium* and *Lactobacillus.*
4. Capable of enhancing the growth of beneficial bacteria such as *Bifidobacterium* and *Lactobacillus,* but not pathogens causing gastrointestinal diseases such as *Clostridium perfringens.*

Prebiotics must be able to withstand acid hydrolysis in the stomach, able to move to large intestine without changes or being absorbed in small intestine so that they can be utilized by the indigenous microflora in the large intestine to enhance their growth. Oligosaccharides that are considered Prebiotics are lactose, lactulose, raffinose, stachiose, and fructooligosaccharide. There are other compounds that can be fermented by *Bifidobacterium* and *Lactobacillus* in the large intestine, e.g., resistant starch, non-starch polysaccharides, which include plant constituents such as pectin, cellulose, hemicelluloses, and xylan.

Naturally Occurring Prebiotics

1. Galactooligosaccharides:

(*a*) Galactooligosaccharides contain galactose.

(*b*) They are found in human milk, cow's milk, yoghurt and may be synthesized from lactose with β-galactosidase.

(*c*) These are non-digestible by gut enzymes and can pass into the large intestine without being digested. However, they can be hydrolyzed by microorganisms in the large intestine, producing short chain fatty acids, e.g., acetic, propionic and butyric acids, and gases, like H_2, CH_4 and CO_2.

(*d*) There may be other compounds from the hydrolysis of galactooligis accharides such as lactate, which can enhance the growth of *Bifidobacteria* and *Lactobacilli.* These microorganisms can help synthesize vitamins, stimulate immunity and prevent stomach upset.

2. Inulin:

(*a*) Inulin is a polysaccharide which is stored in the plants as a nutrient.

(*b*) Inulin is generally found in plants, bacteria, and some fungi.

(*c*) It is found in more than 3600 fruits and vegetables, especially those in the Cichorium family, e.g., chicory, banana, large onion and garlic.

(*d*) Inulin is not digested in small intestine, but parts of it may be digested in the large intestine by its microflora.

(*e*) It has been reported that Inulin reduces both serum and hepatic cholesterol and triglycerides, and may provide improved absorption of minerals such as calcium, magnesium, iron and phosphate.

Table 2.9: Inulin Content (% of Fresh Weight) of Plants that are Commonly Used in Human Nutrition

Source	Edible part	Inulin content (%)
Onion	Bulb	2-6
Jerusalem artichoke	Tuber	14-19
Chicory	Root	15-20
Leek	Bulb	3-10
Garlic	Bulb	9-16
Banana	Fruit	0.3-0.7
Rye	Cereal	0.5-1.0

3. Soybean oligosaccharides (SOS): SOS is a oligosaccharides in soybean, which consists of raffinose and stachiose. They can withstand enzymatic digestion in the stomach and small intestine and are capable of being hydrolyzed by the microflora in large intestine. They can enhance the growth of *Bifidobacteria* in the large intestine.

Non-traditional nutraceuticals: They are the artificial foods prepared by means of biotechnology. They are again categorize as

(*i*) Fortified nutraceuticals

(*ii*) Recombinant nutraceuticals

Fortified nutraceuticals: It constitutes fortified food from agricultural breeding or added nutrients or ingredients. e.g. orange juice fortified with calcium, cereals were fortified with vitamins or minerals and flour with added folic acid. Some examples are milk fortified with cholecalciferol used in vitamin D deficiency. Prebiotic and prebiotic fortified milk with *Bifidobacterium lactis HN019* used for the control of diarrhoea, respiratory infections and severe illnesses, in children. Banana fortified using soybean *ferritin* gene used for control of iron deficiency.

Table 2.10

Recombinant plant	Deficiency	Gene for expression
Gold kiwi fruit	Iron	High level Ascorbic acid, Carotenoids, lutein and Zeaxanthin.
Potatoes	Protein	Tuber-specific expression of a seed protein AmA1 (*Amaranthus Albumin 1*)
Golden mustard	Vitamin A	Soybean *ferritin* gene
Tomato	Folate	(Aminodeoxychorismate synthase At ADCS)
Golden rice	Vitamin A	Two daffodil genes and one bacterial gene
Iron rice	Iron deficiency	Soybean *ferritin* gene

Recombinant nutraceuticals: Energy providing foods such as bread, alcohol, fermented starch, yoghurt, cheese, vinegar are produced with the help of biotechnology.

Factors Responsible for Rapid Emergence of Nutraceuticals

- Consumers dissatisfied with drug costs and conventional health care are turning to unproven and untested natural product for treatment and prevention.
- Chronic diseases with poor therapeutic alternatives
- Desire for personalized medicines.
- Large populations try to get rid off the effects of aging.
- New focus on preventing medicine.
- Public perception that "natural is good".

Benefits of nutraceuticals:

1. May enhance the health value of our diet.
2. May help us live longer.
3. May help us to avoid particular medical conditions.
4. May be perceived to be more "natural" than traditional medicine and less likely to produce unpleasant side effects.

Safety of nutraceuticals: To ensure that nutraceuticals are safe and effective.

1. They need to be tested for purity as well as potency of ingredients.
2. Standardised testing methods need to be in place to verify quality of ingredients and dosage consistency.
3. Better means of producing ingredients and identifying new ingredients.
4. Need for product evaluation.

Table 2.11: Nutraceuticals and Diseases

Types of diseases	Nutraceuticals used
Cardiovascular diseases (CVD'S)	Antioxidants, dietary fibres, Omega-3-PUFA, vitamins and minerals for the prevention and treatment of CVD'S. Polyphenols in grape prevent and control arterial diseases.
Diabetes	Docosahexaenoic acid modulates insulin resistance and is also vital for neurovisual development. Lipoic acid, antioxidants, for treatment of diabetic neuropathy. Dietary fibers from Psyllium have been used for glucose control in diabetic patient and to reduce lipid level in hyperlipidemia.

Cancer	Flavonoids which block the enzymes that produce estrogen reduce of estrogen-induced cancers. To prevent prostate/breast cancer a broad range of phyto-pharmaceuticals with a claimed hormonal activity, called "phyto-estrogens" is recommended. Soyfoods source of isoflavones, curcumin from curry and soya isoflavones possess cancer chemopreventive properties. Saponins (found in peas, soybeans, some herbs, spinach, tomatoes, potatoes, alfalfa and clover) contain antitumor and antimutagenic activities.
Anti-inflammatory activities	Curcumin (diferuloylmethane) which is a polyphenol of turmeric possesses anticarcinogenic, antioxidative and anti-inflammatory properties. Gamma linolenic acid (found in green leafy vegetables, nuts, vegetable oils i.e.-evening primrose oil, blackcurrant seed oil, and hemp seed oil, and from spirulina, cyanobacteria) are used for treating problems with inflammation and auto-immune diseases.
Allergy	Quercetin (found in Onions, red wine and green tea) reduce the inflammation that results from hay fever, bursitis, gout, arthritis, and asthma.
Alzheimer's disease	β-carotene, curcumin, lutein, lycopene, turmerin etc may exert positive effects on specific diseases by neutralizing the negative effects oxidative stress mitochondrial dysfunction, and various forms of neural degeneration.
Parkinson's disease	Vitamin E in food may be protective against Parkinson's disease.

Natural Pigments

These include anthocyanins, betalains, carotenoids, chlorophylls and other pigments are conspicuously found in the plants. These pigments play an important role in ecological and metabolic functions in the plants and are more frequently exploited as the source of nutraceuticals to address a number of human ailments. The nutraceutical value of natural plant pigments such as carotenoids, anthocyanins, chlorophylls and betalains is based on their recognized biologically active properties. These pigments have been implicated in regimes to maintain human health, to protect against chronic disease(s), or to restore wellness by repairing tissues after disease has been established. The natural pigments and related phytochemicals are integral to the plants strategies for survival, serving protective roles (as shields against abiotic stresses like temperature, UV-B radiation, low water potential or mineral stress), active defensive roles (against pathogen or insect attack); attractant roles (inviting pollinators and seed dispersers) or roles in cell-level regulation (as gene expression modulators). The ecological benefits to the plant have at least some bearing on the potential medicinal benefits for humans.

Major Colour Pigments and their Impact on Human Health

Anthocyanins: The term Anthocyanin is derived from the Greek words meaning flower and blue. Anthocyanins are natural pigments belonging to the flavonoid family. They are responsible for the blue, purple, red and orange colour of many fruits and vegetables. Anthocyanins are present in different plant organs, such as fruits, flowers, stems, leaves and roots. These pigments are normally found dissolved uniformly in the vacuolar solution of epidermal cells. However, in certain species, the anthocyanins are localized in discrete regions of the cell vacuole, called "anthocyanoplasts". The main sources of Anthocyanin are red fruits, mainly berries and red grapes, cereals, principally purple maize, vegetables and red wine among drinks. The most common Anthocyanidins in higher plants are: delphinidin, cyanidin, petunidin, pelargonidin, peonidin and malvidin. The glycosides of the three non-methylated Anthocyanidins (delphinidin, cyanidin and pelargonidin) are the most abundant in nature, which represent 80% of leaf pigments. 69% in fruits and 50% in flowers. The distribution of the six most common Anthocyanidins in the edible parts of plants is cyanidin (0%), pelargonidin (12%), peonidin (12%), delphinidin (12%), petunidin (7%) and malvidin (7%). The most widespread Anthocyanin in most fruit is cyanidin-3-glucoside. However, malvidin glycosides are the most characteristic anthocyanins in red grape and derived products. Anthocyanins are interesting for two reasons: the first being technological, namely, their impact on the organoleptic characteristics of food which may influence their technological behaviour during food processes; and the second is Anthocyanin implication in human health through different pathways. Anthocyanins are relatively unstable and easily oxidized. They are sensitive to many factors, apart from pH, that may affect their stability and colour such as temperature and UV radiation) Many studies in recent years have focused on the study of the health properties of anthocyanins from different perspectives.

Antioxidant Characteristics of Anthocyanin Rich Diets and the Enhancement of Cardiovascular Health / Disease Preventive Role of Anthocyanins are given below

Cardiovascular: This is possibly the most studied effect and the one for which a great quantity of epidemiological evidence exists. Anthocyanins are capable of acting on different cells involved in the development of atherosclerosis, one of the leading causes to cardiovascular dysfunction vascular endothelial growth factor (VEGF) is a major pro-angiogenic and proatherosclerotic factor but anthocyanins have been shown to prevent the expression of VEGF in vascular smooth muscle cells. Blackberry anthocyanins inhibit LPS induced nitric oxide biosynthesis. The Anthocyanin extracts from chokeberry, bilberry, and elderberry have shown endothelium- dependent relaxation capacity in porcine coronary arteries and intake of flavonoids, including tannins and anthocyanins, is associated with reduced incidence of coronary heart disease. The rich Anthocyanin pigment content of red wines, as well as associated flavonoids, are purported to be responsible for the well-publicized correlation between red wine consumption and reduced cardiovascular mortality. Because anthocyanins are potent inhibitors of nitrated tyrosine formation *in vitro,* they may have a role in prevention of atherosclerotic lesions in human coronary arteries. Bioflavonoid mixtures derived from fruit sources *(Rubus occidentalis, Sambucus nigra,* bilberry, and *Aronia melanocarpa)* has demonstrated ability to accelerate ethanol metabolism, reduce inflammatory and edematic symptoms, and improve permeability and strength of capillaries. Anthocyanins in red wines and grape juice contributed to the ability of these dietary sources to inhibit heart attacks, by virtue of their antithrombotic potential, and to inhibit platelet function and enhance nitric oxide release. The anthocyanins and related polyphenolics in red wines prevented the development of atherosclerotic lesion.

Cancer Related

It has been suggested that anthocyanins possess anti-inflammatory as well as chemopreventive properties. It has been shown that the Anthocyanin-containing fraction of red wines is capable of suppressing proliferation of human colon cancer cells and gastric adenocarcinoma (AGS) cells. Liu *et al.* (2005) have shown that the proliferation of human hepatocellular liver carcinoma cells (HepG2) is inhibited by raspberry extracts, containing among other flavonoids anthocyanins. (Karko *et al.* (2004) have reported an inhibitory effect of the Anthocyanidins, delphinidin, cyanidin, petunidin, pelargonidin, peonidin and malvidin on cell proliferation in human vulva carcinoma cells and human colon carcinoma cells. Angiogenesis plays a critical role in the development of cancer. Mutagenicity is closely related to carcinogenicity. Yoshimoto and Okuno (1999) have observed that mutagenicity of certain carcinogenic compounds, such as heterocyclic amines, in *Salmonella typhimurium,* is decreased by aqueous extracts of the roots of different varieties of coloured sweet potatoes *(Ipomoea batatas).* Anthocyanins and related flavonoids from berries including cranberry, lingonberry, bilberry and blueberry have demonstrated the ability to inhibit not only the initiation stages of chemically induced carcinogenesis but also the later promotion and proliferation stages (Schmidt *et al.,* 2003).

Diabetes

Basically, anthocyanins may have a beneficial effect on diabetes at two levels. On the one hand, they can interfere with glucose absorption and on the other hand, they may have a protective effect on pancreatic cells. It has been shown that the simultaneous and daily administration of anthocyanins to rats from red wine together with streptozotocin, a diabetogenic compound with betacytotoxic effects, decreases glucose concentration in urine and serum. Additionally, anthocyanins from red wine prevent the generation of free oxygen radicals, and decreases lipid peroxidation (Kong *et al.*, 2003). Jayaprakasam *et al.* (2005) have shown that anthocyanins are also able to stimulate insulin secretion from rodent pancreatic beta-cells.

Eyesight Including Night Vision

The most extensively documented phytomedicinal role of anthocyanin pigments is in improving eyesight, including night vision. Black currant *(Ribes nigrum* L.) anthocyanins concentrated from juice, when administered to humans markedly improved visual adaptation to darkness. Anthocyanin pigments have been administered to remedy vision disorders, enhance visual ability, and increase capillary resistance. Retinopathy and cataracts, serious consequences of diabetes mellitus, can be combated using plant-derived anthocyanin pigments. AGH (a-glucosidase) enzyme normally catalyzes cleavage of glucose from disaccharides, leading to excess glucose absorption and aggravation of diabetes mellitus. Anthocyanin extracts from a wide range of plant species including *Ipomoea batatas* and *Brassica oleracea* have demonstrated ability to inhibit AGH, especially the acylated forms of the anthocyanin pigments prevalent in black carrots. Consumption of black currant based extracts or concentrates of anthocyanins has a positive effect on night vision, i.e., dark adaptation (Nakaishi *et al.*, 2000). In subjects with myopia, it has been shown that the administration of anthocyanins for 4 weeks improved subjective symptoms and objective contrast sensitivity (Lee *et al.*, 2005).

Microbial and Viral Activity

The effect of anthocyanins on microbial pathogens has not been studied in depth up to now. Some few studies exist, however, on the effect of berry extracts on pathogens. Even though many studies have shown that isolated anthocyanins or plant extracts rich in this group of flavonoids have an effect on microbial growth, results are not yet conclusive. Anthocyanins exert significant antimicrobial properties, and (in association with other flavonoids) have demonstrated quite effective inhibition of aflatoxin biosynthesis (Norton, 1999). Puupponen-Pimia *et al.* (2001) showed that extracts from different berries had an inhibitory effect on gram-negative bacterial growth, but had no effect on gram-negative bacteria. Moreover, they showed that blackcurrant extracts stimulated the growth of different strains of *Lactobacillus rhamiiosus* and *Lactobacillus paracasei* but inhibited those of *Escherichia coli.* Recent studies have demonstrated that blackcurrant concentrates inhibit the growth of different strains of *Staphylococcus aureus, Escherichia coli* and *Enterococcus faecium* (Werlein and Kutemeyer, 2005). Different cyanidin glycosides present in extracts of *Ribes nigrum* L. have shown antiviral properties towards influenza A and B viruses and herpes-1 virus (Knox *et al.*, 2003).

Betalains

Betalains have been widely used as natural colourants for many centuries, but their attractiveness for use as colourants of foods (or drugs and cosmetics) has increased recently due to their reportedly high anti-oxidative, free radical scavenging activities and concerns about the use of various synthetic alternatives. The main commercial sources of betalains are powders and concentrates of red beet *(Beta vulgaris)* or cactus pear *(Opuntia ficusindica)* extracts. Commercially, betaxanthin pigments have been introduced as a food supplement in order to fortify processed food products with a nutraceutical natural colourant containing essential amino acids. Betalains reportedly have diverse, desirable activities including anti-inflammatory, hepatoprotective and cancer chemo-preventative activities, and the ability to reduce oxidative stress and protect low density lipoproteins (LDLs) from oxidation. A striking characteristic of betalain pigments is that they can be naturally absorbed by the body; at least 15% of consumers absorb large amounts resulting in temporary red urinary discharge, which indicates minimal transformation during metabolism. In particular, one pigment in the betalain group, betanin, appears to be a potent anticancer compound. Beetroot extract, rich in betalain pigments, has demonstrated chemopreventive properties against both lung and skin cancers (Kapadia *et al.*, 1996). In a study of different beetroot phenotypes, it was the most highly pigmented (betacyanin-rich) beets that were most efficient at free-radical scavenging and inducing quinine reductase in urine hepatoma cells *in vitro*.

Carotenoids

Carotenoids are the second most abundant pigments in nature, and consist of more than 700 members (Britton, 1998). Carotenoids, a large group of fat-soluble compounds, are responsible for many of the yellow, orange and red colours in plant and animal. Carotenoids make up a diverse class of natural pigments that are of interest for pharmaceutical use, as natural food colourants, nutrient supplements and animal feed. Carotenoids play an important role in plant reproduction, through their role in attracting pollinators and in seed dispersal, and are essential components of humans' diets. Several carotenoids protect humans by hindering free radical chain reactions caused by aging, smoking, pollution and other stresses. Beta-carotene is a precursor of vitamin A, and lutein and zeaxanthin have been implicated in the reduction of age-related macular disease (AMD) (Landrum and Bone, 2004). In terms of nutraceutical contribution, carotenoids are best recognized for their antioxidant capacity. Hydrogen peroxide, singlet oxygen, nitrogen oxides, superoxide anion, and other reactive oxygen species can be inactivated by carotenoids; in fact, carotenoids are considered the most potent of biological quenchers of singlet oxygen (Paiva and Russell, 1999), and can react with virtually any radical species likely to be encountered in a biological system. About 50 carotenoids have been identified in the human diet. Beta-carotene, lycopene, and lutein are the most prevalent carotenoids in the diet (Lila, 2004).

Vision and Eye Functions

Also like the flavonoids, carotenoids provide protection to vision and eye function, and against macular degeneration and cataracts. Two carotenoids present within the entire retina and macula, lutein and zeaxanthin (classified together as xanthophylls), account for the yellowish cast in the macular region of the eye. Macular degeneration, caused by blue light-mediated free radical damage to the retina, is the leading cause of irreversible blindness in aging adults over 65. Lutein has been loosely referred to as 'the eye-protective nutrient' and its intake has been shown in epidemiological trials to be inversely associated with ocular diseases such as age related macular degeneration and cataracts (Khachik *et al.*, 2002). Retinoic acids are capable of effectively reducing swelling and destruction of collagen, and hence have been integral to some arthritis therapy regimes. Carotenoids have a photo-protective function in human metabolism, and hence have been used in therapies for photosensitivity diseases. Mechanisms suspected to be involved in the protective effects of these macula carotenoids are filtering blue light, and scavenging reactive intermediates generated in photo-oxidation (Sies and Stahl, 2003).

Inhibition of Cardiovascular Disease

A series of studies have now demonstrated a correlation between high intakes or high serum concentrations of carotenes and lowered risk of coronary artery disease. Inhibition of low-density lipoprotein (LDL) oxidation has been demonstrated, especially with low levels of carotene, although interestingly, the carotenoids lycopene did not protect against oxidation in these tests. Clinical studies show that a 2-week dosage of tomato juice, rich in carotenoids, effectively lowers LDL in male subjects.

Cancer Chemoprevention

Carotenoids enhance cell-to-cell communication because they can up-regulate gap junctions. Carotenoids are able to induce gap junctional communication, although the natural carotenoids are more efficient. Carotenoids are associated with inhibition of several types of cancers including cervical, esophageal, pancreatic, lung, prostate, colorectal and stomach. Less-compelling evidence has been shown for a link between carotenoids and breast cancer; however, observation indicates that very low carotenoid intakes may be associated with increased risk of breast cancer. In particular, the carotenoid lycopene has been extensively researched for its role in cancer inhibition. Lutein and zeaxanthin intake has been linked to reduced risk of prostate cancer. Both α-carotene and vitamin A supplementation indicate that both substances inhibit cell proliferation in carcinogenesis. Lycopene inhibitory effect on prostate cancer cells has been linked to antioxidant mechanisms.

Chlorophylls

Chlorophyll is the most important plant pigment and a 'real life force' that nature uses to explode plants into greenery. It is not a single compound, but made up of two classical components—the bluish black chlorophyll-a and dark green chlorophyll-b. Chlorophyll is photoreceptive, absorbs blue and red spectrum of the visible light (400-700 nm) and reflects the unabsorbed spectrum in the green region. It is the green reflection that makes plant parts look green. The spectacular show of green turning to brilliant shades of yellow and red in autumn before plants shed leaves is nothing but manifestation of pigment change, from one to another. Chlorophyll is present in the membrane of disc-like structures called 'chloroplasts', which are like chemical factories powered by the sun to synthesize carbohydrates. It is one of the greatest miracles of nature that chlorophyll and its companions, sparked by sunlight, produce simple sugar (carbohydrate). The process is called 'photosynthesis', which beyond doubt is the most fundamental of all biochemical reactions and one that helps plants to grow, flower, produce seed and sustain life on earth.

Effect on Human Health Maintenance

Chlorophylls in green foods are credited with numerous interventions in human health maintenance including reduction of blood pressure, blood sugar control, brain activation, antimutagenic and anticholesterolic effects and more. The dark green vegetables are simultaneously excellent sources of carotenoids, in particular lutein, which contribute with the chlorophylls to the health-protective properties.

Cancer Chemoprevention

The anti-mutagenic properties of chlorophylls have been demonstrated in various assays, and clearly, intake of chlorophyll has potential to act as a chemopreventive compound in humans. However, much of the research is equivocal. Chlorophyllin, a water-soluble, food-grade, stable sodium and copper salt of chlorophyll, has shown both anticancer properties and cancer-promoting activity. Dietary consumption of green vegetables has been associated with the protection against mutagenic activity with chlorophyll as the principal protective agent involved. Research supporting chlorophyll's roles in cancer chemoprevention indicates that these pigments are capable of deactivating potential carcinogens in the digestive tract and preventing absorption.

Curcumin

Curcumin available from turmeric is widely consumed, especially in middle-eastern diets, and has a broader range of pharmacological applications. It acts as an anti-inflammatory agent. Low levels of curcumin in the diet of laboratory animals resulted in significant lowering of blood cholesterol levels, and improvement in the LDL/HDL ratios (Suresh-Babu and Srinivasan, 1997). As such, a therapeutic role for turmeric for individuals with diabetes as well as predisposition to coronary heart disease is suggested. Similarly, turmeric has demonstrated anti-mutagenic and anti-carcinogenic properties in both *in vitro* and *in vivo* chemopreventive assays. Curcumin has also been shown to have beneficial effects of drugs and vitamins (Lila, 2004).

Nutraceutical Properties of Different Fruits and Vegetables

It is well-known that fruits and vegetables are an essential part of a healthy diet. The chief reason is that fruits and vegetables are rich sources of important phytochemicals, which provide essential nutrients and enhance the body's ability to prevent and fight disease. There is a multitude of phytochemicals, in unique combinations, in different fruits and vegetables, and each functions differently in the body: as anti-oxidant, as anti-allergenic, as anti-carcinogenic, as anti-inflammatory, as anti-viral, and/or anti-proliferative. Being of natural origin, some of the phytochemical pigments are increasingly sought after as food colourants. Antioxidants are important because they are believed to protect the body against free radicals, the harmful molecules that can cause heart disease, premature aging, Alzheimer's disease, blindness and a variety of cancers. There are many kinds of antioxidants, some are produced by the body and others are derived from the foods we eat. When the body's natural antioxidant defenses are lowered or greater amounts of free radicals are being produced, the body becomes more dependent upon food sources for antioxidants. Some of the nutraceutical rich vegetable crops include red and black carrot, beet root, tomato, chilli, and broccoli. Among the fruits, pomegranate is very rich in antioxidants. Other fruits rich in nutraceuticals include watermelon and Jamun.

Carrot (*Daucus carota* L.)

Carrot is available in red, yellow, purple, or even black colour. The variety of pigments contained in them performs a range of protective functions in the human body. Many of the pigments serve to shield plant cells during photosynthesis. Red carrots derive their colour mainly from lycopene, a type of carotene believed to guard against heart disease and some cancers. Yellow carrots accumulate xanthophylls, pigments similar to β-carotene that support good eye health. Purple carrots possess an entirely different class of pigments—anthocyanins—which act as "powerful antioxidants. Red carrots are thought to have originated in India and China in the eighteenth century. Red strains of carrot contain abundant lycopene in addition to the provitamin A, carotenoids, α- and β-carotene. Tissue specific accumulation of carotenoids in carrot roots has been reported in carrots and related vegetables of Umbelliferae. The red carrot qualifies as a functional food because, in addition to providing essential vitamin

A, it may offer protection against chronic disease through the putative benefits of lycopene. While red carrot and tomato paste contain lycopene, β-carotene concentration is very low in tomato paste compared with red carrots. Studies have revealed that lycopene in the red carrot is about 44% as bioavailable as that from tomato paste. Red carrots, therefore, provide an alternative to tomato paste as a good dietary source of lycopene and also provide bioavailability of a-carotene. Black Carrot Unlike red Carrot, which contains lycopenes and other carotenes, is a rich source of anthocyanins. Anthocyanins have many different functions for the plant. They are antioxidants, protect the plant against UV light, and play an important role in pollination and reproduction. The black carrot extract is being used to colour drinks, pastries and other beverages.

Tomato (*Solanum lycopersicum* L.)

Tomatoes have received significant attention worldwide because of interest in lycopene, the primary carotenoid found in this fruit and its role in cancer risk reduction (Gerster, 1997). Tomato is an excellent source of nutraceuticals such as lycopene, vitamins A, C and E. Lycopene is one of the most powerful natural antioxidants which help prevents prostate cancer and benefit the heart. Tomatoes and tomato based sauces, juices, and ketchup account for more than 85%. The lycopene content of tomatoes depends on species and increases as the fruit ripens. Unlike other fruits and vegetables, where nutritional content such as vitamin C is diminished upon cooking, processing of tomatoes increases the concentration of bioavailable lycopene. Lycopene in tomato paste is four times more bioavailable than in fresh tomatoes. This is because lycopene is insoluble in water and is tightly bound to vegetable fiber. Thus, processed tomato products such as pasteurized tomato juice, soup, sauce, and ketchup contain the highest concentrations 'of bioavailable lycopene. Lycopene is insoluble in water and can he dissolved only in organic solvents and oils. Unlike carotene, lycopene is not converted to vitamin A but is a powerful antioxidant, and an efficient scavenger of singlet oxygen and thus, having anti-cancer effect.

Red Chilli (*Capsicum annuum* L.)

Chillies are the dried red fruits of the genus *Capsicum* and family Solanaceae. The two well known species are *Capsicum annuum* L. and *C. frutenscens* L., the former being widely grown and economically important of the domesticated chilli peppers. India is the largest producer and exporter of chillies. The estimated export of dry chillies was 75,000 metric tonnes valued at 255 crores in 2001. In chilli, pungency and colour are the two main quality attributes. The red colour of chillies is due to the presence of the carotenoid pigment like capsanthin (major, 35%), zeaxanthin, violaxanthin, cryptoxanthin, β-carotene etc. These pigments are present in chillies mainly in the esterified form and to a small extent in non-esterified forms. Chilli oleoresin is used in many Indian processed foods like sausages, meat products to impart desired taint and pungency.

Such pungency is not desired in many food products. Pungency-free food colourants from chilli are, therefore, desired to obtain high value commercial chilli oleoresin. The hot flavour of chillies is due to the presence of a group of seven closely related compounds called capsaicinoids. Capsaicin (S-methyl-N-vanillyl-nonenamide) and dihydrocapsaicin are the two main active components that account for approximately 90% of the pungency. These two compounds are about twice as potent as the minor capsaicinoids nordihydrocapsaicin, homodihydrocapsaicin and homocapsaicin. Capsaicin and capsaicinoids are produced as a secondary metabolite of chilli peppers probably as deterrent against herbivores. Pure capsaicin is a hydrophobic, colourless, odourless crystalline to waxy compound having irritant/pungent properties. Despite popular belief, the seeds do not produce any capsaicins, instead, it is present in large quantities in the placental tissue which holds the seeds, the internal membranes and to a lesser extent in the fleshy parts of the capsicum fruits. Hot peppers are a good source of dietary antioxidants, encompassing, apart from widespread compounds (flavonoids, phenolic acids, carotenoids, vitamin A, ascorbic acid and tocopherols) also specific constituents such as the pungent capsaicinoids (capsaicin, dihydrocapsaicin, and related analogues). In the spice extraction industry, chilli oleoresin is produced by extraction of chilli powder with solvents such as acetone, ethylene dichloride and hexane followed by desolventization to get deep coloured oleoresin. Capsaicin is currently used in tropical ointments in concentrations between 0.025-0.075% to relieve minor aches, muscle pains, joint pains, backache, peripheral neuropathic pains, osteoarthritis pain as well as strains and sprains. Capsaicin is also being explored as a possible cure for diabetes, prostate cancer and as a pesticide to deter pests. Burning and painful sensations associated with capsaicin results from its chemical interaction with sensory neurons and depletion of neurotransmitters.

Pomegranate (*Punica granatum* L.)

The pomegranate fruit possesses a vast ethnomedical history and represents a phytochemical reservoir of medicinal value. It has recently been acclaimed for its health benefits and for its disease-fighting antioxidant potential. The phytochemistry and pharmacological actions of all *P. granatum* components suggest a wide range of clinical applications for the treatment and prevention of cardiovascular protection, cancer, as well as other diseases where chronic inflammation is believed to play an essential role. Studies have shown that pomegranate juice has more polyphenol antioxidants than any other drink, such as red wine, green tea, blueberry juice, cranberry juice and orange juice. Currently, the two common ways of consuming pomegranates are by eating the fleshy arils of the pomegranate and by drinking the juice obtained from the arils. The extract obtained from pomegranate solids consists of the pericarp, inner membrane and seeds. The extract produced differs from commercially-available pomegranate juice in that the extract is substantially derived from the pomegranate solids, whereas pomegranate juice is substantially derived from the sweet, fleshy arils. Punicalagin is a powerful antioxidant, protecting cardiovascular function and accurate cellular replication. While the antioxidant and other beneficial health effects of the extract are due to the presence of polyphenols, the presence of other phytochemical compounds in the extract, or the synergistic effect of these phytochemicals, may also be responsible for the anti-oxidant and other beneficial health effects of the extract. In addition to punicalagin. other high molecular weight polyphenols have been characterized in the extract of pomegranate solids. These high molecular weight polyphenols include ellagitannin and other hydrolysable tannins, such as— punicacortein A, punicalin, pedunculagin, and gallotanin dimmers and trimers. A large number of anthocyanins have also been characterized in the extract of the pomegranate solids. These include pelargonidin 3-glucoside, cyanidine 3-glucoside, delphinidin 3-glucoside, pelargonidin 3,5-diglucoside, cyaniding 3,5-diglucoside, and delphinidin 3,5-diglucoside. Although, these anthocyanins have been characterized in both the pomegranate juice and the extract, these lower molecular weight polyphenols comprise a higher proportion of the total polyphenol content in pomegranate juice (approximately 50%) than in the extract.

Oxidation of LDL has been proposed to play a key role in hardening of the arteries (atherosclerosis) which is linked to heart disease - the cause of about 50 per cent of deaths from heart diseases. Pomegranate juice consumption increases antioxidant enzyme activity, protecting the body from free radicals. It has been suggested that pomegranate juice, rich in polyphenols, protects LDL against oxidation, which is thought to speed up the hardening of the arteries.

Jamun (*Syzygium cuminii* L.)

Jamun is a tropical and sub-tropical evergreen tree that yields purple ovoid fleshy fruit. It is valued for its medicinal and therapeutic properties. In traditional Indian medicine, it is extensively used against diabetes and apart from that, it is also administered against various ailments like carminative, febrifuge, antibacterial, diuretic and diarrhoea. Based on the available ethno-pharmacological knowledge, studies have been conducted to understand the chemical composition and antioxidant activities of three anatomically distinct parts of fruit the pulp, kernel and seed coat. Ethanolic extract of jamun kernel exhibited antioxidant activity superior to catechin and other commercial synthetic antioxidants. Activity has been attributed to the presence of anthocyanin content in the fruits. Some of the bioactives in the fruits have been identified as delphinidin-3-gentiobioside, jambocine, malvidin- 3-laminaribiside and petunidin-3-gentiobioside. Among the 30 volatiles compounds in the fruit, three esters, namely dihydrocarvyl acetate, geranyl butyrate and terpinyl valerate were probably responsible for the characteristic flavour of the jamun fruits. Fruits also yielded citric, malic and Gallic acids. Seeds contain a-sitosterol. Diluted juice of fruits is diuretic and prevents enlargement of spleen. Seed powder of jamun is used as good diabetic medicine.

Beet Root (*Beta vulgaris* L.)

It is a potent and nutritious source of natural energy and vitality. It is important because of its cultivated varieties' sugar-producing ability. Beet root powder is a very popular colouring agent for use in soaps and cosmetic products. The red colour in the Beet root is derived from anthocyanin and the water-soluble, red betaine pigments-betacyanin and betaxanthin. These pigments belong to the betalain-group of colours which are classified on their structure and divided into two groups; betacyanins and betaxanthins, with red-purple and yellow colours, respectively. In beet root, the main betacyanin is betanin and the main betaxanthins are vulgaxantin I and vulgaxanthin II. All betalains are water soluble, which limits the use. Betalains are stable between pH 3.5 and 7.0, which covers nearly all foods with maximum colour stability at pH 5.5. Betanin is susceptible towards light and temperature, which limits the use to fresh foods, foods packed under modified atmosphere, or foods that undergo no heat treatment. It is mainly used in frozen products (ice cream, yoghurt). Dry betanin is more stable and it is used as a colour in instant foods and powdered soft drinks. It is also stable in high sugar conditions and can, thus, be used in candies and fruit gels and fillings.

Some of the other active constituents in beet root include saponiside, phytosterol, betaine, leucine, tyrosine, beta-carotene, and vitamins Bl, B2, B3, B6 and C.

Beet root is believed to boost the body's natural defenses in the liver and regenerate immune cells. It contains soluble fiber which can help reduce high blood cholesterol levels. Its phytochemicals, carotenoids and flavonoids act as cardiotonic and prevent LDL (bad cholesterol) from being oxidized and deposited in the arteries. It is a wonderful cleansing and nourishing tonic that normalizes the blood's pH balance (reducing acidity) and purifies the blood by flushing away fatty deposits and improving circulation.

Broccoli (*Brassica oleracea* var. italica L.)

It is high in vitamin C and its soluble fiber contains the multiple nutrients with potent anti-cancer properties including di-indolylmethane and selenium. The 3,3-Di-indolylmethane found in broccoli is a potent modulator of the innate immune response system with anti-viral, anti-bacterial and anti-cancer activity. Broccoli also contains the compound glucoraphanin, which can be processed into an anticancer compound sulforaphane, though the benefits of broccoli are reduced if the vegetable is boiled. A high intake of broccoli has been found to reduce the risk of aggressive prostate cancer. Broccoli leaf is also edible and contains far more a-carotene than the florets. Broccoli contains important phytochemicals but it is also rich in other nutrients, including calcium, fibre and vitamins. Broccoli is high in antioxidant and anticancer compounds. Phytochemicals in broccoli can protect the eyes against macular degeneration. These compounds have been identified as sulphoraphane and the glucosinolates.

Safety And Efficacy

Consumers desire the increased health control these products offer and the promised health benefits. The danger is that many of these products do not provide consumers with solid information about their safety and effectiveness, possible side effects, interactions with prescription medicines or the impact they may have on existing medical conditions. While acceptance of nutraceuticals is growing among physicians, many members of the medical and scientific communities remain concerned that many products entering the market lack adequate efficacy and safety data. Professionals on both sides of the fence agree there is an urgent need for funding to support high-quality scientific research, testing and clinical trials before nutraceuticals are introduced to consumers. Clinical research on specific nutraceutical products sold would help substantiate the potential medical or health values of these products. As a result, patients and health care professionals would know the facts about the benefit and the safety of the products being taken.

Health Benefits of Different Colour Groups of Fruits and Vegetable Crops

By eating fruits and vegetables of a variety of different colours, one can get the best all-around health benefits. Each different colour fruit and vegetables contains unique health components that are essential to our health. Fruits and vegetables are very important to our health because they are whole foods, created by nature, that are rich in a large amount of nutrients. The processed foods that we so commonly eat, can never compare to the health benefits provided by strawberries or broccoli, which have fiber, vitamins, and enzymes built right in. Eating plenty of healthy vegetables and fruits helps prevent heart disease and strokes, control blood pressure, prevent some types of cancers, and guards against cataract and macular degeneration or vision loss. The phrase *"eating a rainbow "* of fruits and vegetables is a simple way of remembering to get as much colour variety in your diet as possible, so that you can maximize your intake of a broad range of nutrients. By getting a variety of different coloured fruits and vegetables, you are guaranteed a diverse amount of essential vitamins and minerals.

Red fruits and Vegetables

Contain nutrients such as lycopene, ellagic acid, Quercetin and Hesperidin. These nutrients reduce the risk of prostate cancer, lower blood pressure, reduce tumour growth and LDL cholesterol levels, scavenge harmful free-radicals and support joint tissue in arthritis cases.

Orange, Yellow Fruits and Vegetables

Contain β-carotene, zeaxanthin, flavonoids, lycopene, potassium and vitamin C. These nutrients reduce age-related muscular degeneration and the risk of prostate cancer, lower LDL cholesterol and blood pressure, promote collagen formation and healthy joints, fight harmful free radicals, encourage alkaline balance and work with magnesium and calcium to build healthy bones.

Green Fruits and Vegetables

Green vegetables contain chlorophyll, fiber, lutein, zeaxanthin, calcium, folate, vitamin C, and calcium and β-carotene. These nutrients found in these vegetables reduce cancer risks, lower blood pressure and LDL cholesterol levels, normalize digestion time, support retinal health and vision, fight harmful free-radicals and boost immune system activity.

Blue and Purple Fruits and Vegetables

Contain nutrients which include lutein, zeaxanthin, Resveratrol, vitamin C, fiber, flavonoids, ellagic acid and quercetin. Similar to the previous nutrients, these nutrients support retinal health, lower LDL cholesterol, boost immune system activity, support healthy digestion, improve calcium and other mineral absorption, fight inflammation, reduce tumour growth, act as an anticarcinogens in the digestive tract and limit the activity of cancer cells.

White Fruits and Vegetables

Contain nutrients such as beta-glucans, EGCG, SDG and lignans that provide powerful immune boosting activity. These nutrients also activate natural killer B and T cells, reduce the risk of colon, breast and prostate cancers and balance hormone levels, reducing the risk of hormone related cancers.

MEDICINAL PROPERTIES OF SOME COMMON EDIBLE FRUITS

Aonla (*Emblica officinalis*)

Fruit

1. Fruit is the most useful part of Aonla and it is the richest source of vitamin-C (600 mg/100 g).
2. A *sherbet* of Aonla fruit with lemon juice is taken for arresting acute bacillary dysentery.
3. The fresh fruit is refrigerant, antiscorbutic, diuretic and laxative.
4. It is used in fevers, hiccup, vomiting, indigestion and other disorders of digestive system.
5. In combination with iron, dried fruit is used in jaundice, anemia and dysentery.

Seeds

1. An infusion of seeds is given to control fever, diabetes, digestive problems and nausea.
2. Seeds can be used to cure skin diseases like scabies and to control itching.
3. Smoke of seeds is inhaled in asthma and bronchitis.
4. Oil extracted from seeds is used for destroying dandruff and blackening hair.

Banana (*Musa spp.*)

Fruit

1. The fruits are rich in carbohydrates and are cooling, antihelminthic, antiscorbutic.
2. The flour of dried fruit is prescribed in chronic diarrhea, dysentery and dyspepsia.
3. The unripe fruit is used to control diabetes as it is astringent and the unripe fruit is rich source of phenolic compounds.
4. The partially ripe fruits can also be used for the treatment of chronic diarrhea, dysentery and dyspepsia.

Flower

1. The inflorescence axis is specifically used to treat renal problems.
2. The ash obtained from burning the whole plant can be used for the treatment of hyper acidity, heart burn and colitis.

Root and Rhizome

1. The underground parts i.e., roots and rhizomes are used to treat blood and veneral diseases, helminthiasis, scabies, leprosy, skin diseases and in diarrhoea.

Bael (*Aegle marmelos*)

Fruits

1. Fruits contain an alkaloid ''Marmelosin'' and are rich source of Riboflavin (Vitamin B2).
2. A pulp or sherbet of ripe fruit is given for chronic constipation, diarrhoea and dyspepsia.
3. Ripe fruits are good for the heart and brain.
4. It is also prescribed in intestinal disorders and certain forms of dyspepsia characterized by alternate constipation and diarrhoea.

Leaves

1. Leaves contain an essential oil consisting of ''phellandrene'' and bark contains ''coumarin'' and ''umbelliferone''.

2. The oil extracted from bael leaves is known as "bilva oil" and is used to treat deafness.
3. The leaves can also be used to treat opthalmia, inflammations, eye cataract and diabetes.
4. Leaf juice mixed with black pepper is given in jaundice and dropsy.

Ber (*Ziziphus mauritiana*)

Fruits

1. The fruits are sour, sweet, cooling, appetizer and used in tonic.
2. They are used to treat wounds, ulcers, haemorrhages and constipation.

Root and Stem Bark

1. A well known compound "betulinic acid" has been isolated for the treatment of melanoma.

2. They are used to treat cough, fever, wounds and ulcers.

Seeds

1. They are used in the treatment of burned wounds, stomach ulcers and in asthma.

Custard Apple (*Annona squamosa*)

Fruits

1. They are useful in anemia, burning sensation, cough, malignant tumours and as an anti snake venom.
2. The unripe fruit is prescribed in diarrhoea, dysentery and dyspepsia.

Leaves

1. The leaves contain saponin and are insecticidal.
2. They are used for the treatment of ring worm (*Taenia versicolor*) and skin diseases.

Seeds

1. The seeds are abortifacient when applied in the form of paste on uterus.

Roots

1. The roots act as anti snake venom.
2. The root bark contains an alkaloid "Anonaine".
3. They are useful in acute dysentery, mental depression and spinal disorders.

Grape (*Vitis vinifera*)

Fruits

1. The ripe berries are sweet, laxative, rejuvenating, digestive and used in tonics.

2. They are used in the treatment of cough, burning sensation, constipation, haemorrhages, and anemia, leprosy and skin diseases.
3. Unripe fruits contain organic acids like tartaric, malic, oxalic and racemic acids.
4. The juice from unripe fruits is used in throat infections.

Flowers

1. They are useful in the treatment of bronchitis, hepatopathy and anemia.

Stem and Leaf

1. The sap of young branches is used as remedy for skin diseases.
2. The leaves are astringent and diuretic.
3. They are useful to treat scabies, skin diseases, syphilis, haemorrhoides and splenomegaly.

Jamun (*Syzygium spp.*)

Fruits

1. Its juice is used in diabetes, diarrhoea, pharyngitis, splenomegaly and to kill ringworms.
2. The ripe fruits are sweet, acrid, sour, astringent, antiscorbutic and diuretic.

Leaves

1. The leaves are used for strengthening the teeth and gums.
2. The crushed tender leaves are effective to treat diabetes.

Seeds

1. Seeds are rich in a phenolic compound called "ellagic acid" and an alkaloid "jambosine".
2. It is very effective to control Diabetes mellitus and glycosuria.
3. It quickly reduces sugar in urine.
4. The powder of dried seeds is effective in diarrhoea and dysentery.

Acid lime (*Citrus aurantifolia*)

Fruits

1. The fruit juice contains citric acid and fruit rind contains volatile oil containing citral, limonene and linalool.
2. The fruits are sour, bitter, astringent, laxative, appetizer and anti-scorbutic.

Flowers:

1. The flowers are used for the treatment of stomach pains, nausea, vomiting and cough.

Leaf

1. The leaves contain flavoured volatile compound "coumarins" and are used for hepatomegaly due to excessive liquor consumption.

Mango (*Mangifera indica*)

Fruits

1. The unripe fruits are acidic, antiscorbutic, digestive and carminative.
2. Rind of fruit is astringent, stimulative and used in tonic.
3. The ripe fruits are sweet, laxative, haemostatic and cardiotonic.

Stone

1. The seed kernel is rich source of protein (8.5%) and Gallic acid.
2. Fried kernel is given to expected mothers suffering from diarrhoea.
3. The kernel juice, if snuffed can stop nasal bleeding.

Pomegranate (*Punica granatum*)

Fruits

1. The fruits are sweet, sour, astringent, laxative and diuretic.
2. The fruit juice is widely used to treat leprosy patients.
3. Fruits are useful to treat anemia, pharyngitis, diarrhoea and gastralgia.
4. The fruit rind is known as "*dalim chhal*" which is powerful astringent.
5. Fruit rind is used for wound healing, intestinal parasites and as an antidysentery and antidiarrhoeal.

Seeds

1. Dried seeds with aril are known as *anardana*.
2. Seeds are astringent, diuretic and cardiotonic.
3. A paste of the seeds made with milk is used for dissolving stones and gravel in kidneys.

Roots

1. Roots are astringent and antihelminthic.
2. Root and stem bark contains alkaloids "punicine" and "pellertierine" which are highly toxic to tapeworms, so the decoction or powder of freshly dried barks is much effective as taenicide and for expelling round worms.

CONCLUSIONS AND FUTURE STRATEGIES

Since plant pigments have multiple roles in human health protection, maintenance and therapy through a diverse array of biological activities, evidenced through *in vitro, in vivo,* and clinical trials, as well as through extensive epidemiological evidence. The combined evidence of numerous research trials indicates that variety of different pigments in a well-balanced diet is a key to prevention and therapy for a range of chronic human disease conditions. One of the biggest challenges to conclusively determine the biological properties of natural plant pigments in human health maintenance has been the inability to track the fate of these pigments after ingestion. Epidemiological studies have suggested that reduction in cardiovascular disease, cancer risk and a range of other chronic disease conditions is linked to consumption in the diet of anthocyanins, betalains, chlorophylls, and carotenoids. Still, very little is known about accumulation of pigments or pigment metabolites in various organs of the body, or absorption after digestion. Lack of knowledge concerning mechanisms of action, absorption, bioavailability, and metabolic fate hinders the comprehensive demonstration of health benefits. The selective activation of those metabolic pathways involved in the synthesis of more stable or bioactive final products will open up ways for the design of functional foods or new foods with health related claims. Studies involving labelled pigments in feeding or incubation experiments will, therefore, go a long way in providing a much clearer view of the beneficial effect of natural phytochemicals on human health, besides giving clues to their mechanisms of action.

REFERENCES

Cecil, R, Pace-Asciak, Susan Hahn, Eleftherios Diamandis, P, George Soleas, David Goldberg, M. 1995. The Red Wine Phenolics *Trans*-resveratrol and Quercetin Block Human Platelet Aggregation and Eicosanoid Synthesis: Implications for Protection Against Coronary Heart Disease. *Clinica Chimica Acta*. 207-219.

Chang, R.L, Huang, M.T, Wood, A.W, Wong, C. Q, Newmark, H.L, Yagi, H, Sayer, J.M, Jerina, D.M. and Conney, A.H. 1985. Effect of Ellagic Acid and Hydroxylated Flavonoids on the Tumorigenicity of Benzopyrene and 8α-dihydroxy-9α, 10α-epoxy-7, 8, 9, 10-tetrahydrobenzopyrene on Mouse Skin and in the Newborn Mouse. *Carcinogenesis*. 6:1127-1133.

Chemoprevention. *Journal of National Cancer Institute*. 96:662-672.

Dai, Z, Li Y, Quarles L.D, Song T, Pan, W. and Zhou H. 2007. Resveratrol Enhances Proliferation and Osteoblastic Differentiation in Human Mesenchymal Stem Cells via ER Dependent ERK1/2 Activation. *Phytomedicine*. 14:806–14.

Kawakami, K., Aketa, S, Nakanami, M, Iizuka, S. and Hirayama, M. 2010. Major Water-Soluble Polyphenols, Proanthocyanidins, in Leaves of Persimmon (*Diospyros kaki*) and their α-amylase Inhibitory Activity. *Bioscience, Biotechnology, and Biochemistry*, 74:1380–1385.

Sun, S.Y, Hail J. N. and Lotan, R. 2004. Apoptosis as a Novel Target for Cancer

Yu-Lin Kao, Yi-Ming Kuo, Yi-Ru Lee, Shun-Fa Yang, Wen-Rong Chen and Huei-Jane Lee. 2015. Apple Polyphenol Induces Cell Apoptosis, Cell Cycle Arrest at G2/M Phase and Mitiotic Catastrophe in Human Bladder Transitional Carcinoma Cells. *Science Direct*. 384-394.

Zhang, L, Li J, Hogan, S, Chung, H, Welbaum, and Zhou K. 2009. Inhibitory Effect of Raspberries on Starch Digestive Enzyme and their Antioxidant Properties and Phenolic Composition. *Food Chemistry*. *119*:592–599.

Nutraceuticals and Pharmaceuticals from Medicinal Plants
Edited by: Dr. Pawan Kumar 'Bharti'; Dr. M.M. Abid Ali Khan; Dr. Ashok K. Rathoure
ISBN: 978-93-86841-55-1
Edition: 2018
Published by: Discovery Publishing House Pvt. Ltd., New Delhi (India)

3 Valuable Approaches, Important Concerns and Significance of Medicinal Plant Conservation

[1]Dr. Showkat Ahmad Bhat, [2]Dr. Hilal Ahmad Wani, [1]Dr. Tehseen Hassan, [1]Professor Sabhiya Majid, [1]Nisar Ahmad Naikoo

ABSTRACT

For a long time plants have been provide essential nutritional values, medicinal properties and notable physiological effect to life and are a good source of food. Medicinal plants have played an essential role in the development of human culture. Probably the single most important role for medicinal plants in biological conservation is their 'use' to achieve conservation of natural habitats more generally. This stems from the special meanings that medicinal plants have to people, related to the major contributions that they make too many people's lives in terms of health support, financial income, cultural identity and livelihood security. Many types of action can be taken in support of the conservation and sustainable use of medicinal plants. Some of these are undertaken directly at the places where the plants are found, while others are less direct, such as some of those relating to commercial systems, etc. The fair and equitable sharing of benefits from bioprospecting is required under the Convention on Biological Diversity, but it is not always easy to achieve these ideals in practice. While experience is accumulating in how this may practically be achieved, it is important, at the present time, that controls imposed on scientific research to prevent biopiracy or theft of local and indigenous intellectual property do not unduly restrict research that has little or nothing to do with these matters. We recommend that biotechnical approaches (e.g. tissue culture, micropropagation, synthetic seed technology, and molecular marker-based approaches) should be applied to improve yield and modify the potency of medicinal plants.

Keywords: Medicinal plants, conservation, valuable approaches, biological diversity.

---

[1] Department of Biochemistry, Govt. Medical College Srinagar, Karan-Nagar, Srinagar Jammu & Kashmir, India-190010

[2] Multidisciplinary Research Unit (MRU), Govt. Medical College Srinagar, Karan-Nagar, Srinagar Jammu & Kashmir, India-190010

Medicinal Plants and their Conservation Impacts on Humans

Medicinal plants are resources of traditional medicines and many of the modern medicines are produced indirectly from plants. The special significance of medicinal plants in conservation stems from the major cultural, livelihood or economic roles that they play in many people's lives. Various sets of recommendations have been compiled relating to the conservation of medicinal plants (Akerele *et al.* 1991; Bodeker 2002). They include: the need for coordinated conservation action, based on both in situ and ex situ strategies; inclusion of community and gender perspectives in the development of policies and programmes; the need for more information on the medicinal plant trade; the establishment of systems for inventorying and monitoring the status of medicinal plants; the development of sustainable harvesting practices; encouragement for microenterprise development by indigenous and rural communities; and the protection of traditional resource and intellectual property rights. Because so many species of plants are medicinal, medicinal plant conservation is, in some ways, a microcosm of plant conservation as a whole. Similar questions arise concerning identification of the most significant issues and most effective approaches. This is especially so given that, just because a species has been used somewhere medicinally, it does not follow that it is so used everywhere and at all times. In such cases, the challenges facing conservationists are similar to those encountered with other groups of plants singled out by 'plant conservationists' as special, for example because they have been classified by scientists as 'endangered', but which lack any special significance to other people. There can be aspects of medicinal plant conservation which plant conservationists can pursue, working largely outside the normal dynamics of people/plant relationships. Work of this type can sometimes be found, for instance, associated with seed-banks, information systems or 'totally protected' nature reserves. The fact that efforts are made in favour of medicinal plants, rather than plants of any other type, is incidental, except as regards the criteria used for the initial selection of species for attention. Most work by conservationists on medicinal plants should be with those people who own, manage or make use of these species, or else own or manage the land on which they grow. It is in working with such stakeholders that the special meanings of medicinal plants to people can best be 'exploited'. Billions of people in the world rely chiefly on herbal medicine, while millions gain income from their wild harvest or cultivation, or are involved in their trading or processing. Medicinal plants are symbolically significant in many cultures, often being seen as sources of power.

In other words, the significance of medicinal plants to people can be sufficiently great that arrangements made for the conservation and sustainable use of medicinal plants can lay important foundations for the conservation of natural habitats and ecological services more generally. Therefore the 'biological beneficiaries' of 'medicinal plant conservation' are not necessarily only the medicinal plants themselves. This is nowhere more so than in those remoter parts of the world where cultural and biological diversity tend to be most concentrated, and where medicinal plants can assume high importance in cultures and for livelihoods. Working effectively with communities requires conservationists to have an appreciation of the cultures, economies, social structures and dynamics of local societies, in addition to the knowledge that they need about the biology and ecology of the plants themselves. Similar 'lateral engagement' is also necessary for work with other classes of people involved with medicinal plants. For example, the main concerns of conservationists about manufacturers are likely to revolve around questions of the effects of their patterns of obtaining raw materials on the environment. However, manufacturers will often be more interested in other aspects of product quality than biological and ecological sustainability, especially those relating to quality control that involve species authentication, presence of active constituents, limitations to heavy metal content, and residues of pesticides and fertilizers. Conservationists working with manufacturers need to understand these facts of the business, just as they need to understand those of village life when working with communities. However, in doing so, they should never lose sight of their own conservation objectives. There are cultural differences in the ways that plants are classified according to their properties, for example, with less of a distinction between food and medicine in Eastern and African traditions than in the West. Medicinal plants are grouped for many commercial purposes in the broader category of 'medicinal and aromatic plants' (MAPs), covering not only plants used medicinally (as more strictly understood), but also for neighbouring and overlapping purposes, for instance as foods, condiments and cosmetics (Schippmann *et al.* 2002). The term 'botanicals' is becoming commonly used for a wide range of plant-based products.

Values of Medicinal Plants in the World

Plants in traditional medicine It is estimated that 70–80% of people worldwide rely chiefly on traditional, largely herbal, medicine to meet their primary healthcare needs (Pei 2001). The global demand for herbal medicine is not only large, but growing (Srivastava 2000). The market for Ayurvedic medicines is estimated to be expanding at 20% annually in India (Subrat 2002), while the quantity of medicinal plants obtained from just one province of China (Yunnan) has grown by 10 times in the last 10 years (Pei 2002b). Factors contributing to the growth in demand for traditional medicine include the increasing human population and the frequently inadequate provision of Western (allopathic) medicine in developing countries.

There are many traditional systems of medicine. Modified from a practice in China, they may be classified into three broad categories: (I) Traditional

Scholarly Medical Systems, with written traditions of documentation of knowledge, pharmacopoeias for doctors and institutions for training doctors; (II) Traditional Medical Knowledge (Folk Medicine), which is orally transmitted and associated with households, communities or ethnic groups; and (III) Shamanistic Medicine, with a strong spiritual element and which can only be applied by specialist practitioners (shamans). Traditional Scholarly Medical Systems are especially concentrated in Asia. Some of the more widely familiar are Chinese Traditional Medicine, Tibetan Medicine, Ayurveda, Siddha, Unani, and Western Herbal Medicine, the latter being rather ill-defined.

Medicinal Plants as Pharmaceutical Medicine

Plants have contributed hugely to Western medicine, through providing ingredients for drugs or having played central roles in drug discovery. Some drugs, having botanical origins, are still extracted directly from plants, others are made through transformation of chemicals found within them, while yet others are today synthesized from inorganic materials, but have their historical origins in research into the active compounds found in plants. There are undoubtedly many more secrets still hidden in the world of plants (Mendelsohn and Balick 1995).

Worldwide Use and Significance of Medicinal Species

In terms of the number of species individually targeted, the use of plants as medicines represents by far the biggest human use of the natural world. Plants provide the predominant ingredients of medicines in most medical traditions. There is no reliable figure for the total number of medicinal plants on Earth, and numbers and percentages for countries and regions vary greatly. Estimates for the numbers of species used medicinally include: 35 000 – 70 000 or 53 000 worldwide. The great majority of species of medicinal plants are used only in Folk Medicine. Traditional Scholarly Medical Systems employ relatively few: 500–600 commonly in Traditional Chinese Medicine (Pei 2001); 1430 in Mongolian Medicine (Pei 2002b); 1106–3600 in Tibetan Medicine (Pei 2001, 2002b); 1250–1400 in Ayurveda (Dev 1999); 342 in Unani; and 328 in Siddha (Shiva 1996). The number of plant species that provide ingredients for drugs used in Western Medicine is even fewer. It was calculated for an article published in 1991 that there were 121 drugs in current use in the USA derived from plants, with 95 species acting as sources (more than one drug is obtained from some species) (Farnsworth and Soejarto 1991). Despite the small number of source species, drugs derived from plants are of immense importance in terms of numbers of patients treated. The value of medicinal plants to human livelihoods is essentially infinite. They obviously make fundamental contributions to human health, and "is not health dearer than wealth". There is much trade in Medicinal and aromatic plants (MAPs), on scales ranging from the local to the international. Much of this is unrecorded in official statistics or poorly documented reasons why there is typically so little awareness among decision-makers of the significance of the trade to the healthcare and economies of their people, or about problems of unsustainability and the sometimes deleterious impacts of wild collection on natural habitats. Large quantities of MAPs are traded into urban centers from rural areas in developing countries, and also regionally and internationally. China's production of medicinal plants from cultivated and wild-harvested sources, considered together, was calculated at 1.6 million tonnes in 1996, with a total value (excluding exports) in terms of finished products of US$ 3.7 billion (Kuipers 1997). The reported annual imports of MAP material into all countries during the 1990s amounted to an average of 400 000 t, valued at US$ 1.2 billion, showing a 100% rise between 1991 and 1997 (Lange 2000). There are at least 2000 species of MAPs marketed in Europe, these originating from over 120 countries. Although virtually everyone on Earth benefits from medicinal plants, it is the financially poorest who are typically most closely dependent on medicinal plants culturally and for their medicines and income. Only 15% of pharmaceutical drugs is consumed in developing countries (Toledo 1995), and a large proportion of even this small percentage is taken by relatively more affluent people. The poor have little alternative to using herbal medicine, which, anyway, they may prefer at least for certain conditions (Marshall 1998). Medicinal plants can provide a significant source of income for rural people in developing countries, especially through the sale of wild-harvested material. The collectors are often herders, shepherds or other economically marginalised sections of the population, such as landless people and women. Between 50–100% of households in the northern part of central Nepal and about 25–50% in the middle part of the same region are involved in collecting medicinal plants for sale, the materials being traded to wholesale markets in Delhi (Olsen 1997). The money received represents 15–30% of the total income of poorer households. Medicinal plants can be symbolically very important to people. They can be held in special religious, nationalistic or ideological esteem. This can be advantageous for conservation efforts, given that it is an acknowledgement, well rooted in culture, of the worth of a sizeable proportion of the world's flora. But it also carries challenges, in that this can result in dogmatic views about the medicinal properties of plants, resistance to accepting equally effective substitutes, and uncompromising attitudes towards the ownership of the plants and who should benefit from (or pay for) their continuing existence. The subject of 'medicinal plants' can arouse strong feelings, providing opportunities for bringing key conservation debates into the public arena. There is similarity to the emotions surrounding charismatic species, such as elephants and whales, with the difference that medicinal plants carry much more universal appeal.

Important Concerns Surrounding Medicinal Plants

Concerns about loss of biological diversity and the availability of resources

More than one-tenth of plant species are used in drugs and health products, with more than 50,000 species being used. However, the distribution of medicinal plants is not uniform across the world. These concerns exist, for a large part, because most species of medicinal plants are collected from the wild. The total number of species of medicinal plants cultivated on any scale is few, although this does include some species of MAPs that are traded internationally in large volumes, as well as many of the (small) number of species used as starting points for pharmaceutical drugs. China is probably the country with the greatest acreage of medicinal plants under cultivation, but, even here, only 100–250 species are cultivated (Schippmann *et al.* 2002). Only 130–140 of the 1200–1300 species that are both traded in, and native to, Europe are derived predominantly from cultivation (Lange 1998). There are many parts of the world in which there is virtually no cultivation on any significant scale. An estimated 99% of the 400–550 species currently sold for use in traditional medicine in South Africa originate from wild sources (Williams 1996). There is no reliable estimate for the number of medicinal plants that are globally threatened, variously calculated as 4160 or 10 000 (Vorhies 2000; Schippmann *et al.* 2002). There would seem little doubt from theoretical considerations (Menges 1991) that many medicinal plant species that have been listed as threatened, and indeed others that have not, must be suffering from genetic erosion now, or will do so in the near future. This is because populations of many species are in retreat, with outlying populations being destroyed, as the extent and quality of many natural habitats decline (WWF and IUCN 1994–1997). However, genetic erosion among wild plants is very poorly documented. The advantage of maintaining a pool of genetic diversity within a medicinal species can be illustrated with reference to Arnica (Arnica montana), a popular, but endangered, European medicinal plant, in which genes from wild populations have been used successfully to breed superior cultivated strains (Ellenberger 1998). The number of species of medicinal plants known to have become globally extinct is very few and conservationists are advised to avoid exaggerated claims in this respect. It has been estimated that over-exploitation threatens 150 species of MAPs in at least one European country (Lange 1998), but it should not be deduced from this that many, if any, of these species are in danger of complete continental extinction. On the other hand, the seriousness of local, national or regional extinction, or, indeed, of commercial extinction should not be under-estimated. There can be serious consequences for livelihoods and economies, quite apart from issues of genetic conservation. Many of the threats to medicinal plant species are similar to those causing endangerment to plant diversity generally. The most serious proximate threats generally are habitat loss, habitat degradation and over-harvesting (Hamilton 1997). Medicinal plants can have other uses than as sources of medicines, and the threats from over-harvesting may be due, or partly due, to collection for purposes other than medicinal. This is so in the case of the African trees Acacia senegal, Boswellia papyrifera and Pterocarpus angolensis (Marshall 1998). As far as collection for medicines is concerned, there is general agreement that it is collection for commercial trade rather than home-use that is overwhelmingly the problem. One reason why medicinal plants have become increasingly threatened has been the weakening of customary laws that traditionally have regulated the use of natural resources. Such laws have often proved to be easily undermined by modern socioeconomic forces (Pant 2002). In the case of commercial collection of Prunus africana in Cameroon (Cunningham *et al.* 1997; Ekola *et al.* 2000; Schippmann 2001), the collapse of customary institutions seems to have been connected directly to changes in the ways that this plant was exploited, and this may be a widespread phenomenon. Concerns about loss of medicinal plants, considered as material resources, relate to worries about healthcare, livelihood security and financial income. Among those for whom these problems are most acute are the rural poor, reliant on medicinal plants growing close to their homes for their healthcare and sometimes an income. Manufacturers and consumers, higher up commercial systems, are less influenced by local scarcities of resources, often being insulated by manufacturers switching their sources of supply. Unsustainable harvesting practices result in spreading frontiers of resource depletion, with the negative impacts of over-exploitation confined to the local level until such time as regional or global resource scarcity becomes critical. Poorer members of local communities can face additional problems of loss of access to medicinal plants due to the privatization or nationalization of land. There is a major trend today in many developing countries towards stricter individual ownership of land and plant resources, replacing older forms of tenure and resource rights in which poorer people could be less excluded. Loss of access through nationalization can occur with the creation of more strongly protected types of conservation area.

Concerns about Declines in Local Knowledge and Cultural Survival

Knowledge of medicinal plants, as once embedded in tens of thousands of indigenous cultures, is rapidly disappearing. Every year, the sum total of human knowledge about the types, distribution, ecology, methods of management and methods of extracting the useful properties of medicinal plants is declining rapidly a continuation of a process of loss of local cultural diversity that has been underway for hundreds of years. There has, of course, been a great growth in scientific information about medicinal plants in recent decades, but in many ways this has proved poor compensation, because such information is often inaccessible at field level or is irrelevant to the problems faced by land managers, or collectors or growers of medicinal plants. Knowledge of the natural world is typically a very important part of the knowledge-worlds of rural people following more traditional ways of life (Berlin 1992). Further, medicinal plants tend to figure prominently in these galaxies. It is therefore not surprising that the revitalization of traditional systems of medicine can be high on the agendas of those promoting local and indigenous cultures, a political trend in many parts of the world.

Concerns Relating to the Availability and Quality of Healthcare Services

The adequate provision of healthcare is threatened by declines in traditional medical knowledge and related plant resources. There are many people, notably in developing countries, who lack and will continue to lack for the foreseeable future effective access to Western medicine, while even those who do enjoy this privilege will be limited in their choices of alternative therapies. The increasing nationalization of medicine during the 19th and, especially, the 20th century and the rise in the power of pharmaceutical companies have given even further impetus to Western Medicine. Until recently, and then only in some countries, national healthcare systems have devoted all, or nearly all, their resources to the promotion and delivery of Western Medicine, ignoring other traditions. This is now changing, more so in some countries (such as China and India) than others, but, even so, some medical traditions, such as Tibetan Medicine in Nepal, have yet to gain official recognition (unlike Ayurvedic Medicine, which is officially recognised). Lack of official recognition and associated support has implications for conservation, because such recognition can raise the status of practitioners at village level. Since such practitioners are generally the people most knowledgeable about plants in their communities and have an intrinsic interest in their conservation, an increase in their authority has the potential to greatly assist improved management of plant resources. From the point of view of efficient and effective provision of national healthcare, a problem facing those countries which acknowledge the value of traditional medicine is how best to utilise the resources available. One approach is to provide official recognition to traditional medicine, which is then permitted to operate as a separate sector parallel to and largely unconnected with the main Western medical services provided by the state. Other countries, such as China, are attempting synthesis through trying to draw on the best of different traditions. Official recognition has several implications, including the desirability of registering authentic practitioners and supporting their training. There is also the question of how best to develop traditional systems to meet modern challenges. The environment in which traditional medical practitioners are operating today is not the same as in the past (Craig 2002). Payment for treatment is now more frequently being requested, associations of traditional medical practitioners are being formed for networking and political lobbying, and there is a move towards professionalisation, including towards instruction based in schools rather than through lineages. Authentication of traditional medicine is both a cultural and physiological matter and requires more than just trials similar to those used to test pharmaceutical drugs. Sensitive techniques are needed to avoid unnecessary prohibitions. Due attention needs to be given to traditional standards of quality, which, in Ayurveda, for example, classically refer to cultural and tantric use as well as therapeutic qualities (Misra 2002). Concerns relating to the terms of research on medicinal plants This has become the most publicised area of 'policy debate' relating to medicinal plants. It is a field in which "there has been a polarisation and we've ended up arguing over who is in the wrong" (Sanesh Kishore, quoted by Macilwain 1998). In part, the issues can be traced back to the Convention on Biological Diversity (CBD), agreed at the Earth Summit in Rio de Janeiro in 1992. There are also unresolved conflicts concerning intellectual property rights (IPRs) between the CBD and the Trade Related Aspects of Intellectual Property Rights (TRIPS) of the World Trade Organisation (WTO) (Masood 1998). Parties to the CBD accept that biodiversity is the property and responsibility of states, that the components of this biodiversity should be used sustainably, and that there should be a just sharing of the benefits arising out of the utilisation of genetic resources. Some of the concerns have arisen because of knowledge, or suspicion, that some scientists, research institutes or commercial enterprises have taken samples of plants to test for new products, such as pharmaceutical drugs, without due permission or on ethically unacceptable terms [Commonwealth Secretariat 2001, originally from Dutfield (2003) and GRAIN (2000)]. The worry is that there will be no, or inadequate, benefits accruing to the countries and communities from where the materials originate. There are also concerns about the theft of local or indigenous intellectual property, given that the traditional uses of plants as medicines can be useful guides for the development of new drugs (Holmstedt and Bruhn 1995; Balick and Cox 1996). Proponents of local and indigenous rights argue that traditional knowledge of the uses of plants can be based on years, perhaps millennia, of experimentation, and therefore it is not only scientists or pharmaceutical companies that can claim to be inventors (scientists do so through the filing of patents). There is also an argument that local and indigenous communities have acted historically as the keepers, or even developers, of biological diversity, and thus should be 'compensated' by those who benefit later from their care and labour. On the other hand, there are accusations that some countries and territories have over-reacted to the scares of biopiracy and theft of intellectual resources through creating such tight restrictions over research as to potentially cause serious setbacks to conservation and sustainable development (Rohter 2001; Revkin 2002). It is highly likely that issues surrounding medicinal plants (especially) have been largely responsible for these alleged over-reactions. Probably, there are often misconceptions about the relative prominence that research aimed at bioprospecting should have (compared with research having other objectives), the extent of bioprospecting and the amounts of money to be made (Laird 2002).

Medicinal Plant Conservation Approaches

An ecosystem-based approach is endorsed by the CBD and is appropriate for conservation of medicinal plants. It encourages lateral thinking, inter-disciplinarity and prioritisation. The ecosystem-based approach of the CBD, as encompassed in its 12 principles, recognises that:

- humans, with their cultural diversity, form an integral component of biodiversity; the delimitation of ecosystems for conservation action needs to be defined conceptually on scales appropriate to the problems being addressed;
- work can involve all three objectives of the Convention, requiring the striking of a balance between them;
- there are uncertainties in managing ecosystems and, consequently, a need for conservation measures to contain elements of 'learning-by-doing' or feedback from research;
- the approach needs to be used flexibly, so that other approaches to management and conservation can be incorporated, such as protected areas and single-species conservation programmes;
- benefits need to accrue to those responsible for producing and managing the benefits derived from ecosystems, with a special emphasis on local communities; and
- networks are needed for the sharing of experiences and information.

In view of the inherent uncertainties, the CBD recommends an adaptive approach to interventions and management. This requires the establishment of indicators to monitor the effects of new measures, so that the need to make adjustments can be recognized. Conservationists should periodically take time to reflect fundamentally on their work, drawing back from deep immersion in particular matters. The desirability of changes in emphasis or taking on new types of activity may become apparent. Activists (conservationists) will be essential to ensure the success of efforts to conserve medicinal plants. The work should be designed to influence the ways that resource managers, traders, manufacturers, consumers or members of other defined social groups go about their normal business. What is required is the institutionalization of new activities in favour of conservation. The attainment of institutionalization requires the taking of responsibility by the various stakeholders involved, and therefore conservationists need to be careful in how much they take a lead themselves, balancing this with encouraging the development of initiatives by those who are more fundamentally parts of the systems. Conservationists can expect progress normally to be slow, though hopefully with occasional breakthroughs. The systems involved in medicinal plant conservation tend to be complex, with many variables and many types of actual or potential stakeholders. For the sake of presentation, four distinct sub-systems are recognised here, namely (1) production systems and in situ conservation, (2) commercial systems, (3) ex situ conservation, propagation, domestication and the breeding of crop varieties, and (4) new product discovery (Figure 1), though actually all can be closely connected. It is emphasised that the heart of medicinal plant conservation should be aimed at securing robust management systems in favour of conservation or sustainable production (or both) at the sites where the medicinal plants grow. Given the diversity of field contexts, most 'medicinal plant conservation projects' should be field projects rather than projects of any other type. It will be noted from the brief descriptions of approaches that follow that many measures, which can be taken in favour of conservation, are essentially indirect. They include changes in laws and in the purchasing practices of companies and consumers, the compilation of databases, the ex situ preservation of germplasm in seed banks, and so on. What should be borne in mind is that all such measures will be essentially useless for supporting in situ conservation and sustainable development unless they 'feedback' positively to the field level. Unless due attention is paid, then 'distant' conservation measures, taken with good intent, may be ineffective or even backfire. Take the case of medicinal plants and Bwindi Impenetrable forest in Uganda. The upgrading of Bwindi from being a Forest and Game Reserve to a National Park in 1991 was a reaction to the rampant level of illegal activities, such as timber harvesting, hunting and gold-mining, that previously prevailed (Cunningham 1996). Following parks policy at the time, this declaration resulted in a total ban on the collection of all forest produce, including medicinal plants. What was not taken adequately into account, however, was the impact of this tough new regime on local livelihoods and attitudes. One of the items no longer legally available was the bark of Nyakibazi (Rytygynia spp.), a product so highly valued for medicinal purposes that, without it, declared the people, "they would die". Conflict over this and other matters resulted in an increase in cases of deliberate burning of the forest and threats being made against the mountain gorillas, the flagship species of the forest. The conflict was later partially defused through the formulation of agreements on local rights and responsibilities, allowing regulated collection of Nyakibazi and other natural products from the park (Hamilton *et al.* 2000).

Production Systems and in Situ Conservation Approaches

In many ways, the approaches and methodologies used to promote the in situ conservation and sustainable production of medicinal plants differ little, in principle, from those used for conservation and sustainable use of plant diversity generally. In particular, there are many similarities to those used for other categories of wild plants that are harvested as resources, especially those subject to the pressures of commercial trade. The types and levels of activities that are possible will vary greatly between projects, depending on the resources of time and money available, as well as the particular interests and competencies of those involved. In any event, it is desirable for project teams to be multidisciplinary, preferably with coverage of the biological, ecological, cultural, economic and political dimensions of ecosystems. At least some members of project teams should have an understanding of both the biological and social dimensions of the ecosystems. Interventions will stand less chance of being successful if conservation teams consist solely of different types of specialist, without such linking expertise. This is why knowledge of applied ethnobotany is so desirable (Cunningham 2001a; Hamilton *et al.* 2002). (Ethnobotany is the subject that deals with the relationships between people and plants; applied ethnobotany is ethnobotany applied to conservation and sustainable development.) The range of possible actions in favour of in situ conservation and sustainable use is vast (Aumeeruddy-Thomas *et al.* 1999; Cunningham 2001a; Tuxill and Nabhan 2001; Hamilton *et al.* 2002).

The purposes of a project need to be made clear to stakeholders at the outset and revised periodically, as necessary, with local participation as the project proceeds. Because of the interconnections between different components of ecosystems, it will generally be impossible to make progress on matters of prime concern to those instigating a project without some engagement in matters, which, at first sight, might seem peripheral. For example, the objective of a project could be the conservation of local populations of species of MAPs that are globally threatened. However, to achieve this objective might require engagement in a range of 'developmental' activities. Some of these might seem more obviously relevant, such as the strengthening of certain community institutions, but others might seem less so, such as measures to improve livelihood security, healthcare facilities or local income. It is a matter of judgement and experience how far conservation projects should include developmental matters. The experience of FRLHT in southern India is that the involvement of communities in conservation of medicinal plants cannot be achieved without addressing the healthcare concerns of the people.

The failure of many integrated conservation and development projects (ICDPs) in the past should not be interpreted as showing that conservation does not need to be integrated with development nor, indeed, that local communities should not be fundamentally involved in conservation projects (Wells *et al.* 1999; Peterson 2001; Wilshusen *et al.* 2002). Rather, their failure is thought to be due to a delinking of conservation and development ("we will help you with development, if you don't touch the forest") and loss of a sense of purpose (and therefore authority) among some conservation agencies, which have increasingly seen their roles as taking responsibility for structural problems, such as poverty, market failures, corruption and the global economic order, rather than getting on with tackling practical problems on the ground (Brandon *et al.* 1998). Current ICDP thinking tends towards an emphasis on building support for conservation based on local cultural and economic concerns, full use of traditional ecological knowledge, and negotiations about the rights and responsibilities of the various stakeholders (Langton 2000; Naughton-Treves and Weber 2001). The involvement of local communities will almost invariably be a fundamental ingredient of in situ projects aimed at medicinal plant conservation. One reason, crudely stated, is that it is not difficult, in many parts of the world, for collectors of medicinal plants (whether members of local communities or outsiders) to harvest medicinal plants unsustainably or illegally, if the only controls present are those associated with government officials (e.g., Dold and Cocks 2001). It is even easier to avoid detection in the case of many medicinals than with timber, which is illegally harvested on massive scales in some countries. Conservation agencies, such as Park and Forest Departments, often suffer from shortages of resources and sometimes also work in conditions of political instability (Hamilton *et al.* 2000). Apart from the problems that they face in regulating medicinal plants, government agencies, acting alone, are liable to have little control over many other activities that can endanger medicinal plants, which may include excessive grazing by livestock, the harvesting of plants for other purposes apart from medicinal (for fuelwood, fodder, etc.) and excessive burning. The forms of relationships between project teams, local communities and other local stakeholders, established at the onset of work, are critical. These relationships may well be unwritten and relatively informal, but the tone that they set is important if more precise agreements are needed later, including if possibilities of commercial opportunities emerge based on local biodiversity or knowledge (Laird 2002). Projects are also liable to go through a period of confidence-building as trust is established. Whatever the initial purposes of a project, it is important that priorities are periodically re-evaluated. As work proceeds, it will often be found that presumptions about priorities at the onset of projects are inaccurate, for instance concerning the abundance and vulnerability of medicinal or other types of plants (Martin 1995; Lama *et al.* 2001). Successful conservation depends on the existence of rules and regulations, and a reasonable degree of compliance to them. Property rights and terms of access to resources are critical factors (Subedi 2002). It is especially important to ensure that the interests of those people in communities whose lives are most dependent on MAPs are properly accommodated. Despite reported successes of joint or participatory forest management in India and Nepal, the MAP sector has often been inadequately covered. For instance, in Nepal there are frequent difficulties, relating to a general neglect of NTFPs, excessive restrictions on access, heavy taxes and rent-seeking (Subedi 2002).

Both customary and statutory laws will often be relevant to medicinal plant conservation. Each type of legal system has its merits and disadvantages, and a critical question facing conservationists will often be how they can best be combined so that their positive elements are strengthened, while avoiding a process of mutual undermining (Pant 2002). Analysis of the effectiveness of the two types of laws in India and Nepal shows that there can be considerable strength still remaining in customary institutions, but that they often need reinforcement today, as, for example, through their official recognition by government agencies (Wade 1987; Pant 2002). Protected areas, established through statutory law, can be very useful for the conservation of medicinal plants. There are many types (national parks, forest reserves, strict nature reserves, etc.), generally serving various purposes in addition to biodiversity conservation, and with various rules applying to the conservation and collection of medicinal plants. Generally, medicinal plant issues have proved to be low among the priorities of the responsible agencies. In India, for example, the Forest Department is much more interested in timber than non-timber forest products (NTFPs) and, within the broad category of NTFPs, often in other types of products apart from medicinal plants (especially those regarded as being financially more lucrative) (Jain 2000). The range of measures which can be taken to conserve medicinal plants in protected areas differs little from those that can be applied elsewhere, with the essential difference of an extra layer of legal protection. This means that the rights of communities and other 'outside' parties will be more circumscribed than they are in the general landscape (although, it may be noted, the rights of individual people outside protected areas will depend greatly on systems of land tenure and whether they are private landowners). Agreements between communities and agencies responsible for protected areas will be necessary if collection of medicinal plants is to be controlled. This legal necessity can create exceptional opportunities to strengthen biodiversity conservation generally – not just in favour of those particular species of medicinal plants which receive specific attention. This is because of the special status that medicinal plants can hold in local societies, related to their symbolic, healing and economic properties. Agreements on medicinal plants can form firm bases for improved management of protected areas generally. If cultivation is introduced in the support zones of protected areas, then the provision of assistance by agencies to encourage this development can usefully be tied to agreements which enhance the participation of communities in conservation of the protected areas. Various, often isolated, initiatives are being tried to link conservation and livelihoods through a focus on medicinal plants. A project of the WWF-Nepal Programme with the People and Plants Initiative (PPI), at Shey Phoksundo National Park, is developing community-based systems for the sustainable harvesting of medicinal plants, combined with the strengthening of local medical services as provided by amchis (practitioners of Tibetan Medicine) (Lama *et al.* 2001). The amchis are identified as key members of the communities for promotion of conservation, with their allied interests in plant diversity and livelihoods. The Forest Department of the Great Himalayan National Park, India, is promoting cultivation of medicinal plants as an income-generating enterprise linked to conservation (Pandy and Tandon 2002). The emphasis is on women, in recognition of their economically marginalised status and their special interest in plant resources. By 2002, 92 Women Saving and Credit Groups had been formed involving 930 people. FRLHT is active across the southern cone of India with an integrated programme of conservation, health security and livelihood support, centred around medicinal plants and plant-based medicine (Mrudula 2002). FRLHT encourages the foundation of micro-credit groups, and seeks to prioritise health problems and related local remedies. Species in demand, and also endemic and threatened species, are grown in nurseries, and planted out in demonstration plots, home gardens, and for enrichment planting in areas of degraded forest (ca. 200–300 ha in size). Steps are taken to encourage the transmission of medical knowledge between generations. The FRLHT model is proving successful and becoming adopted elsewhere in India. Monitoring is an essential aspect of effective management. A key question in the case of medicinal plants is the selection of species to monitor (Cunningham 2001a; Lama *et al.* 2001). Certain species are of greater cultural or economic significance to communities or agencies, and there is a greater chance that monitoring programmes will give good results if these are included as indicators. The vulnerability of species to commercial collection depends on the parts of plants used and how they are collected. For example, the collection of underground organs, as is the case with many species in the Himalayas (Aumeeruddy-Thomas 2002), is liable to be more damaging that if leaves are targeted, as is the case with many species used in tropical forest areas of Africa. Populations of specialist species associated with habitats of restricted occurrence, as Mecanopsis spp. in the Himalayas, can easily be decimated (Xie *et al.* 2002). Some countries have laws specifically giving protection to wild plants, some of which may be medicinal. The UK Wildlife and Countryside Act (1981) prohibits the uprooting of any species of wild plant, except by landowners and other authorized people. In several Italian regions, Austrian La¨nder and Swiss cantons, not only is the uprooting or the collection of subterranean parts of plants prohibited, but there are restrictions on the gathering of aerial parts as well. The number of flowering stems or branches that may be picked varies from 5 to 20, or a handful, according to local regulations. Only a few countries have laws specifically for medicinal plants (Lange 1998). In Nepal, the collection, sale, transportation and export of Dactylorhiza hatagirea, Juglans regia and Picrorhiza scrophulariifolia are all banned, while other species are specifically banned for export (Aryal 2002).

However, in many parts of the world, for instance Africa and India, laws protecting wild plants are little known by the general public or, indeed, even among those charged with their enforcement (Marshall 1998; Jain 2000). Cultivation is frequently advocated as a measure to take the pressure off wild stocks, especially for species collected in large quantities for trade (Lange 1998; Bodeker 2002). Cultivation can be commercially attractive to companies, because they then have greater control over quality and supply (Harnischfeger 2000). Various factors influence the feasibility of cultivation, its impact on conservation and by whom it is best undertaken. If volumes required and market prices are both high, then cultivation is more likely to be economically feasible. The introduction of medicinal plants into home gardens is seen as a useful means of providing accessible cures for common ailments and supplementary income (Schippmann *et al.* 2002). Medicinal plants have been introduced successfully into traditional farming systems in Guatemala, providing regular income to farmers (Eid 2000). If cultivation is to be introduced, then there can be many problems inhibiting success – for instance, in India, lack of knowledge of cultivation and post-harvest techniques for some species, and lack of availability of planting material of good quality (Uniyal 2000). If a species has not previously been in cultivation, then domestication may be needed, which can prove a difficult, expensive and lengthy process (Kuipers 1997). There should be public funding for domestication programmes for those many species of MAPs which are highly endangered but which economically or otherwise are unlikely to become domesticated, as has been proposed for the Eastern Cape Province of South Africa (Dold and Cocks 2001). There can be advantages to wild collection over cultivation. From the medical viewpoint, there is a widespread belief that wild-harvested material is more efficacious, as is sometimes reflected in higher prices. Asian buyers will pay up to 30 times more for wild-harvested roots of American Ginseng (Panax quinquefolius) than for those from cultivated sources. On the other hand, 82% of healers interviewed in the Eastern Cape Province of South Africa stated that they would readily make use of cultivated plants, possibly (according to the researchers) because they recognise that wild supplies are declining (Dold and Cocks 2001). The social benefits of wild harvest too can be considerable, given that it is generally the most economically and socially marginalised members of communities that are so involved (Lange 1998). Even if cultivation is introduced, then this may be adopted by relatively well-off people, with better access to land, financial capital or information. The landless and other disadvantaged sectors of society may fail to benefit, but rather continue to collect just as before. Another important factor is that individual land-holdings can be very small and farmers are likely to adopt a high risk strategy in terms of livelihood security if they convert from food crops to MAPs. For example, in the Himalayas, topographic and demographic factors limit the size of agricultural land per family often to only 0.4–1 ha (Karki 2002). However, from the conservation viewpoint, perhaps the strongest argument for retaining or promoting wild harvesting is that this will then maintain links between people and the intricacies of their local natural worlds (Hamilton 2001). The successful conservation of biodiversity will always require the existence of people who know about such details and care enough for their existence that they will make efforts to retain them. Without this type of involvement, there is little cultural base at the local level on which to build support for national or global conservation goals.

Commercial System Approaches

Some conservationists interested in MAPs should become engaged with the commercial sector, both because it is the pressures of trade that are responsible for so much MAP endangerment, and also, more positively, because of the opportunities which engagement with industry and consumers presents. Various social groups are involved in commercial systems, including producers (collectors or growers), traders of various types, manufacturers and consumers (Figure 3). Apart from self-regulation, commercial systems for MAPs are subject to many types of standard, statutory or otherwise. Conservationists can become engaged in various ways, including helping to formulate and promote appropriate standards, supplying relevant information to the parties involved, and also putting parties in touch with each other. Because of the connections between different parts of commercial systems, it will often be productive to work simultaneously with different types of stakeholder. Thus, it can make sense to work simultaneously both with producers (to improve their management systems) and manufacturers (to make their purchasing of raw materials more conservation-friendly). In any event, what is vital is that changes in the behavior of those at the 'top' of the trade chains (e.g., traders, manufacturers and consumers) feedback to the production level, otherwise efforts will have been in vain. In many countries, the MAP sector is economically liberalised and in the hands of private enterprise. In such cases, commercial systems tend to be complex, poorly integrated vertically and secretive. There is very little overlap in the UK between the trading systems relating to traditional European herbal medicine, Chinese Traditional Medicine, Ayurveda and Unani (Dennis 1998). Bhutan has a central system which controls the harvesting of medicinal plants – made into medicines in the capital Thimpu and then the distribution of the medicinesto hospitals throughout the country. In China, there is one major business, the state-owned Company of Chinese Medical Crude Drugs, which is responsible for the bulk of the collection and distribution of raw medicinal plant materials, but there are several major manufacturers of Chinese Traditional Medicine, some under national and others under private ownership. The collapse of Communist regimes in eastern Europe resulted in considerable deregulation of state-controlled commerce in MAPs and a weakening of pre-existing quota-controlled harvesting structures (Lange 1998). As a result, the number of traders in MAPs has increased and wild collection has grown in an unregulated fashion, with associated conservation concerns. In Bulgaria, an element of socialist centralisation remains. The main national dealer in MAPs is Bulgarcoop, a co-operative enterprise, but this is joined today by many small, largely family owned, businesses. Both Bulgarcoop and 50–60 of the businesses (the latter acting collectively through the 'Private Herb Exchange') provide help to growers with cultivation and guarantees to purchase harvests (Lange 1998). Standard-setting with regard to MAPs is a complex business, more so than with timber (which will be a point of comparison for some conservationists) (Pierce and Laird, in press). The complexity is due to the variety of harvesting and socioeconomic circumstances, the complexity of the chains of custody through which materials travel, the wide range of markets (local to international) and the numerous types of product. The latter include not only medicines, but also foods, food supplements, fragrances and personal care products. Quite a number of therapeutic products made from MAPs are marketed as food supplements or herbal tonics, rather than medicines, avoiding the stricter regulations that apply to the latter. The main concerns of the industry (and consumers) as regards standards normally relate to medical efficacy and safety (Pierce and Laird, in press). In terms of botanical ingredients, these concerns translate into specific requirements, most basically that MAP materials or products really are made from the right species, but also concerning the parts of the plants used, the times of harvest, the levels of active principles, and the contents of pollutants. It is not unusual for species to be sold incorrectly labelled (Harnischfeger 2000). Aside from these medical concerns, some enterprises (and consumers) are also interested in social justice, for instance relating to the distribution of financial benefits received from the trade, and the fair treatment of women and children. There are major questions of social justice in the MAP sector, because of the very low prices generally paid to collectors and, allegedly, the maintenance of artificially high prices by a monopoly of wholesale distributors (Heywood 2000). Environmental concerns may not be restricted solely to matters strictly related to biological conservation or the sustainability of harvesting. Some environmental standards, such as those relating to organic accreditation, only relate partially to biological conservation. Many manufacturers, at least in some countries, are said to care little about the standards of quality of the material they purchase (Begum 2002). If manufacturers actually are interested in conservation, then they are faced with the problem of knowing whether the raw materials that they purchase are derived from plants harvested or grown in ways that promote this objective. Manufacturers commonly think about conservation, in this context, in terms of sustainability. In general, even the most environmentally inclined manufacturers will find it impossible to guarantee that all their sources of medicinal plants are sustainable. Many manufacturers buy largely from wholesalers (some of the biggest of which, in Europe, are in Germany). They do so because they then can be more certain that stocks of reliable quality are available, prices are relatively low and purchasing is easy. Therefore, a problem for environmentally inclined manufacturers is how to learn about the origins of MAP materials on sale. Some wholesalers are reluctant to provide information about their sources, fearing that manufacturers might use this information to side-step them in the future. It has been suggested that one way that manufacturers might be able to obtain greater assurance of sustainability is through the incorporation of conservation criteria in the specification sheets which they prepare for the formulation of products (Laird *et al.* 2003). They can then require wholesalers to confirm that they have met these standards or lose out to other suppliers. Some manufacturers may be able to encourage higher conservation standards through their more direct sourcing of MAP materials. Likewise, ethical producers may be able to 'jump up' market chains, for instance selling MAP materials directly to manufacturers. Collectors and growers often benefit from being organized into associations of co-operatives, including to increase their negotiating power (Pandy and Tandon 2002; Rastogi 2002). The US-based Rocky Mountain Herbalist Coalition (www.herbcoalition.wildspecies.com) provides a list of ecologically conscious suppliers of botanicals. Direct sourcing or marketing is not without its drawbacks. Manufacturers may be faced with higher costs and reduced reliability in supplies. For communities, social and economic problems can arise if traditional trading relationships are broken. Probably, direct sourcing is likely to remain a preferred option mainly for manufacturers of 'quality' products aimed at specialized markets, in which there is an ability to pay the higher prices required. Nevertheless, there are probably many unrealised opportunities for more direct sourcing awaiting discovery by enterprising communities and manufacturers. Given the concerns of at least some manufacturers and consumers to produce, or use, medicines of good quality, there would seem to be opportunities for communities, perhaps motivated by NGOs, to seek market advantage for themselves through adopting higher environmental standards and establishing direct market linkages. An incremental approach is probably often realistic, starting, for instance, from first meeting organic standards, with full certification of sustainability (a complex undertaking) a more distant possibility. If cultivation is attempted, then it is important to select suitable species from the agronomic and economic perspectives, the number of which may be quite limited for any particular site. An example, which so far is proving successful at promoting a socially and environmentally ethical trade, is the project, mentioned earlier, of the NGO CRIAA SA-DC on Devil's Claw (Harpagophytum procumbens). Devil's Claw has become a very popular remedy in Europe, but the plant has been unsustainably harvested in the past and it has even been held that it could be in danger of extinction (Laird 1999). Between 10 000 and 15 000 harvesters rely on sales from its collection as their only source of cash (Cole and Lombard 2000). In 1998, a sustainably harvested Devil's Claw project was established at one resettlement farm in Namibia and the scheme rapidly expanded. In 1999, the project covered some 307 415 ha of rangeland and 10 210 kg of Devil's Claw were produced, providing local people with a sustainable product at a guaranteed and fair price. Dave Cole and Cyril Lombard (Cole and Lombard 2000) write that: "We have been able to demonstrate through this project that by ensuring good prices, by making information available, by creating options, by strengthening their bargaining position and by providing general support, harvesters are taking responsibility for the management of this resource. Compliance with sustainable harvesting techniques, that is, leaving the tap-root undisturbed and refilling the hole, for example, has increased to between 80 and 85%. This is generally not the case in other areas where Devil's Claw is extensively harvested in Namibia". A lesson from various experiences is the need to involve a wide range of partners from the start, including not only the farmers, but traders, the government, NGOs and scientists as well, so that the necessary linkages and access to technical expertise are established. The involvement of industry from project inception can help ensure that products will be purchased at agreed prices, taking note of required species and standards of quality. Marketing is a critical issue for the success of organised collectors' or growers' schemes (Begum 2002). Obstacles to progress can include cumbersome systems of required permits (relating to permission to grow the plants and transport the products), lack of good quality planting material, problems with cultivation practices and access to markets. The Devil's Claw is a trend-setter. It has demonstrated the need for dedication and persistence with this approach.

There is a wide range of laws, regulations and guidelines (with various degrees of official recognition) relating to MAPs. Some of the foci of standards along the botanical supply chain are shown in Figure 4 (Pierce and Laird, in press). Actually, biological conservation and sustainability rarely figure prominently in these standards, being, for example, mentioned with very little practical detail in recent proposals for good harvesting practice (GHP) for collecting plant material (Harnischfeger 2000). Nevertheless, there can be significant opportunities for conservationists in commenting on standards produced by official bodies, recommending improvements in favour of conservation. The World Health Organisation (WHO) is currently developing good sourcing practice guidelines, which may contain an annex on sustainability; if so, they will provide a global point of reference for more local conservation efforts. WHO first published guidelines for good manufacturing practice (GMP) for medicines and herbal products in 1969, recommending these to member states. The aim was to guarantee the consistent quality of medicinal products. The guidelines contained no provision requiring proof of sustainable production, inclusion of which would have stimulated the development of sustainability criteria (Garg *et al.* 2002). In Europe, the European Herb Growers Association (EUROPAM) is currently developing good agricultural practice (GAP) and good wild harvesting practice (GWHP) guidelines for MAPs (www.europam.net). These might be included in the European Union (EU) Directive on Good Manufacturing Practice for Starting Materials, if and when this directive becomes operational. The GAP guidelines are more or less finalised and have already been endorsed by the European Medicine Evaluation Agency (EMEA). They are weak from the sustainability perspective. There might possibly be a greater chance of incorporating sustainability criteria in the GWHP guidelines, since these are still under active development. There is an EU Directive on Traditional Medicinal Products nearing completion. This deals mainly with issues of efficacy and safety, and apparently will contain nothing on conservation and sustainable production. In the case of China, a new law came into effect in June 2002 relating to the standards of traditional medicines. The main purpose is the regulation of products produced by larger enterprises. The law was introduced because of concerns about inadequate supplies, toxicity (pesticides in the case of cultivated plants; contaminants from plastic wrappings) and lack of standardisation of ingredients (medicines carrying the same name are not always formulated in the same way). The law will require various types of information to be supplied with each batch of MAP material, including the botanical name, the place of origin, the time of harvest and the level of insect contamination. Material of cultivated origin will require information on the fertilisers and pesticides used, and on heavy metal content. Quotas will be set for the quantities of species allowed for wild harvest in particular areas. This is a framework law and regulations for individual species will follow. The current government target in China is to ensure that 50 species of MAPs are cultivated according to GAP by 2010 (Pei 2002b). Some countries have laws that regulate the commercial collection or trade of MAPs. Poland lists species of MAPs that cannot be collected without permit. An Italian law of 1931 stipulates that permits for the commercial collection of species that are listed will only be issued to people who have degrees in herbalism from schools of pharmacy. Bulgaria has established a quota system for the gathering of certain MAPs that is reviewed annually, according to species and region. Countries may also ban exports, as did the Government of India in 1994 for 50 species believed to be endangered in the wild (this list was later reduced by one-third following representations by the herbal industry) (Bodeker 2002).

To return to the matter of standards, it is known that there can be problems in adherence because there are so many types of standards and some of the requirements are cumbersome to meet (Pierce and Laird, in press). Furthermore, the expense involved in meeting some standards means that they can be discriminatory against small producers. Another issue is that conservation organisations have had problems in devising useful messages for consumers, related to the challenge of combining simplicity with accuracy. A general warning that some medicinal plants are threatened (while most are not) is hardly helpful. No unified label exists today that guarantees sustainability. Fortunately, there is a ground-swell in sections of the industry to improve their conservation standards, partly in recognition that, unless they do so voluntarily, they may well be forced to do it by law. There is also a sizeable market, especially in more affluent countries, for environmentally friendly products. At present, the best that can be expected generally is that some manufacturers will gain just recognition for their environmental efforts and will accordingly be rewarded by concerned consumers. It might also be useful for a few species which should be avoided by consumers to be identified and publicised, but these have yet to be authoritatively listed. Because presumably most consumers have some interest in the standards of efficacy and safety of medicines, and at least some of them are concerned also about social justice and the environment, it would be useful for conservationists to explore the possibility of establishing a unitary concept of 'quality', covering all of these matters (Pierce and Laird, in press). If so, this could be followed by the development of a system of labelling, with a chance of general recognition, guaranteeing the quality of products containing MAPs across the board. This would greatly help the ethical consumer. Such labeled products should be third-party certified.

Propagation, Domestication, Ex situ Conservation and the Breeding of Crop Variety Approaches

Plant species can be found away from the sites where they naturally occur in a range of contexts, including in botanic and other types of gardens, nurseries, seed banks, tissue culture units, etc. In fact, ex situ conservation is not always sharply separated from in situ conservation. There are intermediates between the 'purest' forms of in situ and ex situ conservation, as represented possibly, on the one hand, by the total protection of wild populations of species without any other form of management and, on the other hand, by seed banks with specialist scientists situated at a far distance from the places where the plants naturally grow. The term circa situ conservation has been used for a range of practices commonly associated especially with more traditional (and biodiversity-rich) agricultural systems (Hawkes *et al.* 2001). They include the deliberate encouragement of certain species of 'wild' plants (which could include MAPs) in 'natural' habitats, the retention of valued 'wild' plants when land is cleared for agriculture or crops are weeded, the growing of valued 'wild' plants in home gardens, and the selection and storage of seed at household level for later replanting. Circa situ conservation grades into both in situ and ex situ conservation. As an example of how ex situ collections of MAPs can be connected to conservation and livelihoods through circa situ means, consider the case of the Pepperbark tree (Warburgia salutaris), the most highly prized medicinal plant in southern Africa (Cunningham 2001b). This species has been collected to the point of national extinction in Zimbabwe, causing difficulties in obtaining the medicine, a matter of great concern to traditional medical practitioners and patients alike. Dr. Tony Cunningham and the Zimbabwean NGO SAFIRE (Southern Alliance for Indigenous Resources) have managed to successfully re-introduce this species from nurseries in South Africa into Zimbabwe. However, reintroduction was not back into its natural forest habitat, from which it would probably again soon disappear since the causes of its over-collection in these largely open-access areas remain. Rather, rooted cuttings were distributed for the home gardens of local farmers, all of whom knew and valued the species. It is believed that many of these farmers will be prepared to guard the plants with the attention that will certainly be required. Given that such a large proportion of the world's flora is medicinal, it is not surprising that MAPs are well represented in botanical gardens, even though, in most cases, they will not have been selected for growing because of their medicinal properties. This said, there are many botanical gardens with collections of MAPs and, in some parts of the world, such displays are quite commonly also found attached to schools, museums and other institutions. In general, these living collections consist of only one or a few specimens of each species and, while sometimes of value educationally, they are of limited use from the point of view of genetic conservation. Botanic gardens can play further major roles in medicinal plant conservation through developing propagation and cultivation protocols, and undertaking programmes of domestication and variety breeding, all of which can benefit from traditional knowledge.

Seedbanks offer a more attractive way of storing the genetic diversity of many plants ex situ than botanic gardens, at least in terms of cost (except for species with recalcitrant seeds). However, medicinal plants are poorly represented in seedbanks (Heywood 2000). Currently, the International Plant Genetic Resources Institute (IPGRI) is supporting an Economic Crop Protection/ Genetic Resources (ECP/GR) Group for MAPs. However, only few members of the group, which convened for the first time in Slovenia in September 2002, have shown an interest in the conservation of threatened species. More concern was expressed at the meeting with gene-banking common culinary herbs with complicated taxonomy (e.g. mint, oregano and thyme – Mentha, Origanum, Thymus). Unless properly organised, the contribution of ex situ collections to in situ conservation and sustainable development can be limited. In practice, most seedbanks are used mainly as repositories of the genetic diversity of agricultural crops and their main users are agricultural scientists – breeders of 'improved' varieties of crops. Seedbanks will remain of limited use for conservation of MAPs until, and unless, their fundamental purposes and modes of operation are rethought (Richards and Ruivenkamp 1997). It is not just a question of increasing the stocks of MAPs in genebanks. Nor is there much point in reintroducing endangered species from ex situ collections back into natural habitats, unless the factors that caused their endangerment in the first place are reduced or eliminated. What is needed to make ex situ collections more useful for conservation is connection with the socio-economic and cultural dimensions of in situ ecosystems (Richards and Ruivenkamp 1997). This means that ex situ collections must be designed to serve developmental purposes (as locally defined), as well as for cropbreeding and 'strict' biological conservation. There is progress in this field in India, where four genebanks have been established specifically for MAPs, producing considerable quantities of planting materials for conservation and production purposes.

Approaches to New Product Discovery

This subject is covered authoritatively in some recent publications (ten Kate and Laird 1999; Laird 2002; Laird and ten Kate 2002) and partially elsewhere in this paper (see section "Concerns about declines in local knowledge and cultural survival"). Several stages are involved in the process of prospecting the chemical properties of plants to discover drugs or other novel products. First, unless discoveries are fortuitous, decisions are made about which plants to sample and how to sample them. Sampling may be in the field or from ex situ collections, the latter perhaps represented by plants growing in botanical gardens or by dried specimens in herbaria. These decisions are based on published and unpublished information, including sometimes knowledge of local medical uses and about the relative difficulty of undertaking research in different contexts. The next step involves isolation of chemical fractions for automated screening, for example the in vitro testing of activity against cell lines. Promising results may lead to further tests, including perhaps clinical trials, and these may result in the development, including licensing, of marketable products. As an alternative to chemical screening, there is growing interest today in screening extracts from plants for genetic information, a branch of science set to grow spectacularly. Although, according to the CBD, benefits for conservation of biodiversity and sustainable development should accrue from this process, there are often difficulties for researchers, national authorities and communities to agree exactly what these should be. The onus is on all parties to be reasonable, which itself requires a good grasp of the complexities involved. Various types and levels of benefits are appropriate at different stages (Laird 2002). Agreements with communities are likely to prove null and void unless they can demonstrate that they have been made with 'prior informed consent'. The experience of the last 10 years is that the most significant benefits to source countries have resulted from the research process (Laird and ten Kate 2002). The foundation has been partnerships between bioprospecting companies and institutions in source countries, such as research agencies, universities and local businesses. These benefits have so far been (and are likely so to remain) mainly in the form of scientific and technological capacity-building. They have also been channeled chiefly to central government, and to urban-based companies and institutions, often with little (if any) contributions to conservation or sustainable development at the sites at which the plants actually grow. Even when there have been discussions or inclusion of benefits to source areas, much more interest has generally been taken in equity than conservation. Thus, the challenge remains for those interested in conservation of biological diversity or development compatible with this objective to connect biodiversity prospecting to real benefits at field level. It is extremely useful if developing country institutions, which enter into agreements with companies, develop clear and transparent institutional policies to ensure that some benefits really are extended to the field. Similar types of policies are also needed on the parts of protected areas, local and indigenous communities, and other involved parties. On the part of governments, a current challenge is to create a permit system for authorising work by researchers, allowing a fair and equitable distribution of benefits from bioprospecting, while, at the same time, not being over-restrictive and bureaucratic, and thus preventing or delaying useful research (Hawkes 1998).

Knowledge Systems, Learning and Information

Projects concerned with the conservation and sustainable use of MAPs will normally involve interactions between different knowledge systems, including associated knowledge holders, practices and institutions. Interactions between knowledge systems can provide valuable stimuli for learning how to tackle problems better. Thus, the development of improved systems for managing natural habitats, including populations of MAPs, will benefit greatly from collaborative work between scientists and those local people who are expert in traditional ecological knowledge (ethnoscientists) (Cunningham 2001a). The adoption of new cultivation practices for medicinal plants can often best be achieved through building on farmers' own experimental efforts (Uniyal 2000). The development of improved healthcare systems, especially in developing countries (where financial resources are scarce), can usefully draw on both traditional and Western medicine (Berlin and Berlin 2000). Up to now, most projects aimed at promoting the conservation and sustainable use of MAPs have been local efforts, which, if successful, have led to only local improvements. There is a need to scale-up, to analyse why certain approaches and methodologies have been successful and others not, extract general lessons, and convert examples of good practice into government policies, and the standard practices of scientists, NGOs, traders and manufacturers. The identification of such 'wise practices' is a principal purpose of recent work by the Medicinal and Aromatic Plants Programme in Asia (MAPPA) and by the PPI in the Himalayas (Aumeeruddy-Thomas 2002; Karki 2002). The development of wise practices is an hierarchical process. Wise practices will be detailed and specific for every particular location, with increasing degrees of generalisation as the scale of application increases. The ability to learn will depend on how open people are to new ideas. A sense of history helps in understanding the biases contained in knowledge systems, allowing clearer views of their strengths as well as limitations. Economics, religion and ideology all influence how cultures develop, including in determining how dogmatic they become and their willingness to change. Conservationists should also have a reasonable grasp of the power and limitations of science, considered as a knowledge system that has developed according to such influences (Hamilton 2001). A major task of conservationists is to create opportunities for the sharing of knowledge to encourage learning. In doing so, they will sometimes find themselves in positions of trust, as confidants of private knowledge. There are strong reasons why some of those involved with medicinal plants try to guard their knowledge. Harvesters of medicinal plants may wish not to reveal the localities of valued plants, fearing that their disclosure will be used by competitors to their disadvantage. An element of mystique increases the power of traditional medical practitioners (as indeed of doctors of all types); the revelation of certain medical formulae or recipes may cause them to lose their potency. The medicinal plant trade is notoriously secretive, fearing competition. Scientists researching on medicinal plants, concerned with plagiarism, may hide their results until they are published. There is a traditional distinction between attitudes to knowledge on the parts of academia and industry. Knowledge has typically been considered by educators as a public good, and the acquisition and dissemination of knowledge have therefore been encouraged. The same open-minded approach to knowledge is also a feature of some societies. Referring to the amchis of Dolpo, Nepal, Yeshi Choden Lama and her colleagues have written (Lama *et al.* 2001):

"*Transfer of this knowledge (about the medical uses of plants) to the global community* does not pose any ethical problem to the amchis (traditional medical practitioners following the Tibetan Medical Tradition), except regarding specific compounds that have not been fully tested and therefore cannot be used by non-specialists. It is also to be noted that in the context of Buddhism and Bon, the amchis see this knowledge as an asset to be used for the good of all sentient beings, that is, human welfare". A very different attitude is found among many scientists and commercial companies interested in developing new products. They are likely to resort to the patenting system to register their inventions, receiving, if successful, monopolies over the use of their inventions for a number of years (typically 20 in the case of new drugs). Justifications for this privilege include the claim that inventors need such monopolies to recuperate the expenses incurred in their research and, more generally, that society as a whole will suffer unless there are financial incentives for the development of new technologies. In actuality, the traditional distinction in attitudes to knowledge between academia and industry is starting to break down. For example, some universities, botanical gardens and research institutions have entered into agreements with private companies, including sometimes for the purpose of new product discovery, and it can no longer be assumed that all such institutions exist, in principle, entirely for the objective pursuit of knowledge and public edification. A vast quantity of information on medicinal plants is available in publications and on the Internet, but, unfortunately, very little of this serves conservation purposes, especially for managers, collectors and growers at field level. Many topics important for conservation are little covered, and the information is often unavailable, in practice, to those who might best benefit from it, or comes in unusable forms (Marshall 1998; Srivastava 2000). Communities are commonly largely ignorant of market and price information, knowledge of which could sometimes increase their bargaining power. It frequently happens that much material collected by villagers for sale is wasted through lack of knowledge of post-harvest processing, such as techniques of drying and storage. Packages of information developed by research institutes to promote cultivation of MAPs can prove inappropriate under field conditions (Uniyal 2000). It is reported that most pharmaceutical, perfumery and cosmetic companies have little appreciation of the negative effects that their current methods of obtaining bulk materials can have on the environment (Heywood 2000). Manufacturers may be ignorant of substitutes for endangered species (Behrens 2001). Those compiling information on medicinal plants need to consider for whom the information is intended, and then the forms in which it should be delivered to be most useful. There is certainly a need to compile general background information relevant to the conservation of MAPs, such as the regional studies undertaken by TRAFFIC (e.g. Marshall 1998), but these must be taken a further stage through selection, refinement and in terms of presentation if they are to be of much practical use to stakeholders. One practical attempt is that of United Plant Savers in their production of Wildcrafting Guidelines, a 7-point educational guide for harvesters (www.plantsavers.org). On the healthcare side, the organisation Traditional Medicine for the Islands (TRAMIL) has been trying to develop recommendations of simple herbal preparations for home use in the Caribbean and Central America through a programme of validation of traditional remedies. The analysis of information to select priorities for conservation action can be very helpful. A good example is the identification of Aquilaria malaccensis (a tree that produces Agarwood, otherwise known as Gaharu) and Prunus africana as the two taxa of highest priority for action under CITES, a selection based on the fact that they are traded in significant quantities, their collection has had detrimental impacts in a number of exporting countries, and they are inadequately reported by Parties under CITES (Schippmann 2001). Further examples are provided by efforts to identify the most vulnerable species of MAPs (on various geographical scales), based on a range of indicators (Marshall 1998; Cunningham 2001a; Lama *et al.* 2001). As already mentioned, conservationists have found it difficult to provide clear advice to the public relating to their patterns of purchase of botanicals.

CONCLUSIONS

The special significance of medicinal plants in conservation relates to the values that they hold for people. These values concern the contributions that medicinal plants can make to healthcare, financial income, cultural identity and livelihood security. It is believed that these contributions can sometimes be sufficiently great that a focus on medicinal plants has the potential to achieve much more, in terms of conservation and sustainable development, than just conservation of populations of the medicinal plants themselves, or sustainable production of materials for medicines. It would be useful to investigate the geographical relationship between the overall value of medicinal plants to people and the distribution of plant diversity. It is suspected that medicinal plants often achieve their highest relative values in societies found in places richest in plant diversity. If this association is found to hold, then projects at many centers of plant diversity aimed at general biological conservation could often usefully have a focus on medicinal plants. Conservationists need to identify the conditions at field sites that are most favorable for releasing the potential offered by medicinal plants to achieve conservation and sustainable development. It is suggested that the contributions that medicinal plants can make are maximized if local people: (a) - feel that they receive significant health benefits from locally growing medicinal plants (b) - receive an appreciable income from the sale of locally growing medicinal plants (c) - ascribe special cultural significance to medicinal plants (d) - believe that there is reasonable chance that these benefits will persist in the future.

REFERENCES

Akerele O., Heywood V. and Synge H. 1991. The Conservation of Medicinal Plants. Cambridge University Press, Cambridge, UK.

Aryal R.S. 2002. An Overview of Legal Arrangements of Medicinal Plants in Nepal. Paper at a Workshop on Wise Practices and Experiential Learning in the Conservation and Management of Himalayan Medicinal Plants, Kathmandu, Nepal, 15–20 December 2002, Supported by the Ministry of Forest and Soil Conservation, Nepal, the WWF-Nepal Program, MAPPA and PPI.

Aumeeruddy-Thomas Y. 2002. Wild Harvesting and Cultivation, Market Instruments, Institution Capacity Building, Issues of Access and Benefit-sharing. Paper at a Workshop on Wise Practices and Experiential Learning in the Conservation and Management of Himalayan Medicinal Plants, Kathmandu, Nepal, 15–20 December 2002, Supported by the Ministry of Forest and Soil Conservation, Nepal, the WWF Nepal Program, MAPPA and PPI.

Aumeeruddy-Thomas Y.A., Saigal S., Kapoor N. and Cunningham A.B. 1999. Joint Management in the Making – Reflections and Experiences. People and Plants Working Paper no. 7. Division of Ecological Sciences, UNESCO, Paris, France.

Balick M.J. and Cox P.A. 1996. Plants, People and Culture: The Science of Ethnobotany. The Scientific American Library, New York.

Begum F. 2002. Ex situ Conservation of Medicinal Plants for Primary Healthcare in Laxmipur District, Bangladesh. Paper at a Workshop on Wise Practices and Experiential Learning in the Conservation and Management of Himalayan Medicinal Plants, Kathmandu, Nepal, 15–20 December 2002, Supported by the Ministry of Forest and Soil Conservation, Nepal, the WWF-Nepal Program, MAPPA and PPI.

Behrens J. 2001. Can the Utilisation and Conservation of Medicinal Plants Coexist? European Journal of Herbal Medicine 5(3): 18–26.

Berlin B. 1992. Ethnobiological Classification. Princeton University Press, Princeton, New Jersey.

Berlin O.B. and Berlin E.A. 2000. Improving Health Care by Coupling Indigenous and Modern Medical Knowledge: The Scientific Bases of Highland Maya Herbal Medicine in Chiapas, Mexico. In: Cetto A.M. (ed) Science for the Twenty-First Century: A New Commitment. UNESCO, Paris, France, pp. 438–439.

Bodeker G. 2002. Medicinal Plants: Towards Sustainability and Security. Green College, Oxford, UK.

Brandon K., Redford K.H. and Sanderson S.E. 1998. Parks in Peril: People, Politics and Protected Areas. Island Press, Washington, DC.

Cole D. and Lombard C. 2000. The Sustainably Harvested Devil's Claw Project in Namibia. Centre for Research Information and Action in Africa, Windhoek, South Africa.

Commonwealth Secretariat 2001. Bioprospecting/Biopiracy of Biodiversity and Indigenous Knowledge. Commonwealth Secretariat, London.

Craig S. 2002. Himalayan Healers in Transition: Professionalisation, Identity and Conservation among Tibetan Medicine Practitioners in Nepal. Paper at a Workshop on Wise Practices and Experiential Learning in the Conservation and Management of Himalayan Medicinal Plants, Kathmandu, Nepal, 15–20 December 2002, Supported by the Ministry of Forest and Soil Conservation, Nepal, the WWF Nepal Program, MAPPA and PPI.

Cunningham A.B. 1996. People, Park and Plant Use. People and Plants Working Paper no. 4. Division of Ecological Sciences, UNESCO, Paris, France.

Cunningham A.B. 2001a. Applied Ethnobotany: People, Wild Plant Use and Conservation. Earthscan, London.

Cunningham A.B. 2001b. Return of the Pepper-bark. Medicinal Plant Conservation 7: 21–22.

Cunningham M., Cunningham A.B. and Schippmann U. 1997. Trade in Prunus Africana and the Implementation of CITES. German Federal Agency for Nature Conservation, Bonn, Germany.

Dennis F. 1998. The Trade in Medicinal Plants in the United Kingdom. In: First International Symposium on the Conservation of Medicinal Plants in Trade in Europe. TRAFFIC Europe and The Royal Botanic Gardens, Kew, UK, pp. 19–32.

Dev S. 1999. Ancient–modern Concordance in Ayurvedic Plants: Some Examples. Environmental Health Perspectives 107: 783–789.

Dold T. and Cocks M. 2001. The Trade in Medicinal Plants in the Eastern Cape Province, South Africa. TRAFFIC Bulletin 18: 11–13.

Dutfield G. 2003. Developing and Implementing National Systems for Protecting Traditional Knowledge: A Review of Experiences in Selected Developing Countries. In: Proceedings of Expert Meeting on National Systems and National Experiences for Protecting Knowledge, Innovations and Practices. Geneva, 30 October–1 November 2000. UNCTAD, Geneva, Switzerland.

Eid U. 2000. Medicinal Plants in German Development Co-operation. In: Medicinal Utilisation of Wild Species: Challenges for Man and Nature in the New Millennium. TRAFFIC Europe and The Royal Botanic Gardens, Kew, UK, pp. 24–25.

Ekola A., Sutherland J. and Wilson E. 2000. Ancient Medicinal Tree Threatened with Extinction: Tree is Leading Remedy for Prostate Disorders Worldwide. www.futureharvest.org/news/prunusrelease.shtml.

Ellenberger A. 1998. Assuming Responsibility for a Protected Plant: Waleda's Endeavour to Secure the Firm's Supply of Arnica Montana. In: First International Symposium on the Conservation of Medicinal Plants in Trade in Europe. TRAFFIC Europe and The Royal Botanic Gardens, Kew, UK, pp. 127–130.

Farnsworth N.R. and Soejarto D.D. 1991. Global Importance of Medicinal Plants. In: Akerele O., Heywood V. and Synge H. (eds) The Conservation of Medicinal Plants. Cambridge University Press, Cambridge, UK, pp. 25–51.

Garg M., Honnef S. and Melisch R. 2002. Medizinalpflanzen: Rechtliche Rahmenbed Ingungen und Möglichkeiten der verandkerung von Prinzipien der Nachhaltigkeit. WWF-Germany/TRAFFIC Europe-Germany, Frankfurt, Germany.

Govaerts S. 2001. How Many Species of Seed Plants are There? Taxon 50: 1085–1090. GRAIN 2000. Patents on Life: The Final Assault on the Commons. Genetic Resources Action International, Barcelona, Spain.

Hamilton A.C. 1997. Threats to Plants: An Analysis of Centres of Plant Diversity. In: Touchell D.H. and Dixon K.W. (eds) Conservation into the 21st Century. Proceedings of the 4th International Botanic Gardens Conservation Congress (Perth, 1995). Kings Park and Botanic Garden, Perth, Australia, pp. 309–322.

Hamilton A.C. 2001. Human Nature and the Natural World: From Traditional Societies to the Global Age. New Millennium, London.

Hamilton A.C., Cunningham A., Byarugaba D. and Kayanja F. 2000. Conservation in a Region of Political Instability. Conservation Biology 14: 1722–1725.

Hamilton A.C., Pei S., Kessy J., Khan A.A., Lagos-Witte S. and Shinwari Z.K. 2002. The Purposes and Teaching of Applied Ethnobotany. www.rbgkew.org.uk/peopleplants.

Harnischfeger G. 2000. Proposed Guidelines for Commercial Collection of Medicinal Plant Material. Journal of Herbs, Spices and Medicinal Plants 7: 43–50.

Hawkes J.G., Maxted N. and Ford-Lloyd B.V. 2001. The Ex situ Conservation of Plant Genetic Resources. Kluwer Academic Publishers, London.

Hawkes N. 1998. Drug Companies Accused of Pirating Native Plants. The Times, London, 8 May. He S.A. and Gu Y. 1997. The challenge for the 21st Century for Chinese Botanic Gardens. In: Touchell D.H. and Dixon K.W. (eds), Conservation into the 21st Century. Proceedings of the 4th International Botanic Gardens Conservation Congress (Perth, 1995). Kings Park and Botanic Garden, Perth, Australia, pp. 21–27.

Heywood V. 2000. Management and Sustainability of the Resource Base for Medicinal Plants. In: Honnef S. and Melisch R. (eds) Medicinal Utilization of Wild Species: Challenge for Man and Nature in the New Millennium. WWF Germany/TRAFFIC Europe-Germany, EXPO 2000, Hannover, Germany.

Holmstedt B.R. and Bruhn J.G. 1995. Ethnopharmacology – a challenge. In: Schultes R.E. and von Reis S. (eds) Ethnobotany: Evolution of a Discipline. Chapman & Hall, London, pp. 338–342.

Holsinger K.E. and Gottlieb L.D. 1991. Conservation of Rare and Endangered Plants: Principles and Prospects. In: Falk D.A. and Holsinger K.E. (eds) Genetics and Conservation of Rare Plants. Oxford University Press, New York, pp. 195–208.

Jain A.K. 2000. Research on 'Regulation on Collection, Transit and Trade of Medicinal Plants in India'. In: Medicinal Plants Stakeholders' Meeting. TRAFFIC-India, New Delhi, India.

Karki M. 2002. MAPPA's role. Paper at a Workshop on Wise Practices and Experiential Learning in the Conservation and Management of Himalayan Medicinal Plants, Kathmandu, Nepal, 15–20 December 2002, supported by the Ministry of Forest and Soil Conservation, Nepal, the WWF-Nepal Program, MAPPA and PPI.

Kuipers S.E. 1997. Trade in Medicinal Plants. In: Bodeker G., Bhat K.K.S., Burley J. and Vantomme P. Medicinal Plants for Forest Conservation and Healthcare. Non-Wood Forest Products 11: 45–59.

Laird S.A. 1999. The Botanical Medicine Industry. In: Ten Kate K. and Laird S.A. (eds) The Commercial Use of Biodiversity: Access to Genetic Resources and Benefit-Sharing. Earthscan, London, pp. 78–116.

Laird S.A. 2002. Biodiversity and Traditional Knowledge: Equitable Partnerships in Practice. Earthscan, London.

Laird S.A. and Pierce A.R. 2002. Promoting Sustainable and Ethical Botanicals: Strategies to Improve Commercial Raw Material Sourcing. Rainforest Alliance, New York.

Laird S.A. and ten Kate K. 2002. Linking Biodiversity Prospecting and Forest Conservation. In: Pagiola S., Bishop J. and Landell-Mills N. (eds) Selling Forest Environmental Services. Earthscan, London, pp. 151–172.

Laird S.A., Pierce A.R. and Schmitt S.F. 2003. Sustainable Raw Materials in the Botanical Industry: Constraints and Opportunities. Paper given at the 3rd World Congress on Medicinal and Aromatic Plants for Human Welfare, 3–7 February 2003, Chiang Mai, Thailand.

Lama Y.C., Ghimire S.K. and Aumeeruddy-Thomas Y. 2001. Medicinal Plants of Dolpo: Amchis' Knowledge and Conservation. WWF-Nepal Program, Kathmandu, Nepal.

Lambert J., Srivastava J. and Vietmeyer N. 1997. Medicinal Plants: Rescuing a Global Heritage. The World Bank, Washington, DC.

Lange D. 1998. Europe's Medicinal and Aromatic Plants: Their Use, Trade and Conservation: An Overview. TRAFFIC International, Cambridge, UK.

Lange D. 2000. The role of Europe and Germany within the Worldwide Trade in Medicinal and Aromatic Plants. In: Honnef S. and Melisch (eds) Medicinal Utilization of Wild Species: Challenge for Man and Nature in the New Millennium. WWF Germany/TRAFFIC Europe-Germany, EXPO 2000, Hannover, Germany, pp. 48–49.

Langton M. 2000. Indigenous Knowledge and Conservation Policy: Aboriginal Fire Management of Protected Areas. In: Cetto A.M. (ed) Science for the Twenty-First Century: A New Commitment. UNESCO, Paris, France, pp. 435–436.

Macilwain C. 1998. When Rhetoric Hits Reality in Debate on Bioprospecting. Nature 392: 535–540.

Marshall N.T. 1998. Searching for a Cure: Conservation of Medicinal Wildlife Resources in East and Southern Africa. TRAFFIC-International, Cambridge, UK.

Martin G. 1995. Ethnobotany: A Methods Manual. Chapman & Hall, London.

Masood E. 1998. Social Equity Versus Private Property: Striking the Right Balance. Nature 392: 537.

Mendelsohn R. and Balick M.J. 1995. The Value of Undiscovered Pharmaceuticals in Tropical Forests. Economic Botany 49: 223–228.

Menges E.S. 1991. The application of minimum viable Population Theory to Plants. In: Falk D.A. and Holsinger K.E. (eds) Genetics and Conservation of Rare Plants. Oxford University Press, New York, pp. 45–61.

Misra S.S. 2002. Classical Quality Standards in Ayurvedic Medical Sciences. Paper at a Workshop on Wise Practices and Experiential Learning in the Conservation and Management of Himalayan Medicinal Plants, Kathmandu, Nepal, 15–20 December 2002, Supported by the Ministry of Forest and Soil Conservation, Nepal, the WWF-Nepal Program, MAPPA and PPI.

Moerman D.E. 1998. Native North American Food and Medicinal Plants: Epistemological Considerations. In: Prendergast H.D.V., Etkin N.L., Harris D.R. and Houghton P.J. (eds) Plants for Food and Medicine. Proceedings from a Joint Conference of the Society for Economic Botany and the International Society for Ethnopharmacology, London, 1–6 July 1996. Royal Botanic Gardens, Kew, UK, pp. 69–74.

Mrudula V. 2002. On the Work of FRLHT. Paper at a Workshop on Wise Practices and Experiential Learning in the Conservation and Management of Himalayan Medicinal Plants, Kathmandu, Nepal, 15–20 December 2002, Supported by the Ministry of Forest and Soil Conservation, Nepal, the WWF Nepal Program, MAPPA and PPI.

Mulliken T.A. 2000. Implementing CITES for Himalayan Medicinal Plants Nardostachys Grandiflora and Picrorhiza Kurrooa. TRAFFIC Bulletin 18: 63–72.

Naughton-Treves L. and Weber W. 2001. Human Dimensions of the African Rain Forest. In: Weber W., White L.J.T., Vedder A. and Naughton-Treves L. (eds) African Rain Forest Ecology and Conservation. Yale University Press, New Haven, Connecticut, pp. 30–43.

Olsen C.S. 1997. Commercial Non-timber Forestry in Central Nepal: Emerging Themes and Priorities. Ph.D. Thesis, Royal Veterinary and Agricultural University, Copenhagen, Denmark.

Pandy S. and Tandon V. 2002. Great Himalayan National Park: Linking Conservation and Local Livelihoods. Paper at a Workshop on Wise Practices and Experiential Learning in the Conservation and Management of Himalayan Medicinal Plants, Kathmandu, Nepal, 15–20 December 2002, supported by the Ministry of Forest and Soil Conservation, Nepal, the WWF-Nepal Program, MAPPA and PPI.

Pant R. 2002. Customs and Conservation: Cases of Traditional and Modern Law in India and Nepal. Kalpavriksh and International Institute of Environment and Development, Puni, India.

Pei S. 2001. Ethnobotanical Approaches of Traditional Medicine Studies: Some Experiences from Asia. Pharmaceutical Botany 39: 74–79.

Pei S. 2002a. A Brief Review of Ethnobotany and Its Curriculum Development in China. In: Shinwari Z.K., Hamilton A. and Khan A.A. (eds) Proceedings of a Workshop on

Curriculum Development in Applied Ethnobotany, Nathiagali, 2–4 May 2002. WWF-Pakistan, Lahore, Pakistan.

Pei S. 2002b. Ethnobotany and Modernisation of Traditional Chinese Medicine. Paper at a Workshop on Wise Practices and Experiential Learning in the Conservation and Management of Himalayan Medicinal.

Plants, Kathmandu, Nepal, 15–20 December 2002, Supported by the Ministry of Forest and Soilm Conservation, Nepal, the WWF-Nepal Program, MMAPPA and PPI.

Peterson R.B. 2001. Conservation – For whom? A Study of Immigration onto DR Congo's Ituri Forest Frontier. In: Weber W., White L.J.T., Vedder A. and Naughton-Treves L. (eds) African Rain Forest Ecology and Conservation. Yale University Press, New Haven, Connecticut, pp. 355–368.

Phillips O.L. and Meilleur B.A. 1998. Usefulness and Economic Potential of the Rare Plants of the United States: A Statistical Survey. Economic Botany 52: 57–67.

Pierce A.R. and Laird S.A. 2003. In Search of Comprehensive Standards for Non-timber Forest Products in the Botanicals Trade. International Forestry Reviews 5: 138–147.

Rastogi A. 2002. Sustaining farm Based Medicinal Plants Enterprise Admist Globalisation: Initiative of Grower's Forum in Uttaranchal, India. Paper at a Workshop on Wise Practices and Experiential Learning in the Conservation and Management of Himalayan Medicinal Plants, Kathmandu, Nepal, 15–20 December 2002, Supported by the Ministry of Forest and Soil Conservation, Nepal, the WWF Nepal Program, MAPPA and PPI.

Revkin A.C. 2002. Biologists Sought a Treaty; Now they Fault it. New York Times, New York, 7 May.

Richards P. and Ruivenkamp G. 1997. Seeds and Survival: Crop Genetic Resources in War and Reconstruction in Africa. IPGRI, Rome, Italy.

Rohter L. 2001. Brazil Sees Promise in Jungle Plants, but Tribes see Peril. New York Times, New York, 23 December.

Schippmann U. 2001. Medicinal Plants Significant Trade Study. German Federal Agency for Nature Conservation, Bonn, Germany.

Schippmann U., Leaman D.J. and Cunningham A.B. 2002. Impact of Cultivation and Gathering of Medicinal Plants on Biodiversity: Global Trends and Issues. Inter-Department Working Group on Biology Diversity for Food and Agriculture, FAO, Rome, Italy.

Schopp-Guth A. and Fremuth W. 2001. Sustainable Use of Medicinal Plants and Nature Conservation in the Prespa National Park area, Albania. Medicinal Plant Conservation 7: 5–8.

Shiva V. 1996. Protecting our Biological and Intellectual Heritage in the Age of Biopiracy. The Research Foundation for Science, Technology and Natural Resources Policy, New Delhi, India.

Srivastava R. 2000. Studying the Information Needs of Medicinal Plant Stakeholders in Europe. TRAFFIC Dispatches 15: 5.

Subedi B. 2002. Property Rights and Terms of Access to Communities for NTFP Conservation. Paper at a Workshop on Wise Practices and Experiential Learning in the Conservation and Management of Himalayan Medicinal Plants, Kathmandu, Nepal, 15–20 December 2002, Supported by the Ministry of Forest and Soil Conservation, Nepal, the WWF-Nepal Program, MAPPA and PPI.

Subrat N. 2002. Ayurvedic and Herbal Products Industry: An Overview. Paper at a Workshop on Wise Practices and Experiential Learning in the Conservation and Management of

Himalayan Medicinal Plants, Kathmandu, Nepal, 15–20 December 2002, Supported by the Ministry of Forest and Soil Conservation, Nepal, the WWF-Nepal Program, MAPPA and PPI.

Ten Kate K. and Laird S.A. 1999. The Commercial Use of Biodiversity. Earthscan, London.

Toledo V.M. 1995. New Paradigms for a New Ethnobotany: Reflections on the Case of Mexico. In: Schultes R.E. and von Reis S. (eds) Ethnobotany: Evolution of a Discipline. Chapman & Hall, London, pp. 75–88.

Tuxill H. and Nabhan G.P. 2001. People, Plants and Protected Areas. Earthscan, London.

Uniyal R.C. 2000. Research for 'Medicinal Plants Cultivation in India – A Reference Book'. In: Medicinal Plants Stakeholders' Meeting. TRAFFIC-India, New Delhi, India.

Uniyal S.K., Awasthi A. and Rawat G.S. 2002. Current Status and Distribution of Commercially Exploited Medicinal and Aromatic Plants in Upper Gori Valley, Kumaon Himalaya, Uttaranchal. Current Science 82: 1246–1252.

Vorhies F. 2000. The Global Dimension of Threatened Medicinal Plants from a Conservation Point of View. In: Honnef S. and Melisch R. (eds) Medicinal Utilization of Wild Species: Challenge for Man and Nature in the New Millennium. WWF Germany/TRAFFIC Europe-Germany, EXPO 2000, Hannover, Germany, pp. 26–29.

Wade R. 1987. The Management of Common Property Resources: Collective Action as an Alternative to Privatisation or State Regulation. Cambridge Journal of Economics 11: 95–106.

Wells M., Guggenheim S., Khan A., Wardojo W. and Jepson P. 1999. Investing in Biodiversity: A Review of Indonesia's Integrated Conservation and Development Projects. The World Bank, Washington, DC.

Wild R.G. and Mutebi J. 1996. Conservation Through Community Use of Plant Resources. People and Plants Working Paper no. 5. Division of Ecological Sciences, UNESCO, Paris, France.

Williams V.L. 1996. The Witwaterrand Muti Trade. Veld and Flora 82: 12–14.

Wilshusen P.R., Brechin S.R., Fortwangler C.L. and West P.C. 2002. Reinventing a Square Wheel: Critique of a Resurgent "Protection Paradigm" in International Biodiversity Conservation. Society and Natural Resources 15: 41–64.

WWF and IUCN 1994–1997. Centres of Plant Diversity: A Guide and Strategy for their Conservation. IUCN Publications Unit, Cambridge, UK.

Xiao P.-G. and Yong P. 1998. Ethnopharmacology and Research on Medicinal Plants in China. In: Prendergast H.D.V., Etkin N.L., Harris D.R. and Houghton P.J. (eds) Plants for Food and Medicine. Proceedings from a Joint Conference of the Society for Economic Botany and the International Society for Ethnopharmacology, London, 1–6 July 1996. Royal Botanic Gardens, Kew, UK, pp. 31–39.

Xie Y., Xu J. and Fang Z. 2002. Conservation Biology of Himalayan Poppy (Mecanopsis spp.): In situ and Ex situ Cultivation in Northwest Yunnan, China. Paper at a Workshop on Wise Practices and Experiential Learning in the Conservation and Management of Himalayan Medicinal Plants, Kathmandu, Nepal, 15–20 December 2002, supported by the Ministry of Forest and Soil Conservation, Nepal, the WWF-Nepal Program, MAPPA and PPI.

Nutraceuticals and Pharmaceuticals from Medicinal Plants
Edited by: Dr. Pawan Kumar 'Bharti'; Dr. M.M. Abid Ali Khan; Dr. Ashok K. Rathoure
ISBN: 978-93-86841-55-1
Edition: 2018
Published by: Discovery Publishing House Pvt. Ltd., New Delhi (India)

4

Role of Vegetable Biochemical Compounds in Human Health and Their Improvement

[1]G. Koteswara Rao, P. Ashok, K. Sasikala, T. Thomson

ABSTRACT

Bio-chemicals are chemical compounds that occur naturally in plants are responsible for color and other organoleptic properties. These chemicals may have biological, pharmacological or toxicological effects in man and animals. There are different commercially exploited major biochemical compounds present in vegetables such as β-Carotene, Allicin, Lycopene, Capsaicin, Solanine, Glucosinolates and Cucurbitacins. Phytochemicals (Biochemical compounds) are chemical compounds that occur naturally in plants (phyto means "plant" in Greek). Some are responsible for color and other organoleptic properties, such as the deep purple of blueberries and the smell of garlic. Phytochemicals may have biological significance, for example carotenoids or flavonoids. Phytochemicals in plants are compounds produced by plants having pharmacological or toxicological effects in man and animals. Although nutrients elicit pharmacological or toxicological effects when ingested at high dosages. There are commercially exploited major compounds present in vegetable crops.

Keywords: Vegetables, Biochemicals, Human Health.

INTRODUCTION

Phytochemicals (Biochemical compounds) are chemical compounds that occur naturally in plants (phyto means "plant" in Greek). Some are responsible for color and other organoleptic properties, such as the deep purple of blueberries and the smell of garlic. Phytochemicals may have biological significance, for example carotenoids or flavonoids. Phytochemicals in plants are compounds produced by plants having pharmacological or toxicological effects in man and animals. Although nutrients elicit pharmacological or toxicological effects when ingested at high dosages. There are commercially exploited major compounds present in vegetable crops.

[1] Department of Vegetable science, College of Horticulture, Dr. YSR Horticultural University, Venkataramannagudem-534101, Tadepalligudem, West Godavari, Andhra Pradesh, India.

They are,

1. β-carotene.
2. Allicin.
3. Lycopene.
4. Capsaicin.
5. Solanine.
6. Glucosinolates.
7. Cucurbitacins.

Now We can discussed about above mentioned major vegetable biochemical compounds in detailed below regarding their occurrence, functions and their improvement.

α-Carotene

α-Carotene is a strongly colored red-orange pigment abundant in plants and fruits. It is an organic compound and chemically is classified as a hydrocarbon and specifically as a terpenoid (isoprenoid), reflecting its derivation from isoprene units.

Biosynthesis Pathway of β-Carotene

β-Carotene is biosynthesized from geranylgeranyl pyrophosphate. It is a member of the carotenes, which are tetraterpenes, synthesized biochemically from eight isoprene units and thus having 40 carbons. Among this general class of carotenes, β-carotene is distinguished by having beta-rings at both ends of the molecule. Absorption of β-carotene is enhanced if eaten with fats, as carotenes are fat soluble. Carotene is the substance in carrots, pumpkins and sweet potatoes that colors them orange and is the most common form of carotene in plants. When used as a food coloring, it has the E number E160a. The structure was deduced by Karrer *et al.* in 1930 Isolation of β-carotene from fruits abundant in carotenoids is commonly done using column chromatography. It can also be extracted from the beta-carotene rich algae, *Dunaliella Salina*. The separation of β-carotene from the mixture of other carotenoids is based on the polarity of a compound. β-Carotene is a non-polar compound, so it is separated with a non-polar solvent such as hexane. Being highly conjugated, it is deeply colored, and as a hydrocarbon lacking functional groups, it is very lipophilic. In nature, β-carotene is a precursor (inactive form) to vitamin A via the action of beta-carotene 15,15′-monooxygenase.

Carotene Rich Vegetables

Carotene is the organic substance in many vegetables that colors them orange and is the most common form of carotene in plants. It is mainly useful for the prevention of various health related diseases such as cancer, cataracts, AIDS and some age related macular diseases. Some of the β-Carotene rich vegetables which are available in the nature to maintain good health conditions they are, pumpkin (50 mg/100g), Sweet potato (0.5-20 mg/100g), Carrot (1.89 mg/100g) and Tomato (0.44 mg/100g).

Dietary Requirement of β-Carotene

To maintain good helath conditions we need to take β-Carotene in the form of fruits and vegetables in our daily diet those which are available β-Carotene rich vegatables like carrot, pumpkin, tomato etc. so we need to take the average daily intake of β-carotene is in the range of 2–7 mg as estimated from a pooled analysis of 500,000 women living in the USA, Canada, and some European countries (The United State Department of Agriculture (USDA) Recommendation).

Dietary Sources

β-Carotene contributes to the orange color of many different fruits and vegetables. Sweet gourd and crude palm oil are particularly rich sources, as are yellow and orange fruits, such as cantaloupe, mangoes, pumpkin and papayas, and orange root vegetables such as carrots and yams. The color of β-carotene is masked by chlorophyll in green leaf vegetables such as spinach, kale, sweet potato leaves, and sweet gourd leaves. Vietnamese gac and crude palm oil have the highest content of β-carotene of any known plant source, 10 times higher than carrots, for example. However, gac is quite rare and unknown outside its native region of Southeast Asia, and crude palm oil is typically processed to remove the carotenoids before sale to improve the color and clarity.

β-Carotene in Human Health

β-Carotene plays a major role in human health to cure various health hazards. It is an substitute for allelopathic medicines. Beta-carotene is used to decrease Asthma symptoms. To prevent certain cancers, like Breast cancer and Skin cancer. To prevent Heart diseases, Cataracts. To prevent Age related macular degeneration (AMD). To treat AIDS. To treat Alcoholism, depression, headache, heartburn, Sunburn, high blood pressure, infertility, rheumatoid arthritis. To cure the skin disorders including Psoriasis and Vitiligo. Beta-carotene is also in used in malnourished (underfed) women to reduce the chance of death and night blindness during pregnancy, as well as diarrhea and fever after giving birth.

Adverse Effects of β-Carotene

Generally the recommended dose of β-Carotene is 2-7 mg/day, if we consume more than that it will leads to some of the negative effects in human health. Overconsumption can cause Carotenosis, a begin condition in which the skin turns orange. The proportion of carotenoids absorbed decreases as dietary intake increases. Excessive intake of β-carotene leads to yellowish skin. Chronic high doses of β-carotene supplementation increases the probability of lung cancer in cigarette smokers.

Crop Improvement in Tomato

The cultivated tomato (*Lycopersicon esculentum* Mill.) is one of the versatile and widely consumed vegetables in fresh, cooked and processed forms throughout the world. In India, the total area under tomato cultivation was 8.65 lakh hectares and production was 168.30 lakh metric tons while in Maharashtra, it was grown on an area of 0.52 lakh hectares with annual production of 73.80 lakh metric tons. The tomato fruit is also rich in vitamins like A, B and C, minerals (calcium, sodium, magnesium, manganese, potassium, iron, phosphorus, boron and zinc) and carotenoid pigments like lycopene and beta carotene, precursor of vitamin A. From nutritional point of view, tomato is popularly known as "The Poor Man's Apple", which is one of the chief vegetable crops in India. The French people called it as 'The Apple of Love' whereas the Germans as 'The Apple of Paradise '.

Vitamin A deficiency is a public health problem in 118 countries where over 200 million pre-school children are suffering from 'hypovitaminosis'. Adding vitamin A to the diet could reduce child mortality by 23 per cent in developing countries while helping to prevent blindness and general infectious diseases. But disseminating vitamin pills would be costly and not suitable. Therefore, efforts were made in developing countries to incorporate beta carotene into crops like tomato converting into cell factory for antioxidant carotenoids which are presently available only through chemical synthesis. The cultivation of high beta carotene tomatoes may be one of the significant and noticeable steps to overcome the widely prevalent vitamin A deficiency in India.

Evidence from epidemiological studies have suggested that higher intake of beta carotene may reduce the risk of cancer and beneficial effect in prevention of numerous chronic diseases including cancer, cardio and cerebro-vascular, ocular and neurological diseases .The popularity of tomato is mainly due to dark red colour i.e. lycopene content. It is one of the carotenoids that cannot be converted into vitamin A, but it is a powerful antioxidant that reduces the risk of heart attack, cancer and chronic diseases. Till the date, no commercial cultivars developed in India especially for enrichment of vitamin A content. The extensive research work has been carried out in India regarding development of new tomato varieties with resistance to pests and diseases and high yield potential. However, not much systematic research work has been reported so far to improve the nutritional value of tomato. Audrius *et al.* (2009) conducted a study on evaluation of ten different tomato cultivars for nutrition quality, revealed that highest amount of Beta carotene was found in cultivars Ranij-310 followed by Elbrus. And also Ana *et al.* (2008) conducted a study on Quality of two tomato cultivars grown under different agronomical conditions. They revealed that highest levels of beta carotene was found in the cultivar 'V_1'. And Vishnu and Patil (2014) revealed that, the highest beta carotene content was noticed in orange fruited tomato cv. 34A-1-1(7.03 mg/100 g).

Crop Improvement in Pumpkin

Pumpkin is one of the vegetables that meet the requirements of healthy nutrition. It is a tasty and valuable vegetable crop, containing a lot of biologically active substances and distinguished for dietary qualities. The name 'pumpkin' is commonly used for cucurbits of some species, similar in botanical characteristiscs. In Central Europe countries pumpkins belonged to *Cucurbita pepo* L. (called also 'squash'), *Cucurbita maxima* Duch. (called 'winter squash') and *Cucurbita moschata* Duch. ex Poir species are mostly grown. Since pumpkin species and cultivars differs in nutritional and technological value of fruits, breeders and scientists seek genotypes of the highest suitability for human nutrition.

The quality of vegetables consists of some properties, which can be evaluated using physical and chemical methods. One of important quality traits of food is biological activity of a product, and especially its antioxidative activity. Antioxidants are compounds that protect cells against the damaging effects of reactive oxygen species. Some of antioxidant agents are found in vegetables. Products high in vitamin A, vitamin C, vitamin E, and β-carotene content are believed to be the most beneficial. Carotenoids are red, orange or yellow fat-soluble plant pigments. These nutrients are commonly found in fruits and vegetables, those with the strongest colors being healthiest. In human organism, carotenoids play two primary roles: exert antioxidant activity, but some are also converted into the vitamin A. Of the 600 carotenoids that have been identified, about 30 to 50 are believed to have vitamin A activity. The best known of this group are β-carotene and α-carotene. At present, there is no officially recommended dietary intake of carotenoids, but recommended dietary intake of vitamin A is about 1-3 mg per day of retinol equivalent. It is assumed that processing of vegetables improves the bio-availability of carotenoids, since it breaks down the cellulose structure of the plant cell.

Experimental studies suggest that a higher dietary intake of carotenoids offers protection against developing certain cancers (e.g., lungs, skin, uterine, cervix, gastrointestinal tract), macular degeneration, cataracts, and other health conditions linked to oxidative or free radical damage. Special physiological activity of these compounds in human organism as the vitamin A precursors and also as antioxidants, causes increasing interest among researchers in determining their content in different products. Gajewski *et al.* (2008) conducted an experiment on Quality of Pumpkin Cultivars in Relation to Sensory Characteristics, revealed that highest carotenoids content, highest antioxidant activity was found in the cultivar 'Kroshka' (6.59 mg/100g).

Crop Improvement in Sweet Potato

Sweet potato (*Ipomoea batatas L.*) is one of the most traditional root crops in many countries. It is traditionally regarded as a 'poor man's crop as it is consumed by poor households. It gives satisfactory yield under adverse climatic and soil conditions, as well as under low or non-use of external inputs. The plant is a herbaceous perennial vine having alternate heart-shaped or palmately lobed leaves and medium-sized sympetalous flowers. The edible tuberous root is long and tapered, with wide ranges of skin colour such as yellow, orange, red, brown, purple, and beige. Its flesh colour ranges from beige through white, red, pink, violet, yellow, orange, and purple. Sweet potato varieties with white or pale yellow flesh are less sweet and moist than those with red, pink or orange flesh.

Vitamin A deficiency is a wide spread nutritional and health problem affecting most people in the developing countries including. The deficiency increases children's risk to common illnesses, impaired growth, development, vision and immune systems, and in severe cases results in blindness and death. In women, vitamin A deficiency increases risk of dying during pregnancy, as well as giving birth to low weight children, and may increase the spread of HIV/AIDS virus infection. New research findings suggest that vitamin A can have important effects on maternal mortality and can protect infants from the effects of maternal tochild transmission of HIV/AIDS Virus.

Approximately one million children have clinical signs of vitamin A deficiency, and more than 0.9 million children under 6 years of age suffer from some degree of Xerothalmia and 30 thousand children become blind every year due to severe vitamin A deficiency in the country. It is estimated that about 29% of the population suffer from protein, while people suffering from vitamin A, B and C are 89, 81 and 93%, respectively. Childrens also suffer from high rates of micronutrient deficiencies, particularly vitamin A, iron, iodine and zinc deficiency. A recent survey reported a decline in the prevalence of night blindness among preschoolage children in rural areas from 3.6% in 1982/83 to 0.67. Among women of reproductive age, clinical vitamin A deficiency continues to be a serious problem. More than 2.7% of pregnant women, 2.4% of lactating women and 2.0% of non pregnant/non lactating women reported being night blind in 1997.

There is a clear need to diversify food sources both in terms of land/ environmental sustainability, development of the rural economy and increased consumption to achieve improvements in the nutritional status of the people of country. Orange fleshed sweet potato is quite rich in β-Carotene. To combat malnutrition and vitamin A deficiency, orange fleshed sweet potato (OFSP) may be a suitable item. Therefore, the present investigation was undertaken to select the suitable orange fleshed sweet potato clones having higher yield potentiality. Rahman *et al.* (2013) evaluated four orange fleshed sweet potato genotypes. Recorded that highest amount of Beta carotene was found in CIP 440267.2.

Inheritance of Beta Carotene

There is a need of study on the inheritance of Beta carotene from wild species to cultivated species. Stommel and Haynes (1994) conducted a study on inheritance of Beta carotene from wild tomato species to cultivated species they are *L. esculentum* cv. Floradade and *L cheesmanii* f. *minor* LA 317 (Tomato Genetics Stock Center) were used as female (P_1) and male (P_2) parents, respectively. *L. esculentum* cv. Floradade served as the recurrent parent in the backcross populations. Seed of F_1, F_2 and BC_1 populations were produced on greenhouse grown plants. These plants were grown in 5-liter pots in a 6:3:2 (v:v:v) steam-treated soil, peat, and perlite mixture with regular applications of water-soluble fertilizer. Controlled cross-pollinations were performed via transfer of pollen to emasculated flowers of the cultivated parent for production of F_1, and BC_1, generation seed. F_1, plants were allowed to self-pollinate for F_2 seed production.

During off season of various Beta carotene rich fruits and vegetables there are some artificial Beta carotene formulations are available in the market they are Bio carotene capsules, Lycomb Plus capsules, Natural beta carotene gel, Beta carotene tonic etc.

Sources of Beta Carotene

Some of the Beta carotene rich lines and varieties are there to use in the future breeding programmes they are in tomato (caro red), carrot (HCO-4 and HCO-1), pumpkin (Arka chandan) and sweet potato (sree rethna, sree kanaka, kiran, samrat, pusa sunheri, pusa bharati, CO-3 and gouri).

ALLICIN

Allicin is an Organo Sulphur compound obtained from garlic and onion, a species in the family Alliaceae. It was first isolated and studied in the laboratory by Chester J. Cavallito and John Hays Bailey in 1944.

Structure and Biosynthesis of Allicin

Allicin features the thiosulfinate functional group, R-S-(O)-S-R. The compound is not present in garlic unless tissue damage occurs, and is formed by the action of the enzyme alliinase on alliin. Allicin is chiral but occurs naturally only as a racemate. The racemic form can also be generated by oxidation of diallyl disulfide. When fresh garlic is chopped or crushed, the enzyme alliinase converts alliin into allicin, which is responsible for the aroma of fresh garlic. The allicin generated is very unstable and quickly changes into a series of other sulfur containing compounds such as diallyl disulfide. generally the allicin is mainly present in bulb crops which are belongs to the family alliaceae they are onion, garlic, leek. The allicin content may be varied from the species to species for example in onion (20-25 mg/100 g) and garlic (20.73-24.31 mg/100 g).

Allicin in Human Health

Allicin has several medicinal properties in human health it is mainly useful for the traeatment of various diseases. To treat the high blood pressure, high cholesterol, coronary heart disease, heart attack. Garlic actually may be effective in slowing the development of atherosclerosis and seems to be able to modestly reduce blood pressure.To prevent colon cancer, rectal cancer, stomach cancer, breast cancer, prostate cancer, and lung cancer and bladder cancer. Garlic has been tried for treating diabetes, osteoarthritis, hay fever (allergic rhinitis), traveler's diarrhea, high blood pressure late in pregnancy (pre-eclampsia), cold and flu. It is also used for building the immune system, preventing tick bites, treating bacterial and fungal infections. To treatment of fever, coughs, headache, stomach ache, sinus congestion, gout, rheumatism, hemorrhoids, asthma, bronchitis, shortness of breath, low blood pressure, low blood sugar, high blood sugar, and snakebites. It is also used for fighting stress and fatigue, and maintaining healthy liver function. Some people apply garlic oil to their skin to treat fungal infections, warts, and corns. While garlic is a common flavoring in food, some scientists have suggested that it might have a role as a food additive to prevent food poisoning.

During off season of bulb crops there is a availability of artificial allicin formulations which are available in the market to meet the average daily allicin requirement for good health condition, the available formulations are allicin max capsules and allicin max gels, creams and ointments etc.

Biosynthesis Pathway of Allicin

For the point of allicin improvement we need to have a clear cut idea regarding the bio synthesis of allicin. When fresh garlic is chopped or crushed, the enzyme alliinase converts alliin into allicin, which is responsible for the aroma of fresh garlic. The allicin generated is very unstable and quickly changes into a series of other sulphur containing compounds such as diallyl disulfide in Garlic and Allyl Propyl Disulphide incase of Onion.

Dietary Requirement of Allicin

To maintain good health condition there is a need to take the average daily requirement of allicin for good healthy condition. The daily requirement may be varied depending on the health condition. The dietary requirement may be varied for various diseases For high blood pressure people : Garlic extract 600-1200 mg divided and given three times daily. For cancer people : For prevention of colon, rectal, and stomach cancer: fresh or cooked garlic 3.5-29 grams weekly. General : Fresh garlic 4 grams (approximately one clove) once daily has also been used. Fresh garlic typically contains 1% alliin.

Adverse Effects of Allicin

The average daily requirement is 4 g/day for optimum good health condition. If we take or consume more than that it will leads to some negative or adverse effects in human beings. Garlic is notorious for causing halitosis, or bad breath. The sulfur-based medicinal compounds in garlic bulb can coat the saliva, teeth, gums and oral tissues, leading to an unpleasant odor. Because the sulfuric compounds in garlic distribute throughout the body, garlic odors may emanate from the sweat glands and soft tissue causes bad odor. When taken by mouth, garlic can cause bad breath, a burning sensation in the mouth or stomach, heartburn, gas, nausea, vomiting, body odor, and diarrhea. Garlic may also increase the risk of bleeding during surgery. Asthma has been reported in people working with garlic, and other allergic reactions are possible.

Crop Improvement in Onion and Garlic

Garlic (*Allium sativum* L.) occupies a prominent position among human foods, not only as a condiment, but also due to its therapeutic properties, attributed to the presence of bioactive compounds .Garlic is a bulb from the Liliacerae family and is widely consumed all over the world. Its beneficial properties have been recognized for over 5000 years. It is indicated as an adjuvant agent in the therapy for prevention of various chronic infirmities such as heart diseases, infections, and atherosclerosis. Most of garlic's health benefits have been attributed to the antioxidant activity of organosulphurous compounds, predominantly allicin.

Garlic is the food with the highest number of organosulfurous compounds. Thirty-three of these compounds have been identified, and the biological activity of several is known. On average, 1 g of fresh garlic contains 11 to 35 mg of total organosulfurous compounds, representing a level approximately four times greater (per gram of fresh weight) than that of other sources such as onions, broccoli, cauliflower, turnip, cabbage and other crucifers.

Onion (*Allium cepa* L.) and garlic (*Allium sativum* L.), among the oldest cultivated plants, are used both as a food and for medicinal applications. In fact, these common food plants are a rich source of several phytonutrients recognized as important elements of the Mediterranean diet, but are also used in the treatment and prevention of a number of diseases, including cancer, coronary heart disease, obesity, hypercholesterolemia, diabetes type 2, hypertension, cataract and disturbances of the gastrointestinal tract (e.g. colic pain, flatulent colic and dyspepsia). These activities are related to the thiosulfinates, volatile sulfur compounds, which are also responsible for the pungent of these vegetables. Besides these low-molecular weight compounds, onion and garlic are characterized by more polar compounds of phenolic and steroidal origin, often glycosilated, showing interesting pharmacological properties. These latter compounds, compared to the more studied thiosulfinates, present the advantages to be not pungent and more stable to cooking. Recently, there has been an increasing scientific attention on such compounds. In this paper, the literature about the major volatile and non-volatile phytoconstituents of onion and garlic has been reviewed. Particular attention was given to the different methodology developed to perform chemical analysis, including separation and structural elucidation.

So there is a need to identify the highest allicin containing lines both in garlic and onion through selection process.

Long-storage onions for temperate latitudes are typically more pungent than short-storage 'short-day' types (Hassan *et al.*, 2014). Preliminary evaluation of onion pungency genetics indicates incomplete dominance for low levels and selection for low pungency has been exercised in varietal development. Beyond these few generalizations, little is known about the potential for genetic improvement of onion flavor. The development of pungent onions may yield onions with greater health benefits to consumers than would mild onions. Potential for improvement of garlic quality is less understood than that for onion. Pseudostem diameter was found to be significantly positively correlated with allicin content (Sandhu *et al.*, 2014). Hassan *et al.* (2015) conducted a study on Impact of Genetic Factor and Geographical Location on Allicin Content of Garlic (*Allium sativum*) Germplasm from Egypt and China. This study was conducted to explore the Genetic variation of allicin content among Chinese and Egyptian garlic germplasm. The role of genetic improvement in allicin content enhancement and the combined influence of genetic and environmental factors on allicin contents in Egyptian garlic germplasm grown in Egypt and China respectively. UPLC method was used for quantification of allicin in garlic bulbs (Wang *et al.*,2010). As the result of cluster analysis based on allicin content, all garlic germplasm (104 accessions) were divided into four groups. Finally what they conclude means from the results presented in this study, we can conclude that the allicin content in garlic bulbs was influenced by both genetic and environmental factors. There was a wide range of genetic variation in allicin content among all germplasm studied, which could be classified into four groups based on allicin content. Clonal selections could obviously improve allicin content in garlic bulbs. The accessions 8N499 and 8N239 from China and 8N497, 8N498, 8N516 and 8N521 from Egypt with high allicin content could be used in future breeding programs aiming at improvement of garlic quality. All garlic varieties grown in China had lower allicin content than those grown in Egypt with the allicin content reduction of 16~63.7%, which proved that production area choice for high allicin is important. Sandhu *et al.* (2015) conducted a study on variability of agronomic and quality characteristics of garlic ecotypes. In order to identify large size bulbs having large clove diameter and high allicin content, 40 diverse genotypes of garlic genotypes were tested at Vegetable Research Farm and Biochemistry Laboratory, Department of Vegetable Science, Punjab Agricultural University, Ludhiana, during 2012-13 so that the suitable genotype should be identified for cultivation in Punjab state. Finally what revealed is the genotypes CSRG-1143 and CSRG-1153 have high bulb weight, high bulb and clove diameter, average number of cloves/bulb and moderate allicin content i.e. it can be released as a variety after multi-location testing. The line CSRG-1149 has highest allicin.

Sources of Allicin

There is a wide range of highest allicin containing lines are available to used in the future breeding programmes. They are in onion giza-6, giza-20, EC-200937, No.799, Bangalore rose, jalgaon vari, No.5 and barwad and in garlic 8N499, 8N239, 8N497, 8N498, 8N52 and CSRG-1149.

LYCOPENE

Lycopene is a member of a group of naturally occurring pigments called carotenoids. Carotenoids usually occurs in plants and not in animals, hence animals rely on ingestion for their source of these biomolecules. In plants the main function of these carotenoids is to serve as light absorbing oxidative pigment and also protect cells against photo oxidative damage during the process of photosynthesis. Tomatoes and tomato-based products are the major sources of natural lycopene in the human diet. It is the major colouring pigment of tomato usually occurs in all trans form (35-96% of the total lycopene) and low levels of *cis*-lycopene (1-22% of the total lycopene). Lycopene for food use can also be manufactured by chemical synthesis or can be produced by fermentation of *Blakeslea trispora*. Lycopene is a bright red carotene and carotenoid pigment and phytochemical found in tomatoes and other red fruits and vegetables. Like all carotenoids, lycopene is a polyunsaturated hydrocarbon. Lycopene from the neo-Latin *lycopersicum*, the tomato species, is a bright red carotene and carotenoid pigment and phytochemical found in tomatoes and other red fruits and vegetables, such as red carrots, watermelons, gac, and papayas, although not in strawberries, or cherries. Although lycopene is chemically a carotene, it has no vitamin A activity. Foods that are not red may also contain lycopene, such as brown beans or parsley. In plants, algae, and other photosynthetic organisms, lycopene is an important intermediate in the biosynthesis of many carotenoids, including beta carotene, which is responsible for yellow, orange, or red pigmentation, photosynthesis, and photo-protection. Like all carotenoids, lycopene is a polyunsaturated hydrocarbon, i.e. an un substituted alkene. Structurally, lycopene is a tetraterpene and assembled from eight isoprene units that are composed entirely of carbon and hydrogen. It is insoluble in water. Lycopene's eleven conjugated double bonds give its deep red color and its antioxidant activity.

Lycopene Rich Vegetables

It is a phytochemical compound found in various fruits and vegetables like tomatoes (8.8–42 μg/g) and other red fruits and vegetables, such as red carrots, watermelons (23-72 μg/g), gac (2,000-2,300 μg/g), and papayas. Although lycopene is chemically a carotene, it has no vitamin A activity. Foods that are not red may also contain lycopene, such as brown beans or parsley.

Biosynthesis Pathway of Lycopene

It is a very important step to improve the quality of any vegetable. It will be helpful in the understanding of metabolism of lycopene. The unconditioned biosynthesis of lycopene in eukaryotic plants and in prokaryotic cyanobacteria is similar, as are the enzymes involved. Synthesis begins with mevalonic acid, which is converted into dimethylallyl pyrophosphate. This is then condensed with three molecules of isopentenyl pyrophosphate (an isomer of dimethylallyl pyrophosphate), to give the twenty-carbon geranylgeranyl pyrophosphate. Two molecules of this product are then condensed in a tail-to-tail configuration to give the forty-carbon phytoene, the first committed step in carotenoid biosynthesis. Through several desaturation steps, phytoene is converted into lycopene. The two terminal isoprene groups of lycopene can be cyclized to produce beta-carotene, which can then be transformed into a wide variety of xanthophylls.

Lycopene in Human Health

Lycopene plays a major role in human health because it has a capacity to cure the various health hazards. It is mainly Used for treatment of cardiovascular diseases and prostate cancer. Studies prove that it has been useful in lowering of hypertension, in particular mild hypertensive patient. Naturally lycopene is useful in the manufacturing of vitamin A. So, it is also helpful in the improved eyesight. It increases the High Density Lipid levels (HDL) which are useful for the absorption of Lower Density Lipids (LDL), thus preventing atherosclerosis, hypercholestremia. People take lycopene for preventing heart disease, "hardening of the arteries" (atherosclerosis). To prevent the cancer of the prostate, breast, lung, bladder, ovaries, colon, and pancreas. Lycopene is also used for treating human papilloma virus (HPV) infection, which is a major cause of uterine cancer. Some people also use lycopene for cataracts and asthma. As an anti oxidant it also helps cholesterol from being oxidised. Lycopene is also useful in treating oral leukoplakia, a condition which is precancerous mucous membrane condition, which is manifested by white patches.

Dietary Requirement of Lycopene

It is very important step and very beneficial for the maintenance of good health condition. So we need to consume on an average the daily intake of lycopene should be 120 mg/day. And also during off season or non availability of lycopene rich fruits and vegetables some of the lycopene formulations are available in the market such as Lycocor capsules, Lycocomb plus capsules, Lycopene bio capsules, Lypen red tonic, Dolly rich tonic, Lycovit plus tablets.

Dietary Sources

There is a wide range of lycopene rich products are available to provide lycopene requirement such as tomato juice, tomato sauce, tomato ketchup, pink grape fruit, pink guava, papaya, rose hip puree and apricot etc.

Adverse Effects of Lycopene

Generally the average daily requirement of lycopene is 120 mg/day but if we consume more than that it will leads to some of the negative effects. In a middle-aged woman who had prolonged and excessive consumption of tomato juice, her skin and liver were colored orange-yellow and she had elevated levels of lycopene in her blood. This discoloration of the skin is known as lycopenodermia. There are also cases of intolerance or allergic reaction to dietary lycopene, which may cause diarrhea, nausea, stomach pain or cramps, gas, vomiting, and loss of appetite.

Crop Improvement in Tomato

Consumers tend to make initial purchases of tomatoes based on external features such as color and appearance, making tomato fruit color an important trait. While red fruit color is dominant in most of the cases, there is a special demand for different colored tomatoes, especially: pink, bicolor (combination of two colors), yellow, orange, green and blue. Tomato fruit color can largely be explained by mutations in the carotenoid pathway. A brief overview of the pathway follows (for a more complete review see Lu and Li: yellow flesh (*r*-mutants) caused by a mutation in phytoene synthase (*PSY*), tangerine flesh color (*t*-mutants) caused by mutations in prolycopene isomerase (*CrtISO*), accumulation of lycopene resulting in deep red fruit (*og/ogc*) caused by mutations in β-cyclase and pink tomatoes caused by the *y* mutation which makes the fruit epidermis clear instead of yellow. Lycopene is an important color pigment since the amount of lycopene is determined based on color intensity, particularly red component of the tomato. Lycopene has been shown to have: anti-cancer and anti-oxidant properties, and prevent cardio-vascular diseases and diabetes. The increased consumer awareness and the demand for food containing bioactive compounds, make lycopene a key trait for tomato breeders to select for. As the importance of the interrelated traits of color and bioactive compounds increase for consumers, the genetics of fruit color becomes increasingly important for tomato breeders a subject that has not been thoroughly investigated outside of the laboratory. While tomato is rich in lycopene, isomer type and availability upon consumption of fresh fruit are under discussion. It has been reported that the *cis*-isomer of lycopene is more readily absorbed than the *trans*-isomers, the major form in raw tomato. Tomato breeding challenges include increasing lycopene content and *cis* lycopene isomers. It has been realized by consumers as well as researchers for a long time that fruit quality including lycopene is the important trait to improve. Realizing this fact, some efforts have been made in the past at NC State University, which resulted in some improved varieties released with improved fruit color. It has been reported that there is a positive correlation between fruit color and lycopene concentration. used tomato genotypes with tangerine (*t*-mutant: LA3183), old gold (*og*-mutant: LA3179), yellow flesh (*r*-mutant: LA3691) and a control genotype (Alisa Craig) with red fruit. Carotenoid profiles and amounts differed among mutants. The *r*-mutant did not have any carotenoids whereas the *t*-mutant and *og*-mutant had a reduced level of β-carotene but an increased level of *trans*-lycopene, respectively.

Hence there is a need to identify the high lycopene contain varieties for the sake of good human health conditions, it is mainly done evaluation of different varieties and hybrids in different vegetables.

Ibitoye *et al.* (2009) conducted a study on agronomic and lycopene evaluation in tomato (*Lycopersicon lycopersicum* Mill.) as a function of genotype. they reported that agronomic evaluation of crop genotypes is essential in identifying the genetic variability that exists within crop germplasm and it is also the starting point for genetic improvement of any crop species. To this end, nine tomato genotypes were evaluated for the variability in their agronomic characteristics and lycopene content. The content of Lycopene an important phytonutrient was also evaluated among the genotypes and it ranged from 70.25 to 147.29 μg/g. They revealed that The highest amount of lycopene content was recorded in 'NHLeader' (147.29 μg/g), followed by NHBig local (100.41) and lowest was recorded in NHLindo (70.25). and F.A. Al-Said *et al.* (2007) conducted a study on field evaluation of high lycopene tomato breeding lines. Eight tomato accessions acquired from AVDRC Taiwan were grown under local Omani field conditions. Significant differences were observed in each the parameters studied. The germplasm varied significantly for yield and fruit quality. The high yielding 279 CLN 2366C was low in TSS and lycopene contents. CLN 2366A produced highest lycopene contents but low TSS. CLN 2070A was the high TSS accession, which produced second highest yield among the 8 entries. The work on selection of high lycopene and stress tolerant varieties required special attention and efforts should be continued towards developing improved tomatoes with these qualities.

Breeding for Color and Lycopene Content in Adapted Tomato Germplasm

There is a need of breeding for the improvement of colour and lycopene content in tomatoes still the research is going on but Francis *et al.* (2001)conducted a wonderful experiment on this aspect. This project aimed to develop strategies and tools to improve the efficiency of breeding for color and lycopene content within breeding lines and varieties adapted to the Great Lakes region.The main specific goals were to develop a sampling strategy to accurately measure the genetic contribution to fruit color in adapted varieties and breeding lines and to measure the genetic contribution to lycopene content. Finally what they concluded is year, location, genotype, between fruit, and within fruit differences significantly contribute to variation for color. Genotype explains up to 28% of the variation, and it is this variation that we can use to improve the genetic potential of tomato varieties. Lycopene is correlated with color genotype explains 29-43% of the variation for lycopene content. Unexplained (Error) variation accounts for the rest.

Sources of lycopene

There are some of the lines are available which contain highest amount of lycopene in tomato and watermelon they are, in tomato High pigment and crimson and in watermelon EC-39240 and EC-393243.

CAPSAICIN

Capsaicin (chemical name 8-methyl-*N*-vanillyl-6-nonenamide) is an active component of chili peppers, which are plants belonging to the genus *Capsicum*. It is an irritant for mammals, including humans, and produces a sensation of burning in any tissue with which it comes into contact. Capsaicin and several related compounds are called capsaicinoids and are produced as secondary metabolites by chili peppers, probably as deterrents against certain mammals and fungi. Pure capsaicin is a volatile, hydrophobic, colorless, odorless, crystalline to waxy compound.

Properties of Capsaicin

Capsaicin has various properties which are capsaicin has no taste or odor. Also It's detectable at 16 ppm by humans and used as an additive to analgesics.

Where it is Present and Examples

Capsaicin is present in large quantities in the placental tissue (which holds the seeds), the internal membranes and, to a lesser extent, the other fleshy parts of the fruits of plants in the genus *Capsicum.* In *Capsicum fruitescens* 19.73 mg/g will be there.

Uses of Capsaicin

Capsaicin used for treatment of various aspects such as repellant for squirrels, dogs and cats. Also to treats arthritis pain, psoriasis and it has been shown to reduce cancerous growth. They stimulate nerve cells to increase the flow of calcium. Used to treat minor aches and pains of the muscles/joints (e.g., arthritis, backache, sprains) and may also be used to treat nerve pain.

Not only these but it also used in various areas such as food industry, research, pepper sprays and control of pests and also used in equestrian sports etc.

Food

Because of the burning sensation caused by capsaicin when it comes in contact with mucous membranes, it is commonly used in food products to provide added spice or "heat" (piquancy). In high concentrations, capsaicin will also cause a burning effect on other sensitive areas, such as skin or eyes. The degree of heat found within a food is often measured on the scoville scale. In some cases, because people enjoy the heat, there has long been a demand for capsaicin-spiced products like hot sauce or salsa.

It is common for people to experience pleasurable and even euphoriant effects from ingesting capsaicin. Folklore among self-described "chiliheads" attributes this to pain-stimulated release of endorphins, a different mechanism from the local receptor overload that makes capsaicin effective as a topical analgesic.

Research

Capsaicin is used as an analgesic in topical ointments, nasal sprays (Sinol-M), and dermal patches to relieve pain, typically in concentrations between 0.025% and 0.25%. It may be applied in cream form for the temporary relief of minor aches and pains of muscles and joints associated with arthritis, backache, strains and sprains, often in compounds with other rubefacients. It is also used to reduce the symptoms of peripheral neuropathy such as post-herpetic neuralgia caused by shingles.

Although capsaicin creams have been used to treat psoriasis for reduction of itching, a review of six clinical trials involving topical capsaicin for treatment of pruritus concluded there was insufficient evidence of effect.

The American Cancer Society warns "available scientific research does not support claims for the effectiveness of capsicum or whole pepper supplements in preventing or curing cancer at this time". Other uses not supported by evidence are: "addiction, malaria, yellow fever, heart disease, stroke, weight loss, poor appetite, and sexual potency".

Pepper Spray and Pests

Capsaicin is also an active ingredient in riot control and personal defense pepper spray agents. When the spray comes in contact with skin, especially eyes or mucous membranes, it produces pain and breathing difficulty, discouraging assailants. Refer to the Scoville scale for a comparison of pepper spray to other sources of capsaicin.

Capsaicin is also used to deter pests, specifically mammalian pests. Targets of capsaicin repellants include voles, deer, rabbits, squirrels, insects, and attacking dogs. Ground or crushed dried chili pods may be used in birdseed to deter rodents, taking advantage of the insensitivity of birds to capsaicin. The Elephant Pepper Development Trust claims the use of chili peppers to improve crop security for rural African communities. Notably, an article published in the Journal of Environmental Science and Health in 2006 states that "Although hot chili pepper extract is commonly used as a component of household and garden insect-repellent formulas, it is not clear that the capsaicinoid elements of the extract are responsible for its repellency."

The first pesticide product using solely capsaicin as the active ingredient was registered with the U.S. Department of Agriculture in 1962.

Equestrian Sports

Capsaicin is a banned substance in equestrian sports because of its hyper-sensitizing and pain-relieving properties. At the show jumping events of the 2008 Summer Olympics, four horses tested positive for the substance, which resulted in disqualification.

Dietary Requirement of Capsaicin

On an average the daily capsaicin content we should be taken at the rate of 13 grams daily/150 pound person.

The capsaicin formulations which are available in the market are capsaicin cream, capzasin HP pain relief gel and capsaicin gels etc.

Adverse Effects of Capsaicin

Generally the average daily intake of capsaicin is 13 g/day if we consume more than that it will leads to some of the negative effects or adverse effects. In large amounts this can cause nerve damage and burns. If ingested in large amounts by adults or small amounts by children, can produce nausea, vomiting, abdominal pain, and burning diarrhea. When used for weight loss in capsules, there has been a report of heart attack. Eye exposure produces intense tearing, pain and eye burn.

Crop Improvement in Chilli

One of traditional plant that has so many pharmacology effects is chili fruit (*Capsicum sp*). Around the world is known five varieties of *Capsicum* sp, which are *C. annuum*, *C. frutescens*, *C. chinense*, *C.baccatum*, *C. pubescens*, meanwhile in Indonesia only known 2 varieties, *C. annuum* also known as red chili, paprika, gendot until curly chili, and *C. frutescens* (rawit). Shape and color variation of *C. annuum* is similar with *C. frutescens*. Chili fruit has a hot taste, this comes from capsaicinoid compounds that are amide acids from vanilinamine and fatty acid chain branched at C9 and C11. Capsaicinoid consists of capsaicin, dihydrocapsaicin, homocapsaicin, and homodihydro-capsaicin. 69% of Capsaicinoid is capsaicin, which is a marker compound and has an affect on stimulating hair growth. Capsaicin is lead in bitterness chilli fruit, thus red chili more hot taste than green chili, because the content of capsaicin of red chili two or three fold more than green chili fruits. In modern ways, capsaicin has been made in *oleoresin* (ethanol or acetone extract) form and has effect as carminative, neuron stimulant and *counterirritant* for lumbago, neuralgia and rheumatoid. *Capsicum sp.* marker compound analysis has been carried out so many times before because of its pharmacological effects. Experiment of capsaicin quantitative analysis on ethanol extract of several *Capsicum sp.* varieties needs to be carried out to determine the best chili fruit variety as raw material to produce capsaicin. Ethanol extract has a mixture of capsaicinoid compounds. One of many methods that can separate and identify compound in a mixture is High Performance Liquid Chromatography method. HPLC method was applied for analysis capsaicin in chili by some publication. However, the preparation sample for analysis capsaicin using solid phase extraction has been yet published. *Solid Phase Extraction* is a very important technique in chromatography sample preparation. This method can reduce contaminant disturbing capsaicin analytical process. The current study, high-speed countercurrent chromatography is applied to rapidly separate capsaicin in Capsicum sp. In this study, capsaicin of Capsicum sp cultivar from Bandung, West Java (Indonesia) was analyzed to give scientific information about capsaicin content quantitative data on ethanol extract that can be used to determine the best chili fruit variety as raw material of capsaicin. So because of these many properties still there is a better need of research for improving the high capsaicin content. And also the selection process is helpful in the identification of high capsaicin containing lines in chilli. Krishnamurthy *et al.* (1999) conducted a study on evaluation of capsaicin content in red and green chillies. They revealed that among red chillies kolhapur (0.22) recorded highest capsaicin followed by Madras (0.21), among green chillies lavangi (0.165) recoded highest capsaicin followed by madras (0.114). and Musfiroh *et al.* (2013) conducted a study on capsaicin levels of various capsicum fruits. They revealed that highest amount of capsaicin was found in green rawit (cayenne) 2.11%, followed by red rawit (1.85%) and red curly (1.14%)(w/w).

Sources of Capsaicin

Some of the lines are available in chilli which contain highest amount of capsaicin which may be useful for breeding programmes to develop high capsaicin containing varieties and hybrids. In chilli EC-347263 and *Capsicum chinense.*

Solanine

Solanine is a glycoalkaloid poison found in species of the nightshade family (Solanaceae), such as the potato and the tomato. Solanine was first isolated in 1820 from the berries of the European black nightshade (*Solanum nigrum*), after which it was named.

Where it is Present and Examples

It can occur naturally in any part of the plant, including the leaves, fruit, and tubers. Toxin is found throughout the plant. Higher levels in green areas of potatoes and in sprouts (eyes of potato). Greening is strongly affected by light, age, and damage. The solanine content may be varied from species to species within the family of solanaceae. In potato it may be (10 mg/100 g) it should not contain more than 20 mg/100 g, it will leads to toxicity in human beings and in tomato it may be (7.7-9.2 mg/100 g).

Solanine in Human Health and Agriculture

Solanine plays an important role in the field of agriculture as well as in human health it has many uses in medical science. Solanine has fungicidal and pesticidal properties, and it is one of the plant's natural defenses. solanine hydrochloride (a salt of solanine) has been used as a commercial pesticide, but never on a large scale. Solanine has sedative and anticonvulsant properties, and has been used as a treatment for asthma, as well as for cough and cold medicines.

Dietary Requirement of Solanine

The solanine requirement is not standardized up to now but there are some research studies are given some doses. One study suggests that doses of 2 to 5 mg per kilogram of body weight can cause toxic symptoms, and doses of 3 to 6 mg per kilogram of body weight can be fatal.

Dietary Sources of Solanine

Solanine mostly found in solanaceae family, it conatains various species in this family. The solanine content may be varied from species to species within the family. Solanine can also be found in nightshade (*Solanum nigrum* and *S. americanum*), eggplant (*Solanum melongena*), and green peppers (*Capsicum anuum*). The common nightshade can contain as much as 7.6 to 8.2 mg/100g. Common peppers from 7.7 to 9.2 mg/100g of solanine. Eggplant solanine content varies from 6.1 to 11.33 mg/100g.

Adverse Effects of Solanine

Over consumption of solanine will leads to negative effects in huaman beings. In the human alpha-solanine and alpha-chaconine(another glycoalkaloid in potatoes) toxicity begins with gastrointestinal disturbances, vomiting, diarrhea, abdominal pain, then followed by neurological disorders at higher doses, low blood pressure, fever, rapid weak pulse. Solanine "poisoning" has a variety of symptoms. These symptoms may include: nausea, diarrhea, abdominal cramps, fever, headache, rapid breathing, hallucinations, delirium, and induce a coma. Other Symptoms include burning of the throat, loss of sensation, paralysis, jaundice.

Crop Improvement in Potato

Potato tubers contain a small amount of naturally occurring steroidal glycoal-kaloids–potentially toxic compounds which are present throughout the family *Soloanaceae.* Approximately 95% of the total glykoalkaloids present in potatoes are accounted for α-solanine and α-chaconine, both of which are structurally similar, being different glycosylated forms of aglycone, solanidine The level of glycoalkoloids in potato tubers can be influenced by several factors: genotype or variety (cultivar), climate, storage environment, maturity, damage, temperature and exposure to light. Potato varieties vary with regard to their inherited glycoalkaloid content; at low level it may enhance potato flavour, so it is acceptable. Higher concentration of glycoalkaloids (above 15 mg 100 g-1 fresh weight) can develop bitterness. Content above 20 mg 100 g-1 fresh weight (FW) is considered unsuitable for human consumption because of toxicity. Glycoalkoloids content in tubers of potato varieties vary quite widely. The varieties with genetically high levels are apparently more susceptible to excessive glycoalkaloids production in extreme conditions. The research of German's potato varieties showed glycoalkaloids content in range from 2 to 22 mg 100 g-1 FW, American varieties – 2 to 13 mg 100 g-1 FW, United Kingdom varieties – 3.6 to 14.2 mg 100 g-1FW. This trait in different investigations demonstrated quite high broad sense heritability (0.50 – 0.89%). Estimation of the glycoalkaloid levels of varieties used as parental genotypes and in the progenies should become an important criterion to take into consideration with aim to provide tuber glycoalkaloids content within accepted safety levels. Different methods for determination of separate glycoalkaloids and total glycoalkaloid (TGA) content were developed during more than 80 years. The first methods were only aware of solanine as the glycoalkaloid in tubers and the method for determination involved extraction, purification and weighing. The developed quantitative assay of potato glycoalkaloids depends on the method of primary extraction, the work-up procedure and the ultimate quantitative assay. The ways for primary extraction are: hot alcoholic extraction, extraction with bi-solvent mixture and extraction with aqueous acidic alcohol. The work-up procedures vary from the classical precipitation in alkaline solution to absorption and hydrolysis and extraction of the aglycones. Several techniques were used for quantitative assay: gravimetric, colorimetric, titrimetric, polarographic and chromatographic. For determination of glycoalkaloids with chromatographic analysis several ways can be used, for example, gas chromatography can be applied for analyses of glycoalkaloids. Some authors for routine determination suggested high-performance liquid chromatography suggested as a better choice. The problem in the practical use of most of these methods is the need for special equipment and many steps involved, therefore, they are money and time consuming. In this case the aims of the investigation were adaptation of a rapid and rather cheap TGA detection method and TGA content evaluation of varieties included in Latvia potato genetic resources. The potato steroidal glycoalkaloids (SGAs) are important components of plant resistance against pests and pathogens but can be toxic to humans at high levels (Idit Ginzberg *et al.*, 2009) The glycoalkaloid content in potato tubers can be influenced by several factors: variety, climate, storage environment, maturity, damage, temperature and exposure to light (Skrabule *et al.*, 2010). Skrabule *et al.*, 2010 conducted a study on adaptation of glycoalkaloids detection method for evaluation of latvia potato genetic resources. The TGA content in tubers of potato varieties was different. For most of the genotypes TGA content in tubers was below 20 mg 100 g FW, considered acceptable for human consumption. Some genotypes contained higher amount of TGA in tubers than accepted as suitable for human consumption. The influence of potato genotype on TGA content in tubers was significant, but the impact of growing conditions or year on TGA content in tubers was not significant.

GLUCOSINOLATES

The cruciferae are the family of plants that include the various familiar members of the species *Brassica oleracea*. Examples include: Broccoli, cabbage, cauliflower, kale, Brussels sprouts. A striking and characteristic chemical property of cruciferous plants is their high content of glucosinolates. Glucosinolates and their isothiocyanate hydrolysis (breakdown) products are well-known protectors against carcinogenesis, suggesting that greater intakes of these vegetables may lower the risk of several types of cancer.

The Unusual Phytochemistry of Crucifers

Glucosinolates are the precursors of isothiocyanates (mustard oils). Glucosinolates play protective and evolutionarily important roles in plants, including: Allelopathy,(Suppression of growth of neighbouring plants). Broad antibiotic properties Including nematocidal, antimicrobial, antifungal, antiprotozoal and insecticidal activities.

Dietary Requirement of Glucosinolates

Although only few attempts have been made to assess human glucosinolate consumption, some estimates are as high as 300 mg/d.

Crop Improvement in Cruciferous Vegetables

Glucosinolates are alkyl-N-hydroximine sulphate esters with a β-Dthio-glucopyranoside group attached to the hydroximine carbon in Z-configuration relative to the sulphate group. These compounds are allelochemicals biosynthetically derived from amino acids and they occur in all plants of the Capparales order and in some other plants. Glucosinolates co-occur with myrosinase isoenzymes (Thioglucosidase; EC 3.2.1.147), which catalyze the hydrolysis of the β-Dthioglucopyranoside bond. The released aglucones form a variety of biologically active products with structures defined by the type of glucosinolate and the reaction conditions Palmieri. These breakdown products can be chemically very reactive, and they have for a long time been known for their biologically active characteristics, such as antinutritional, fungicidal or bactericidal properties. The compositions and contents of GSs varied significantly among and within species and cultivars. The contents of total GSs were 100 to 130 mg/100 g fresh weight (FW) in turnip (*B. rapifera*), 50 to 70 mg/100 g, in purple cai-tai (*B. chinensis* var. *purpurea*), and 14 to 35 mg/100 g FW in Chinese cabbage (*B. pekinensis*), choysum (*B. chinensis* var.*utilis*), and pakchoi (*B. chinensis* var. *communis*) (Xinjuan Chen *et al.*, 2007). Natalia Bellostas *et al.* (2004) conducted a study on qualitative and quantitative evaluation of glucosinolates in cruciferous plants during their life cycles. They reported that reproductive tissues of Brassica Sp. showed highest glucosinolate concentration when compared to the rest of the plant parts. In the three species at the top of U-triangle, reproductive tissues showed the highest glucosinolate concentration when compared to the rest of the plant parts, while in *B. rapa*, the roots were the organs with the highest glucosinolate concentration.

CUCURBITACINS

Cucurbitacin is a class of biochemical compounds that some plants notably members of the family Cucurbitaceae, that includes the common pumpkins and gourds,developed in order to defend themselves from herbivores. Cucurbitacins are chemically classified as steroids, formally derived from cucurbitane, a triterpene hydrocarbon, hence they are called tetracyclic triterpenes.

Uses of Cucurbitacins

(*a*) To prevent cancer.

(*b*) They are used to treat and prevent constipation.

(*c*) They are used as a strong purgative.

(*d*) They are used to treat the diabetes.

(*e*) They are used to giving cooling effect to the body.

(*f*) Purifies the blood.

(*g*) Good for sore eyes, scabies and itches.

(*h*) They are used in Ayurveda and Unani for ulcers, asthama, jaundice, bronchitis and anaemia.

Crop Improvement in Cucurbits

Cucurbits contain cucurbitacins they are mainly useful for the treatment of various diseases and problems which are caused by low cucurbitacins content. So there is a need to improve these biochemical compounds in cucurbits, not only for health but it also useful for against pest resistance also. The breeding methods like selection process are need to be adapted to identify the best and high cucurbitacin containing lines and hybrids so that we can easily used these things in future breeding programmes. Still the research is going on for improving the cucurbitacins content in cucurbits. Still much more research is needed for improvement of these biochemical compounds. Marie Shoorooei *et al.* (2012) conducted a study on Screening of some cucumber accessions to two-spotted spider mite (*Tetranychus urticae*) reported that the Cucumber accessions having highest Cucurbitacin content showed resistance against red spider mite.

Not only these but also other useful vegetable biochemical compounds are present in vegetables are listed below.

Vegetables	Compounds	Role in Disease Prevention
Cole crops	Indoles and dithiolthiones	Prevention of cancer
Bitter gourd	Cheratin	Effective against diabetes
Onion	Diphenyl amine	Effective against diabetes
Celery	3-n-butyl pthalide	Effective against hypertension
Yams	Diosgenin	Manufacture of contraceptive drugs
Lettuce	Lutein	Nutritional antioxidant
Cabbage	Indole-3-carbinol	Against bowl cancer
Broccoli	Sulphoraphane	anticancer activity
Brinjal	Nasunin	Anticancer activity
Broccoli	Glucoraphinanin	Anticancer activity

Other Useful and Toxic Compounds Present in Vegetable Crops

Toxic substances	Crops
Trypsin inhibitors	Soyabean
Phytic acid (Inositol hexaphosphoric acid)	Peas and beans (mature seeds)
Oxalic acid and oxalates	Amaranth, portulaca, celosia, basella, and colocasia
Calcium oxalate	Elephant foot yam and colocasia
Hydrocyanic acid	Tapioca (more in leaves)
Dioscorine	Yam *(Dioscorea spp.,)*
Solasodine	Brinjal
Serotonin	Watermelon
Choline esterase	Pumpkin
Sinigrin	Cole crops
Saponine	Spinach, asparagus, tomato
Cucurbitacins	Cucurbits
Apiin	Celery
Haemaglutine	French bean
Vicine and covicine	Broad bean

CONCLUSION

The breeding lines and hybrids were identified so far can be utilized to cure human health hazards. So far the role of biochemical compounds in vegetables for human health has been exploited to a limited extent. Breeders are using different breeding methods like selection and backcross to improve their abundance. At present the genes regulating these compounds were poorly understood. Hence there is a need to understand the metabolism of these biochemical compounds at molecular level for further utilization of humankind.

REFERENCES

Al-Said, F.A. Al-Farsi, K. A. Khan, A. and A. Ali, A.2007. Field Evaluation of High Lycopene Tomato Breeding Lines in Oman. *Acta Hort.*277-280.

Ana C Agulheiro-Santos, Maria J Bernalte, Mercedes Lozano, Francisco Machado, Ana Sinogas. 2008. Quality of Two Tomato Cultivars Grown Under Different Agronomical Conditions. *Environmentally Friendly and Safe Technologies for Quality of Fruits and Vegetables*. 98-103.

A Textbook of Glaustas Olericulture. *New Vishal Publications*. Selvakumar, R. 2014.

Audrius radzevicius, Rasa karkleliene, Ceslovas bobinas, Pranas Viskelis. 2009. Nutrition Quality of Different Tomato Cultivars. *Zemdirbyste-Agriculture*. 96(3) : 67-75. Hassan, H.A. Mostafa, Wang Haiping, Liu Xinyan and Li Xixiang. 2015. Impact of Genetic Factor and Geographical Location on Allicin Content of Garlic (*Allium sativum*) Germplasm from Egypt and China. *International Journal of Agriculture & Biology*.17:156-162.

David M. Francis, Barb Franchino, Troy Aldrich, and Brenda Schult. 2001. Breeding for Color and Lycopene Content in Adapted Tomato Germplasm. Ohio Agricultural Research and Development Center.

Gajewski marek, Jadwiga radzanowska, Honorata danilcenko, Elvyra jariene, Judita cerniauskiene. 2008. Quality of Pumpkin Cultivars in Relation to Sensory Characteristics. *Not. Bot. Hort. Agrobot.* Cluj 36 (1) : 73-79.

Heterosis breeding. Nagendra Rai and Mathura Rai, 2006. *New India Publishing Agency*.

Krishna murthy, R. Malve, M.K. and Shinde, B.M. 1999. Evaluation of Capsaicin Content in Red and Green Chillies. *Journal of Scientific and Industrial Research*. 58:629-630.

Ibitoye,D.O. Akin-Idowu, P.E. and Ademoyegun, O.T. 2009. Agronomic and Lycopene Evaluation in Tomato (*Lycopersicon lycopersicum* Mill.) As a Function of Genotype. *World Journal of Agricultural Sciences*. 5 (S): 892-895.

Ida musfiroh, Mutakin mutakin, Treesye angelina, Muchtaridi muchtaridi. 2013. Capsaicin Level of Various Capsicum Fruits. *International Journal of Pharmacy and Pharmaceutical Science*. 5(1): 2013.

Marie Shoorooei, Mostafa Nasertorabi, Amanollah Soleimani, Ecehagh Moghbeli, Esmaeil Madadkhah, Hamid Moghbeli, 2012. Screening of Some Cucumber Accessions to Two-Spotted Spider Mite (*Tetranychus urticae*). *International Research Journal of Applied and Basic Sciences*. 3 (8): 1580-1584.

Modern Technology in Vegetable Production. 2011. *New India Publishing Agency*.

Natalia Bellostas, Jens C. Sorensen, Hilmer Sorensen, 2004. Qualitative and Quantitative Evaluation of Glucosinolates in Cruciferous Plants During their Life Cycles. *Agroindustria* 3 (3):5-10.

Penelope Perkins-Veazie and Angela R. Davis.2004. In Search of High Lycopene Watermelon. *Cucurbit Genetics Cooperative Report* 27:51-53.

Prarthana Mohanthy, Ashok, P. Swami, D.V Sasikala, K. 2014. *Msc Horticulture Thesis* Submitted to the *Dr. YSR. Horticultural University.* Venkataramannagudem, West Godavari District.

Rahman, M.H. Alam Patwary, M.M. Barua, H. Hossain, M. and Nahar, S. 2013. Evaluation of Orange Fleshed Sweet Potato (*Ipomoea batatas L.*) Genotypes for Higher Yield and Quality. *A Scientific Journal of Krishi Foundation.* 11(2): 21-27.

Sandhu, S.S. Brar, P.S. and Dhall, R.K. 2015. Variability of Agronomic and Quality Characteristics of Garlic (*allium sativum l.)* Ecotypes. *Sabrao Journal of Breeding and Genetics* 47 (2): 133-142.

Skrabule, I. Grauda,D. A. Mikelsone, A. Vasariete, A.2010. Adaptation of Glycoalkaloids Detection Method for Evaluation of Latvia Potato Genetic Resources. *State Research Programme in Agrobiotechnology* 1-6.

Stommel, J.R. and Haynes, K.G. 1994. Inheritance of β-carotene Content in the Wild Tomato Species *Lycopersicon Cheesmanii. The Journal of Heredity.* 85(5):401-404.

Vegetable Crops. Bose, T.K. Som, M.G. Kabir, J. *Nayaprokash Calcutta.*

Nutraceuticals and Pharmaceuticals from Medicinal Plants
Edited by: Dr. Pawan Kumar 'Bharti'; Dr. M.M. Abid Ali Khan; Dr. Ashok K. Rathoure
ISBN: 978-93-86841-55-1
Edition: 2018
Published by: Discovery Publishing House Pvt. Ltd., New Delhi (India)

5

Scenario of Cancer and Medicinal Plants as A Source of Its Treatment

[1]Dr. Showkat Ahmad Bhat, [2]Wasim Qureshi, [1]Prof. Sabhiya Majid, [1]Dr. Tehseen Hassan

SUMMARY

Cancer is one of the leading and most fatal diseases in the present decade, every year millions of people die because of various types of cancers as it is a dreadful disease and any practical solution in combating this disease is of paramount importance to public health. Many aspects relate to the cause of disease besides heredity, food habits, smoking, nutritional behaviours, radiation etc. The successful cancer therapy till now has been under research, only chemotherapy and radiation treatments are at times successful and much times toxic and lethal. Alternative and less toxic medication is very much in need towards the disease. Nature shows overabundance of medicinal plants with anticancer activities which may suppress the disease completely. The search for cancer drugs from natural sources like medicinal plants started in late 1960s. Keeping the fact, an attempt has been made to write a book chapter on the work being carried out all over the world about the cancer, its causes and different medicinal plants and there parts as anticancerous agents for this deadly disease.

Keywords: Cancer, Medicinal Plants, Treatment, Source

INTRODUCTION

Cancer is a major public health burden in both developed and developing countries. Cancer is a general term applied to the series of malignant diseases that may affect different parts of the body. It is a group of diseases characterized by the uncontrolled growth and spread of abnormal cells. If the spread is not controlled, it can result in death. Cancer is caused by external factors, such as tobacco, infectious organisms and an unhealthy diet and internal factors, such as inherited genetic mutations, hormones and immune conditions. These factors may act together or in sequence to cause cancer. Ten or more years often pass between exposure to external factors and detectable cancer. Treatments

[1] Department of Biochemistry, Govt. Medical College (GMC), Karan-Nagar, Srinagar, Jammu & Kashmir, India

include surgery, radiation, chemotherapy, hormone therapy, immune therapy and targeted therapy (drugs that specifically interfere with cancer cell growth). Cancer is one of the most common leading causes of mortality worldwide. Cancer is an uncontrolled growth of cells resulting in lack of differentiation and ability to invade local tissues and metastasis which are proliferate individually throughout the body. During metastasis, cancer cells enter the blood stream and are carried to distant parts of the body where they form other similar growths. Synthetic drugs are available for the treatment of cancer but they are not free from adverse effects. Chemotherapy and radiation therapy are major clinical treatment used for the control of early stages of tumor but these methods has serious side effects. Nature has provides human a variety of useful sources mainly plants for discovery and development of drugs against dreadful diseases. Traditional herb as an effective system of treatment of cancer and many diseases. Drugs from medicinal plants are found to be comparatively less toxic and side effects. The group of chemicals that cause cancer in human and animals are collectively referred to as carcinogens. Environmental pollution is associated with increased risk of cancer. Prevention of cancer and other related diseases can be pursued by avoiding exposure to recognized carcinogens, by favoring the intake of protective factors and by fortifying physiological defense mechanisms. Moreover, there is an increasing awareness that certain naturally occurring substances in plants and other source have protective effects against environmental carcinogens and also endogenous carcinogens. Hence research work related to the discovery, characterization and use of anticarcinogenic agents is receiving considerable attention. A large number of experimental reports have begun to appear in the scientific literature, wherein increasingly more natural anticarcinogens have been identified, isolated and found to possess significant cancer chemopreventive properties. Cancer is major health problem in both developed and developing countries. Cancer after cardiovascular disease is the second leading cause of death. Cancer is the abnormal growth of cells in our bodies that can lead to death. Because of high death rate associated with cancer

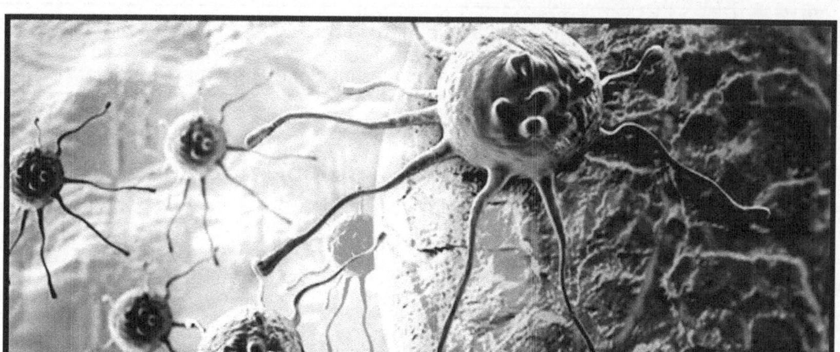

How Cancer Spreads

and because of serious side effects of chemotherapy and radiation therapy, many cancer patients seek alternative complementary methods of treatment. Plants have been used for treating diseases since time immemorial. More than 50% of modern drugs in clinical use are of natural products. In the present review, an attempt has been made to study the plants that have been used in the treatment of cancer.

The Whole Story About Cancer

- Cancers figure among the leading causes of morbidity and mortality worldwide.
- The number of new cases is expected to rise by about 70% over the next 2 decades.
- Among men, the 5 most common sites of cancer diagnosed in 2012 were lung, prostate, colorectum, stomach, and liver cancer.
- Among women the 5 most common sites diagnosed were breast, colorectum, lung, cervix, and stomach cancer.
- Around one third of cancer deaths are due to the 5 leading behavioral and dietary risks: high body mass index, low fruit and vegetable intake, lack of physical activity, tobacco use, alcohol use.
- Tobacco use is the most important risk factor for cancer causing around 20% of global cancer deaths and around 70% of global lung cancer deaths.

Types of Cancer

Table 5.1: Types of Cancer

Type	Site of cancer
Carcinomas	Cells that cover internal and external parts of the body such as lung, breast, and colon cancer.
Sarcoma	Bone, cartilage, fat, connective tissue, muscle and other supportive tissues.
Lymphomas	Lymph nodes and immune system tissues.
Leukemias	Bone marrow and often accumulate in the bloodstream.
Adenomas	Thyroid, the pituitary gland, the adrenal gland and other glandular tissues.

Sign and Symptoms

You should know some of the general signs and symptoms of cancer. But remember, having any of these does not mean that you have cancer-many other things cause these sign and symptoms, too.

- Unexplained weight loss
- Fever
- Fatigue
- Pain

- Skin changes (Darker looking skin, yellowish skin and eyes, reddened skin, itching, excessive hair growth)
- Change in bowel habits or bladder function
- Sores that do not heal
- White patches inside the mouth or white spots on the tongue
- Unusual bleeding or discharge
- Thickening or lump in the breast or other parts of the body
- Indigestion or trouble swallowing
- Nagging cough or hoarseness
- Breathlessness
- Unexplained vaginal bleeding
- Persist hearburn or indigestion
- Croaky voice or hoarseness
- Looser poo or pooing more often
- Persistent bloating
- Difficulty swallowing
- Mouth or tongue ulcer that wont heal
- Heavy night sweats
- Unusual breast changes
- Blood in your poo
- Blood in your pee
- Other symptoms

Diagnosis of Cancer

If you have a symptom or your screening test result suggests cancer, the doctor must find out whether it is due to cancer or some other cause. The doctor may ask about your personal and family medical history and do a physical exam. The doctor also may order lab tests, scans, or other tests or procedures.

- **Lab Tests:** High or low levels of certain substances in your body can be a sign of cancer. So, lab tests of the blood, urine, or other body fluids that measure these substances can help doctors make a diagnosis. However, abnormal lab results are not a sure sign of cancer. Lab tests are an important tool, but doctors cannot rely on them alone to diagnose cancer.
- **Imaging Procedures:** Imaging procedures create pictures of areas inside your body that help the doctor see whether a tumor is present. These pictures can be made in several ways.
- **CT scan:** An x-ray machine linked to a computer takes a series of detailed pictures of your organs. You may receive a dye or other contrast material

to highlight areas inside the body. Contrast material helps make these pictures easier to read.

- **Nuclear scan:** For this scan, you receive an injection of a small amount of radioactive material, which is sometimes called a tracer. It flows through your bloodstream and collects in certain bones or organs. A machine called a scanner detects and measures the radioactivity. The scanner creates pictures of bones or organs on a computer screen or on film. Your body gets rid of the radioactive substance quickly. This type of scan may also be called radionuclide scan.
- **Ultrasound:** An ultrasound device sends out sound waves that people cannot hear. The waves bounce off tissues inside your body like an echo. A computer uses these echoes to create a picture of areas inside your body. This picture is called a sonogram. A strong magnet linked to a computer is used to make detailed pictures of areas in your body. Your doctor can view these pictures on a monitor and print them on film.
- **PET scan:** For this scan, you receive an injection of a tracer. Then, a machine makes 3-D pictures that show where the tracer collects in the body. These scans show how organs and tissues are working.
- **X-rays:** X-rays use low doses of radiation to create pictures of the inside of your body.
- **Biopsy:** In most cases, doctors need to do a biopsy to make a diagnosis of cancer. A biopsy is a procedure in which the doctor removes a sample of tissue. A pathologist then looks at the tissue under a microscope to see if it is cancer. The sample may be removed in several ways.
- **With a needle:** The doctor uses a needle to withdraw tissue or fluid.
- **With an endoscope:** The doctor looks at areas inside the body using a thin, lighted tube called an endoscope. The scope is inserted through a natural opening, such as the mouth. Then, the doctor uses a special tool to remove tissue or cells through the tube.
- v **With surgery:** Surgery may be excisional or incisional. In an excisional biopsy, the surgeon removes the entire tumor. Often some of the normal tissue around the tumor also is removed. In an incisional biopsy, the surgeon removes just part of the tumor.

Factors Influencing Cancer

Age: Cancer most commonly develops in older people; 78% of all cancer diagnoses are in people 55 years of age or older. Anyone can develop cancer. However, the risk of being diagnosed with cancer increases substantially with age. In economically developed countries, 78% of all newly diagnosed cancer cases occur at age 55 and older compared to 58% in developing countries. The difference is largely due to variations in age structure of the populations. The populations of developing countries are younger and have a smaller proportion of older individuals in whom cancer most frequently occurs.

(*a*) **Obesity and Physical activity:** Obesity and lack of physical activity are associated with increased risk at various cancer sites, including breast and endometrial cancer. In India, increases in the rates of obesity, central adiposity, and waist-hip ratio associated with urbanization are seen in every region and are highest among those with the highest levels of education and income. Energy balance, which includes maintaining ideal weight through physical exercise, has been associated with decreased risk of breast cancer. There are few large cross-sectional studies of energy balance in India. Among urban populations, energy intake has increased at the same time that energy expenditures have decreased, due in part to employment in industries reliant on mechanization. No comprehensive study of physical activity in India has been done, but small studies of selected populations suggest that levels of physical activity are inadequate to meet recommendations for prevention of chronic diseases.

(*b*) **Tobacco and Smoking:** The consumption of tobacco is the leading cause of cancers in India. The regular use of tobacco via smoking, chewing, snuffing etc. in some areas of the country (India), which is responsible for 65% to 85% cancer incidences in men and women, respectively. The various cancers produced by the use of tobacco are of oral cavity, pharynx, esophagus, larynx, lungs and urinary bladder. Smoking is the most notorious factor for the causation of lung cancer. Approximately, 87 and 85% males and females have been found to have lung cancer due to tobacco smoking in the form of bidi and cigarette in India.

(*c*) **Alcohol consumption:** Alcohol consumption has been considered as one of the major causes of colorectal cancer as per a recent monograph of WHO. Annually, about 9.4% new colorectal cancer cases are attributed to the consumption of alcohol, globally. An increased risk of 10% was observed with consumption of more than two drinks per day, which suggests a causative role of alcohol consumption in colorectal cancer. Relationship between alcohol consumption and high risk of oesophageal cancer was first known in 1910. However, chronic alcohol consumption has been found to be a risk factor for the cancers of the upper respiratory and digestive tracts, including oral cavity, hypopharynx, larynx and esophagus as well as liver, pancreas, mouth and breast cancers. The mechanism of carcinogenesis due to alcohol consumption is not exactly known, however, it is thought that ethanol being a co-carcinogen might play a crucial role in the carcinogenesis.

(*d*) **Radiation:** In the developed and developing countries, the radiations are also notorious carcinogens. About 10% cancer occurrence is due to radiation effect, both ionizing and non-ionizing. The major sources of radiations are radioactive compounds, ultraviolet (UV) and pulsed electromagnetic fields. The main series of cancers induced by exposure to the adequate doses of the carcinogenic radiations include thyroid, skin, leukemia, lymphoma, lung and breast carcinomas.

(*e*) **Vegetarian diets:** A large percentage of Indians, particularly Hindus, practice vegetarianism and avoid meat and fish products in their diet. Vegetarian diets have been associated with decreased risk for prostate cancer. Case-control studies that compared non-vegetarian and vegetarian diets and alcohol and tobacco use in India have reported that vegetarians have a reduced risk of oral, oesophageal and breast cancers. Vegetarians diets rely on pulses (e.g. beans, chickpeas and lentils) as a source of protein and pulses have been significantly associated with reduction in cancer.

(*f*) **Dietary fats and fiber:** Diets high in saturated fats have been associated with increased risk for cancer. Fat intake, especially saturated fat, is increasing in the middle class in India, although some rural residents traditionally have had a high intake of ghee (clarified butter, high content of saturated fat), as well. Studies have given equivocal results regarding the link between fat intake and the risk of cancer. Large epidemiological studies have identified a possible association between increased dietary fibre and a decreased risk for cancers of the colon and breast. No large studies on dietary fibre have been conducted in India, and rates of colon and breast are low compared to those in western societies. The Indian diet, which generally includes adequate levels of vegetables, fruits and fiber-rich grains, may provide some protection against increased risk for these cancers.

(*g*) **Spices and additives:** Diet in India developed over thousands of years and is based on a mix of religious and secular beliefs. Among the most studied in recent years is turmeric, an ingredient in the common Indian curry and a spice that has been shown to be a potent antioxidant and anti-inflammatory agent with additional promise as a chemo-preventive agent. In a study in human blood cancer cell lines, turmeric suppressed and destroyed blood cancer cells. Turmeric has been shown to suppress tumour initiation, promotion and metastasis in experimental studies. Turmeric also has been found to inhibit the growth of 19 clinical strains of Helicobacter pylori, a carcinogenic bacterium linked to the increased risk of adenocarcinoma of the stomach and colorectal adenomas. Amrita Bindu, a dietary supplement that is a salt-spice-herbal mixture, was found to protect rats against cancer induced by N-methyl-N-nitrosoguanidine, a potent carcinogenic nitro-samine. Studies on spices and food additives have been conducted in vitro and in animal studies. Because of intriguing findings from these studies, there is a need to investigate these dietary factors in human studies.

(*h*) **Micronutrients:** Micronutrients play a significant role in maintaining health and preventing disease, including cancer, through a wide range of mechanisms: anti-oxidation, anti-proliferation and repair of DNA damage. Direct and indirect relationships between micronutrients and health have been described in experimental, epidemiological and clinical trials, Vitamin deficiencies, specifically of vitamins A, C and E may contribute to the high prevalence of oral cancers in India. A study carried out in rural India found that the presence of lesions was associated in patients with oral pre-cancerous lesions with low plasma levels of vitamins E and β-carotene. A study of Kuchias (a tribal population in Kerala, India, who consume a diet high in micronutrients and have a low prevalence of CHD and other chronic diseases of aging, including cancer) found that levels of serum vitamins A and E were inversely related to levels of lipid peroxides and CHD risk factors. Micronutrient deficiencies of iodine, iron and vitamin A are highly prevalent in Indian children. Among 6-14 year-old, goiter, caused by iodine deficiency and related to thyroid cancer, has a prevalence rate of 0.33 to 2.4%.

Leading Sites of New Cancer Cases 2015 Estimates

Table 5.2: Estimated New Cancer Cases 2015.

Male		Female	
Prostate	26%	Breast	29%
Lung & bronchus	14%	Lung & bronchus	13%
Colon & rectum	8%	Colon & rectum	8%
Urinary bladder	7%	Uterine corpus	7%
Melanoma of the skin	5%	Thyroid	6%
Non-Hodgkin lymphoma	5%	Non-Hodgkin lymphoma	4%
Kidney & renal pelvis	5%	Melanoma of the skin	4%
Oral cavity & pharynx	4%	Pancreas	3%
Leukemia	4%	Leukemia	3%
Liver & interhepatic bile duct	3%	Kidney & renal pelvis	3%
All sites	100%	All sites	100%

Leading Sites of New Cancer Deaths 2015 Estimates

Table 5.3: Estimated New Cancer Deaths 2015. Estimated Deaths

Male		Female	
Lung & bronchus	28%	Lung & bronchus	26%
Prostate	9%	Breast	15%
Colon & rectum	8%	Colon & rectum	9%
Pancreas	7%	Pancreas	7%
Liver & interhepatic bile duct	5%	Ovary	5%
Leukemia	5%	Leukemia	4%
Esophagus	4%	Uterine corpus	4%
Urinary bladder	4%	Non-Hodgkin lymphoma	3%
Non-Hodgkin lymphoma	4%	Liver & interhepatic bile duct	3%
Kidney & renal pelvis	3%	Brain & other nervous system	2%
All sites	100%	All sites	100%

The Mechanism on Cancer Therapy

- Inhibiting cancer cell proliferation directly by stimulating macrophage phagocytosis, enhancing natural killer cell activity.
- Promoting apoptosis of cancer cells by increasing production of interferon-I, nterleukin-2, immunoglobulin and complement in blood serum.
- Enforcing the necrosis of tumor and inhibiting its translocation and spread by blocking the blood source of tumor tissue.
- Enhancing the number of leukocytes and platelets by stimulating the haemopoietic function.
- Promoting the reverse transformation from tumor cells into normal cells.
- Promoting metabolism and preventing carcinogenesis of normal cells.
- Stimulating appetite, improving quality of sleep, relieving pain, thus benefiting patient's health.

Carcinogenesis, Carcinogens and Anticarcinogens

Carcinogenesis is a complex multi-stage process induced by various types of carcinogens that ultimately lead to the development of cancer. The common consensus among cancer researchers is that carcinogenesis, the process of malignant growth of normal cells, proceeds through a series of steps involving spontaneous changes in genetic material DNA which is prone to damage by environmental agents especially radiation and chemical mutagens. Many intrinsic and extrinsic factors, interacting with one another, influence this process of carcinogenesis. Carcinogenesis includes three main phases: initiation, promotion and progression.

Initiation: The first stage of carcinogenesis has been labelled initiation since 1947. The conclusions reached from several experiments enabled the conclusion to be drawn that initiation is caused by irreversible genetic changes which predispose susceptible normal cells to malign evolution and immortality. Neoplasia initiation is essentially irreversible changes in appropriate target somatic cells. In the simplest terms, initiation involves one or more stable cellular changes arising spontaneously or induced by exposure to a carcinogen. This is considered to be the first step in carcinogenesis, where the cellular genome undergoes mutations, creating the potential for neoplastic development, which predisposes the affected cell and its progeny to subsequent neoplastic transformation. The human DNA sequences responsible for transformation are called oncogenes. Although the activation of more than one oncogenes appears to be necessary for neoplastic transformation, the data imply that initiation may be induced with one hit kinetics. However, the full expression of such neoplasia initiating mutations invariably requires interaction with other later arising gene mutations and/or changes to the cellular environment, but the initiating mutation creates the stable potential for pre-neoplastic cellular development in cells with proliferative capacity. The transformed cell undergoes continuous division with fidelity to the transformed karyotype and, possibly, with further mutations, before a malignant lesion is manifested. Each oncogene is closely associated with a normal DNA sequence present in the cellular genome, the proto-oncogene. At least five different mechanisms are considered for the conversion of proto-oncogenes to active oncogenes (*i*) Overexpression of proto-oncogene following acquisition of a novel transcriptional promoter. The oncogene then acquires activity because their transcripts are produced at much higher levels than those of the related normal proto-oncogene. (*ii*) Over-expression due to amplification of the proto-oncogene or oncogene. The increased gene copies cause corresponding increases in transcript and gene product. (*iii*) Influences on the levels of transcription and, in turn, the amount of gene product. (*iv*) Juxtaposition of the oncogene and immunoglobulin domains, following chromosomal translocations, that appears to result in deregulation of the gene. (v) Alteration in the structure of the oncogene protein. This is the most well documented mechanism in the case of the oncogene proteins encoded by the ras genes.

Promotion: The concept of promotion was introduced when chemical substances with low carcinogenic activity were discovered, which were still able to induce the development of cancer under experimental conditions Promoter compounds do not interact directly with DNA and unchain biological effects without being metabolically activated. These agents increase cell proliferation in susceptible tissues, contribute towards fixing mutations, enhance alterations in genetic expression and cause changes in cellular growth control. The transformed (initiated) cell can remain harmless, unless and until it is stimulated to undergo further proliferation, upsetting the cellular balance. The subsequent changes of an initiated cell leading to neoplastic transformation may involve more than one step and requires repeated and prolonged exposures to promoting stimuli. Expression of the initial mutation will depend not only on interaction with other oncogenic mutations but also on factors that may temporarily change the patterns of specific gene expression, eg. cytokines, lipid metabolites, and certain phorbol esters. This may result in an enhancement of cellular growth potential and/or an uncoupling of the intercellular communication processes that restrict cellular autonomy and thereby coordinate tissue maintenance and development.

Progression: is the process through which successive changes in the neoplasm give rise to increasingly malignant sub-populations. Molecular mechanisms of tumor progression are not fully understood, but mutations and chromosomal aberrations are thought to be involved. The process may be accelerated by repeated exposures to carcinogenic stimuli or by selection pressures favoring the autonomous clonal derivatives. The initiated cells proliferate causing a fast increase in the tumor size. As the tumor grows in size, the cells may undergo further mutations, leading to increasing heterogeneity of the cell population. In the first phase of progression, sometimes referred to as neoplastic conversion, the pre-neoplastic cells are transformed to a state in which they are more committed to malignant development. The dynamic cellular heterogeneity, a feature of malignant development, may, in many instances, be a consequence of the early acquisition of genespecific mutations that destabilize the genome. Examples are mutations of the p53 gene or DNA mismatch repair genes. Many tumor types develop transforming sequences in their DNA during their progression from the normal to the cancerous state. An elevated mutation rate established relatively early in tumor development may, therefore, provide for the high-frequency generation of variant cells within a premalignant cell population. Such variant cells, having the capacity to evade the constraints that act to restrict proliferation of aberrant cells, will tend to be selected during tumorigenesis. The mechanism of promotion is not well understood. These changes trigger cell proliferation, an apparently necessary process in the "fixation" or expression of tumor initiation. Molecular genetics mechanisms are implicated in tumor progression, leading to chromosomal rearrangements or mutations that activate proto oncogenes. Thus, it appears that of the three stages of carcinogenesis initiation, promotion and progression. Initiation most certainly, and progression most likely, involve molecular genetic changes and leads to particular cancer to a person.

Mechanism of Anticarcinogenesis

The major mechanisms of anticarcinogenesis can be broadly described as under:

A. Chemical or enzymatic inactivation.

B. Prevention of formation of active species.

C. Scavenging.

D. Antioxidant or free radical scavenging.

A: Chemical or enzymatic inactivation: Many carcinogens, which are reactive, acting not only on DNA but also on proteins and enzymes, can be directly inactivated by a range of different chemicals. Anticarcinogenic properties have been associated with both inhibitors and inducers of cytochrome P-450 enzymes such as indole-3-carbinol. Inducers of phase-II metabolic enzymes such as glutathione transferase tend to inhibit a wide range of target carcinogens. e.g. isothiocyanates such as benzyl isothiocyanate and antioxidants such as 2, 3-tert butyl-4-hydroxy-anisole (BHA).

B: Prevention of formation of active species: Many genotoxic mutagens or carcinogens require metabolic activation or bio-activation to an electrophilic from (the active species) that can react with the DNA. Although these processes commonly occur in the liver, there is increasing evidence for metabolic activation by other tissues also, especially for the GIT. N-nitro compounds are often formed in the stomach through a reaction from nitrite and secondary or tertiary amines.

C: Scavenging: A number of anticarcinogens are able to scavenge dietary carcinogens through binding or adsorption. In general, the carcinogen remains intact during this process but is unable to react with DNA. Chlorophyllin and some dietary fibers appear to act in this way.

D: Antioxidant and free radical scavenging: Free radicals can damage DNA and cause mutagenicity and cytotoxicity and thus play a key role in carcinogenesis. It is believed that reactive oxygen species (ROS) can induce mutations and inhibit DNA repair process, that result in the inactivation of certain tumor suppressor genes, leading to cancer. This appears to be the most commonly operative anticarcinogenesis mechanism of medicinal plant constituents. A wide range of anticarcinogenic agents from medicinal plants have excellent antioxidant or free radical scavenging activity e. g. carotenoids, flavonoids and phenolic compounds. These agents can directly scavenge most oxidative and nitrosative free radicals generated during carcinogenesis process thus reduce oxidative stress and prevent carcinogen-toxicity to the vital organs like liver, heart, kidney and brain. These agents can also mediate anticarcinogenesis by augmenting the endogenous both non-enzymatic (glutathione) and enzymatic (glutathione S-transferase, glutathione reductase, superoxide dismutase, catalase) antioxidant defense mechanisms prevalent in the body thereby ameliorating the oxidative impact generated due to carcinogenesis.

Plant As A Source of Anti-cancer Compounds

Natural products of folk medicine have been used for centuries in every culture throughout the world. Scientists and medical professionals have shown increased interest in this field as they recognized the true health benefits of these remedies. While searching for food, the ancient found that some foods had specific properties of relieving or eliminating certain diseases and maintaining good health. It was the beginning of herbal medicine. For thousands of years, cultures around the world have used herbs and plants to treat illness and maintain health. Many drugs prescribed today in modern medicinal system are derived from plants. Herbs and plants are valuable not only for their active ingredients but also for their minerals, vitamins, volatile oils, glycosides, alkaloids, acids, alcohols, esters etc., Complementary and alternative medicine (CAM) can be defined as any treatment used in conjugation (complementary) or in place of (alternative) standard medical treatment. In alternative medicine, medicinal plant preparations have found widespread use particularly in the case of diseases not amenable to treatment by modern method. Plants are the reservoirs of a large number of imperative organic compounds and they have long been used as the sources of medicines. Dependence on plants is prevalent in developing countries where the traditional herbal medicine plays a major role in health care and in the treatment of many infectious diseases. The rural population of a country is more disposed to traditional ways of treatment because of its easy availability and cheaper cost. Herbal therapies although, still an unwritten science is well established in some cultures and tradition and have become a way of treatment in almost 80% of the people in rural areas, especially those in Asia, Latin America and Africa. In this present review article an attempt has been made to compile the information on anticancer properties of five commonly available medicinal plants. The details of which have been mentioned below along with their uses and active principles.

Plant derived compounds, which are the important source of clinically useful anti-cancer drug, has shown to have potential for treatment or prevention of cancer in humans. In the treatment of cancer, plant has a long history; more than 3000 plant species have been reported by Hartwell which are used in treatment of cancer. Plants as well as plant derived compounds have played significant role in the development of a number of clinically used anti-cancer agents. These include vinblastine, vincristine, the camptothecin derivatives, topotecan and irinotecan, etoposide, derived from epipodophyllotoxin, and paclitaxel. Quite a lot of promising new agents are in clinical development based on selective activity against cancer-related molecular targets, including flavopiridol and combretastin A4 phosphate, and some agents which failed in earlier clinical studies are stimulating renewed interest. Also there are some of the semi synthetic plant derivatives which are clinically used as potential anti caner agents. The traditional and the preliminary scientific work on these plant products are giving promising results, further research in the same is to be continued to derive potent anti caner agents from medicinal plants. Chemotherapy, being a major treatment modality used for the control of advanced stages of malignancies and as a prophylactic against possible metastasis, exhibits severe toxicity on normal tissues. Plants have been used for treating various diseases of human beings and animals since time immemorial. They maintain the health and vitality of individuals and also cure diseases, including cancer without causing toxicity. More than 50% of all modern drugs in clinical use are of natural products, many of which have the ability to control cancer cells.

List of Anticancer Plants

Table 5.4: List of Anticancer Plant.

S. No.	Plant name	Family	Chemical responsible for anticancer activity
(a)	Ashwagandha	Solanaceae or nightshade	Isopelletierine, anaferine, withanolides, withaferins
(b)	Turmeric	Zingiberaceae	Curcumin
(c)	Golden root or Arctic root	Rhodiola	Organic acids, flavonoids, tannins, and phenolic glycosides
(d)	Vinca	Apocynaceae	Vinblastine, Vincristine, Vinorelbine, and Vindesine
(e)	Wheat grass	Grasses	Chlorophyll, Selenium and Lactrile
(f)	Neem	Meliaceae	Flavonoids (Rutin and Quercetin)
(g)	Taxus	Taxaceae	Paclitaxel, Taxol
(h)	Aloe vera	Xanthorrhoeaceae	Aloeemodin, Emodin

(*a*) Ashwagandha: Ashwagandha is reported to have anti-carcinogenic effects in animal and cell cultures by decreasing the expression of nuclear factor-kappa-B, suppressing intercellular tumor necrosis factor, and potentiating apoptotic signalling in cancerous cell lines. To investigate its use in treating various forms of cancer, the antitumor and radio sensitizing effects of W. somnifera have been studied. In one study, W. somnifera was evaluated for its anti-tumor effect in urethane-induced lung adenomas in adult male albino mice. Simultaneous administration of W. somnifera (ethanol extract of whole plant, 200 mg/kg daily orally for seven months) and urethane (125 mg/kg without food biweekly for seven months) reduced tumor incidence significantly (tumor incidence: untreated control, 0/25; urethane treated, 19/19; W. somnifera treated, 0/26, and W. somnifera plus urethane treated, 6/24,

$p < 0.05$). The histological appearance of the lungs of animals protected by W. somnifera was similar to those observed in the lungs of control animals. No pathological evidence of any neoplastic change was observed in the brain, stomach, kidneys, heart, spleen, or testes of any treated or control animals.

(*b*) **Turmeric:** Provides anti-Tumor support Curcumin is undergoing clinical trial as an alternative for cancer treatment. Curcumin extract could be beneficial in many kinds of cancer such as breast cancer, colon cancer, skin cancer as well as prostate cancer. Based on its distinct chemical properties, curcumin interacts with numerous extracellular and intracellular molecules that are actively involved in cancer initiation and progression, thereby inhibiting cancer progression. Increasing evidence suggests that deregulated inflammatory pathways play a pivotal role in a multitude of chronic diseases, including cancer. The mechanism by which chronic inflammation drives cancer initiation and progression is via increased production of pro-inflammatory mediators, such as cytokines, chemokines, reactive oxygen species (ROS), over expression of oncogenes, cyclooxygenase (COX-2), matrix metalloproteinase (MMPs), intracellular signaling pathway mediators, transcription factors such as nuclear factor κB (NF-κB), signal transducer and activator of transcription 3 (STAT3), protein kinase B (AKT), and activator protein 1 (AP1) that drive tumor cell proliferation, transformation, invasion, metastasis, angiogenesis, chemo resistance and radio resistance.

(*c*) **Golden Root or Arctic Root:** Twenty-eight compounds have been isolated from the roots and above-ground parts of R. rosea, including 12 novel compounds. The roots contain a range of biologically active substances including organic acids, flavonoids, tannins, and phenolic glycosides. Significant free-radical scavenging activity has been demonstrated for alcohol and water extracts of Rhodiola sps. and is attributed to the variety of antioxidant compounds. p-Tyrosol has been shown to be readily and dose-dependently absorbed after an oral dose, and appears to produce a significant antioxidant and modest 5-lipoxygenase inhibitory activity in vivo. Salidroside (rhodioloside), the additional salidroside-like glycoside compounds (rhodiolin, rosin, rosavin, rosarin, and nrosiridin), and p-tyrosol are thought to be the most critical plant constituents needed for therapeutic activity. Administration of *R. rosea* appears to have potential as an anticancer agent, and might be useful in conjunction with some pharmaceutical antitumor agents. In rats with transplanted solid Ehrlich adenocarcinoma and metastasizing rat Pliss lymphosarcoma, supplementation with *R. rosea* extract inhibited the growth of both tumor types, decreased metastasis to the liver, and extended survival times. Administration of *R. rosea* extract also directly suppressed the growth of and the extent of metastasis from transplanted Lewis lung carcinomas. When *R. rosea* extract was combined with the antitumor agent cyclophosphamide in these same tumor models, the antitumor and antimetastatic efficacy of drug treatment was enhanced. The authors have commented that, "complete abrogation of the haematotoxicity of cyclophosphamide" was observed. The chemotherapeutic drug Adriamycin is known to induce pronounced liver dysfunction, generally reflected by an increase in transaminase levels. In animal experiments, adding *R. rosea* extract to a protocol with Adriamycin resulted in an improved inhibition of tumor dissemination (as compared to that found with Adriamycin alone), and the combined protocol prevented liver toxicit.

(*d*) Vinca: Vinca alkaloids belong to an important class of anti-cancer drugs. The mechanism of action of Vinca alkaloids is that they inhibit the cell proliferation by affecting the microtubular dynamics during mitosis and this causes a characteristic block during mitosis leading to apoptosis. Vinca alkaloids include Vinblastine (VLB) and Vincristine (VCR), Vinorelbine (VRLB) and Vindesine (VDS) are obtained from the Madagascar periwinkle, Catharanthus roseus G. Don. (Apocynaceae). The main mechanisms of Vinca alakaloid cytotoxicity is due to their interactions with tubulin and disruption of microtubule function, particularly of microtubules comprising the mitotic spindle apparatus, directly causing metaphase arrest. However, they can do many other biochemical activities that may or may not be related to their effects on microtubules. Many of the effects that do not include microtubule interruption happen only after treatment of cells with clinically irrelevant doses of the vinca alkaloids. Nevertheless, the vinca alkaloids and other antimicrotubule agents also have an effect on both non-malignant and malignant cells in the non-mitotic cell cycle, because microtubules are involved in many non-mitotic functions.

***(e)* Wheatgrass:** Many dietary compounds have been suggested to contribute to the prevention of cancer, there is a strong likelihood that wheatgrass extract, which contains chlorophyll, an antioxidant, may affect cancer prevention. Additionally, selenium and lactrile present in wheatgrass have anti-cancer properties. Selenium builds a strong immune system, and can decrease the risk of cancer. Wheatgrass contains at least 13 vitamins (several of which are antioxidants) including B12, abscisic acid, superoxide dismutase (SOD), cytochrome oxidase, mucopolysaccharide. SOD converts two superoxide anions into a hydrogen peroxide molecule, which has an extra oxygen molecule to kill cancer cells. Wheatgrass juice may also inhibit hematological toxicity related to chemotherapy in breast cancer patients. It is also observed that people undergoing chemotherapy, who are on wheatgrass, have sailed through this treatment and have not required hospital admission, while side effects such as nausea, vomiting and mouth ulcers have been virtually non-existent. In another study, in vitro cytotoxic and antiproliferation activities of two extracts–the wheatgrass and the mixture of fibers, were tested and demonstrated anti-leukemia potential with less or no toxic effects towards the healthy immune system. Wheatgrass and fiber methanol extracts have successfully exhibited to be cytotoxic towards HL60 cell lines without causing toxicity towards normal human PBMC. Thus, these health products can be a potential alternative supplement for cancer patients.

(f) **Neem:** Azadirachta indica (neem tree) has been used successfully to reduce tumors by herbalists from centuries. Recent studies indicated that an ethanolic extract of neem has been shown to cause cell death of prostate cancer cells (PC-3) by inducitng apoptosis as evidenced by a dose-dependent increase in DNA fragmentation and a decrease in cell viability. Different studies indicate its use against buccal carcinogenesis, skin carcinogenesis, prostate cancer, mammary carcinogenesis, gastric carcinogenesis, Ehrlich carcinoma and B16 melanoma. A. indica (Neem) has also revealed a chemo preventive capability by regressing the hepat-carcinogenesie induced by DEN/AAF carcinogens. The biological activity of Neem leaves was due to its rich content of flavonoids. Flavanoids have been reported to possess both antioxidant activity and anti-inflammatory activities via scavenging free radicals and inhibition of lipid peroxidation. Antitumor activity of flavonoids, isolated from several sources other neem, has been reported. That compounds have been shown to have anti-proliferative effects on human squamous cell carcinoma.

(g) Taxus: Taxol, Docetaxol are the active constituents of Taxus which belong to Taxaceae. These drugs are given to treat breast cancer, after combination anthracycline and cytoxan therapy. Taxol is also used to treat ovarian cancer, lung cancer, head and neck cancer, bladder cancer. A cyclodecane isolated from the bark of the Pacific yew tree, Taxus brevifolia. It stabilizes microtubules in their polymerized form leading to cell death. ABI-007 (Abraxane) is the latest attempt to improve upon paclitaxel, one of the leading chemotherapy treatments. Use of an inhibitor against an activating mutation of signaling molecule in combination with a standard chemotherapeutic agent such as Paclitaxel showed synergistic activity in mutant human endometrial cancer cell lines. A study performed to evaluate the cytotoxic effects of Paclitaxel in combination with Etoposide in Osteosarcoma cells to thermo chemotherapy showed that the apoptosis inducing capacity of the drug combination was stronger than the effect of drugs when used individually. Taxol is an important anticancer drug used widely in the clinical field. Taxol is a diterpenoids, which was first extracted in the bark of yew (Taxus brevifolia). It can kill tumor cells by enhancing the assembly of microtubules and inhibiting their depolymerisation. This compound is the world s first billion dollar anticancer drug and it is used to treat breast, lung, ovarian cancer and other human tissue proliferating disease.

(h) Aloe Vera: Aloe vera contains aloeemodin, which activates the macrophages to fight cancer. Aloe vera also contains acemannan, which enhances activity of the immune cells against cancer. Aloe vera is found to inhibit metastases. There is early evidence that oral Aloe may reduce the risk of developing lung cancer. The role of Aloe in carcinogenicity has not been evaluated well. The chronic abuse of anthranoid-containing laxatives has been hypothesized to play a role in colo-rectal cancer; however, no causal relationship between anthranoid laxative abuse and colorectal cancer has been demonstrated and. Aloe vera juice enables the body to heal itself from cancer and also from the damage caused by radio and chemotherapy that destroys healthy immune cells crucial for the recovery. Aloe vera emodin, an anthraquinone, has the ability to suppress or inhibit the growth of malignant cancer cells making it to have anti-neoplastic properties.

CONCLUSION

Since the dawn of human civilization medicinal plants have been considered to be the best source of curing various dreaded disease and cancer is one among those diseases. Cancer is the abnormal growth of cells in our bodies that can lead to death. There is lot of medicinal plants available in nature which has the anticancerous properties and majority of them are still to be exploited. For treatment of cancer there are very synthetic compounds present but they have many adverse effects as compared to medicinal plants that have anticancer activity. Medicinal plants that have anticancer activity has role in treatment as well as chemopreventive purpose for cancer. Some medicinal plant like turmeric, vinca, taxus, neem, aloe vera, broccoli, etc that have chemical constituents as curcumin, vincristine, vinblastine, taxol and various anticancer classes of constituents like vitamins, flavonoids, phenolic compounds, anthraquinones, carotenoids, diterpenoids, coumarins, tannins, saponins and other miscellaneous compounds have their important role in treatment and/or in prevention of cancer. So, considering the facts it is strongly recommended that there is an urge for these plants to be discovered so that the cancer could be totally eradicated.

REFERENCES

Showkat Ahmad Bhat, Manzoor R. Mir, Sabhiya Majid, *et al.* Environmental Factors in Etiology of Gastric Cancer. Advances in Biochemistry: 2015; 3(5): 51-56.

S. Rajeshkumar, M. Nagalingam, M. Ponnanikajamideen, and M. Vanaja, C Malarkodi, "Anticancer Activity of Andrographis Paniculata Leaves Extract against Neuroblastima (Imr-32) and Human Colon (Ht-29) Cancer Cell Line WJPPS, 2015; 4(06): 1667-1675.

Sanjib Bhattacharya, "Anticarcinogenic Property of Medicinal Plants: Involvement of Antioxidant Role" Research Signpost, 2012; 83-96.

Rajandeep Kaur, Jagpreet Singh, Gagandeep Singh, Harpreet kaur, "Anticancer Plants: A Review" J. Nat. Prod. Plant Resour., 2011; 1(4): 131-136.

Global Cancer Facts and Figures 2008, Second Edition, American Cancer Society, Pg. No. 1-57.

Trosko JE. 2003. Commentary: is the Concept of "Tumor Promotion" a Useful Paradigm? Mol Carcinog 30: 131–137.

Shactere and Weitzman SA. 2002. Chronic Inflammation and Cancer. Oncology 6: 217–226.

Aula A. Oliveira, Aura Colaco, Raquel Chaves, Henrique Guedes. Chemical Carcinogenesis. (Annals of the Brazilian Academy of Sciences. (2007) 79(4): 593-61.

Thomas N Seyfried and Laura M Shelton. Cancer as a Metabolic Disease. Nutrition & Metabolism 2010, 7:7.

Hossein Mozdarani. Biological Complexities in Radiation Carcinogenesis and Cancer Radiotherapy: Impact of New Biological Paradigms. Genes 2012, 3, 90-114

Hunter Shain and Boris C. Bastian. From Melanocytes to Melanomas. Nature Reviews Cancer, doi:10.1038/nrc.2016.37.

Mort, R. L., Jackson, I. J. & Patton, E. E. The Melanocyte Lineage in Development and Disease. Development 142, 620–632 (2015).

Land H, Parada LF and Weinberg RA (1983). Cellular Oncogenes and Multi-step Carcinogenesis. Science, 222, 771-778.

Weisburger JH. 1998. Worldwide Prevention of Cancer and Other Chronic Diseases Based on Knowledge of Mechanisms. Mutat Res 402: 331–337.

Williams gm. 2001. Mechanisms of Chemical Carcinogenesis and Application to Human Cancer Risk Assessment. Toxicology 161: 3–10.

Gomes-Carneiro MR, Ribeiro-Pinto LF and Paumgartten FJ. 1997. Environmental Risk Factors for Gastric Cancer: The Toxicologist's Standpoint. Cad Saúde Pública 13 (Suppl): 27–38.

Mehta R. 1995. The Potential for the Use of Cell Proliferation and Oncogene Expression as Intermediate Markers during Liver Carcinogenesis. Cancer Lett 93: 85–102.

Douglas Hanahan and Robert A. Weinberg. Hallmarks of Cancer: The Next Generation. Cell 144, 4, 2011.

Leron Katsir, Kelli A. Davies, Dominique C. Bergmann, Thomas Laux. Peptide Signaling in Plant Development. Curr Biol. 2011, 10; 21 (9): 56–64.

Arif A. Bhat, Hilal A. Wani, Mushtaq A. Beigh, Showkat A. Bhat. Epigenetic Promoter Methylation of Hmlh1 gene in Human Gut Malignancies. 2:2, 101-10, 2013.

Hartwell LH and Kastan MB. (1994). Cell Cycle Control and Cancer. Science, 266, 1821-1828.

H.A.Wani, M.A.Beigh, S. Amin, A.A. Bhat, S. Bhat, H. Khan, Masood, S. Majid. Methylation Profile of Promoter Region of p16 Gene in Colorectal Cancer Patients of Kashmir Valley. Journal of Biological Regulators & Homeostatic Agents. 27:2, 399-408, 2013.

Wilson S, Jones L, Coussens C & Hanna K (eds.) (2002) Cancer and the Environment: Gene-Environment Interaction. Washington, DC: National Academy Press.

Shah Alam, Pooja Satpathy, Aditi Thosar, "Plants and Its Parts As A Source of Anti-cancer Compounds: A Review" IRJP, 2014; 5(4): 244-245.

Ratnakaram Satya Teja, Bibhukalyan Prasad Nayak, "Anticancer Property of Plant Products" IJRAP, 2011; 2(1): 111-113.

Singh N, Singh SP, Nath R (1986). Prevention of Urethane-induced Lung Adenomas by Withania Somnifera (L.) Dunal in Albino Mice. Int. J.

R. Gowri, N. Narayanan, A. Maheswaran, G. Harshapriya, Siji Mathachan, "Curcumin – A Salubrious Asset To Immune System" International Journal of Pharmacy Review and Research, 2014; 4(2): 75-79.

Muthu K. Shanmugam, Grishma Rane, Madhu Mathi Kanchi, Frank Arfuso, Arunachalam Chinnathambi, M. E. Zayed, Sulaiman Ali Alharbi, Benny K. H. Tan, Alan Prem Kumar and Gautam Sethi, "The Multifaceted Role of Curcumin in Cancer Prevention and Treatment" Molecules, 2015; 20: 2728-2769.

Bonanome A, Pagnan A, Caruso D (2000). Evidence of Postprandial Absorption of Olive Oil Phenols in Humans. Nutr. Metab. Cardiovasc. Dis., 10:111-120.

Udintsev SN, Schakhov VP (1991). Decrease of Cyclophosphamide Haematotoxicity by Rhodiola Rosea Root Extract in Mice with Ehrlich and Lewis Transplantable Tumors. Eur. J. Cancer, 27: 1182.

Udintsev SN, Krylova SG, Fomina TI (1992). The Enhancement of the Efficacy of Adriamycin by using Hepatoprotectors of Plant Origin in Metastases of Ehrlich's Adenocarcinoma to the Liver in Mice. Vopr. Onkol., 38: 1217-1222.

Maryam Moudi, Rusea Go, Christina Yong Seok Yien, Mohd. Nazre "Vinca Alkaloids" International Journal of Preventive Medicine, 2013; 4(11): 1231-1235.

Satyavati Rana, Jaspreet Kaur Kambooj, and Vandana Gandhi, "Living Life the Natural Way – Wheatgrass and Health" Nov. Open Access Functional Foods in Health and Disease, 2011; 447-448.

Fatheya M. Metwally, Hatem A. El-Mezayen, Ahmed E. Abdel Moneim and Nevin E. Sharaf, "Anti-Tumor Effect of Azadirachta indica (Neem) on Murine Solid Ehrlich Carcinoma" Academic Journal of Cancer Research, 2014; 7(1): 38-45.

Neha Agarwal, Amrish Chandra and Lalit Kumar Tyagi, "Herbal Medicine: Alternative Treatment for Cancer Therapy" IJPSR, 2011; 2(9): 2249-2258.

Priyadarshini K and Keerthi Aparajitha U, "Paclitaxel against Cancer: A Short Review" Med Chem, An Open Access Journal, 2012; 2(7): 139-141.

Sonaimuthu Visalakchi and Johnpaul Muthumary, "Taxol (Anticancer Drug) Producing Endophytic Fungi: An Overview" International Journal of Pharma and Bio Sciences, 2010; 1(3): 1-9.

Kharb Manju, Jat R.K. and Gupta Anju, "A Review on Medicinal Plants Used As A Source of Anticancer Agents" International Journal of Drug Research and Technology, 2012; 2(2): 177-183.

K. P. Sampath Kumar, Debjit Bhowmik, Chiranjib, Biswajit, "Aloe vera: A Potential Herb and its Medicinal Importance" Journal of Chemical and Pharmaceutical Research, 2010; 2(1): 21-29.

Pankaj K. Sahu, Deen Dayal Giri, Ritu Singh, Priyanka Pandey, Sharmistha Gupta, Atul Kumar Shrivastava, Ajay Kumar, Kapil Dev Pandey, "Therapeutic and Medicinal Uses of Aloe vera: A Review" Pharmacology & Pharmacy, 2013; 4: 599-610.

Nutraceuticals and Pharmaceuticals from Medicinal Plants
Edited by: Dr. Pawan Kumar 'Bharti'; Dr. M.M. Abid Ali Khan; Dr. Ashok K. Rathoure
ISBN: 978-93-86841-55-1
Edition: 2018
Published by: Discovery Publishing House Pvt. Ltd., New Delhi (India)

6

Pharmacological Properties of 6-Gingerolan Active Ingredient of Ginger

[1]Bilal Ahmad Mir, [1]Insha Amin, [1]Muneeb U Rehman, [1]Showkeen Muzamil, [1]Sheikh Bilal, [1]Ishraq Hussain, [1]Manzoorur-Rehman Mir1

ABSTRACT

Health is a precious gift given by nature to the human being but disease occurrence is no more miraculous. To treat the disease is a key to survive in the world. However the currently available allopathic drugs although represents principle agents for treatment of various metabolic and infectious disease but they are having full package of adverse effects on health. Humans have been using plant based natural compounds since ancient times. Certain phytocompounds present in plants are mainly responsible for their therapeutic effects. Thus in current era of advanced science we should move to explore the extraction, structure and biological properties of phytocompounds present in plants. Ginger is one of the most famous medicinal plants used in all over the world as a spice to add zest to our food. Phytochemistry of ginger is strongly associated with its therapeutic properties. Various phytocompounds like gingerol, shogals and zingerone have been extracted and thoroughly studied recently. 6-Gingerol belongs to gingerol series and is present in abundant amount in fresh ginger.6-Gingerol is having potent antioxidant, anti-inflammatory, antidiabetic, hepatoprotective, neuroprotective and anticancer properties. Besides, it exhibits potent lipolytic activity. This review summarize the mechanistic effects of 6-gingerol involved in its pharmacological activities.

Key words: 6-Gingerol, NFκB, GLUT, Diabetes, Cancer.

INTRODUCTION

Ginger is the commonly used medicinal plant worldwide.It is used as a spice to add typical aroma and taste to our food. The phytochemistry of ginger is associated with its pharmacological and therapeutic activities. It has been used for immemorial time in traditional medicine for the treatment of various

[1] Molecular Biology Lab, Division of Veterinary Biochemistry, Faculty of Veterinary Sciences & Animal Husbandry, Sheri Kashmir University of Agricultural Science & Technology (SKUAST-K), Srinagar, J & K, India 190006.

disorders like indigestion, pain, nausea,vomition and cold induced syndromes (White, 2007). The natural therapeutic power lies in ginger is remarkable in its own. Currently ginger is being recommended for digestive disorders, respiratory disorders (throat), atherosclerosis, hypertension, cancer and diabetes it has potent antibiotic and anthelmintic properties (Ali *et al.*, 2008 and Nicoll and Henein, 2009). India occupies first position in the production of ginger and contributes 35% of the world ginger production (Sajeev*et al* 2011). The active constituents present in ginger are numerous and diverse depending on the origin of place and physical form of the plant; dry or fresh. It contains various vitamins, minerals and few enzymes like zingibain an enzyme having potent proteolytic activity (Jolad *et al.*, 2004). The components of ginger have been broadly divided into two broader groups. Volatile and nonvolatile compounds sesquiterpene and monoterpenoid hydrocarbons are among the volatile compounds imparting the typical aroma to the ginger gingerols, shogaols, paradols and zingerone are among nonvolatile compounds found in ginger. 6-Gingerol is the major gingerol found in ginger besides 8-gingerol and 10-gingerol, zingerone is also found in significant amount in dry ginger, cooking of ginger converts ginerol into zingerone by retro aldol reaction.

6-Gingerol

Gingerols are the series of homology of chemical structures different by length of their unbranched alkyl chains (Govindarajan, 1982). Gingerol mostly exists in two common forms 6-gingerol and 10-gingerol different in methoxygroup positions.Both the forms are present in fresh ginger however 6-gingerol is found in most abundant quantity in gingerol series. It has been reported that 6-gingerol is the main active phytocompound present in ginger which consists antioxidant, anti-inflammatory and anticancer properties (Surh, 2003). Xanthine oxidase enzyme is inhibited by 6-gingerol which plays an important role in generation of reactive oxygen spiecies (Chang *et al.*, 1994).

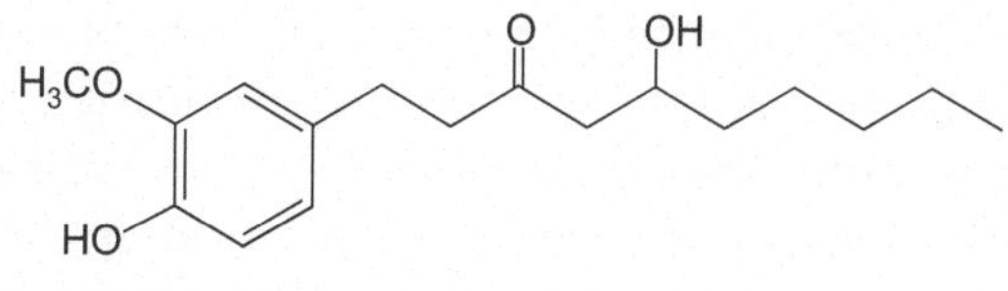

Antioxidant Effect of 6-Gingerol

Antioxidants are the agents which neutralize the free radicals and oxidants mediated oxidative stress. Antioxidant system of our body normally neutralizes the free radicals up to optimum level by its defense activities (Shyur *et al.*, 2005). However any imbalance between free radical production and scavenging of reactive oxygen species leads to oxidative stress (Ceriello *et al.*, 2001; Brownlee, 2000). Several plants have strong antioxidant phytocompounds and play a key role in attenuating oxidative stress and progression of diseases.

Ginger is rich in compounds having potent antioxidant activity and decreases the oxidative stress induced lipid peroxidation. 6-Gingerol present in ginger have strong antioxidant activity due to the presence of unsaturated ketone moiety in its chemical struchure (Dugasani *et al.*, 2010). 6-Gingerol have been reported to inhibit ascorbate/ferrous mediated lipid peroxidation in the liver microsome of wistar rats (Reddey and Lokesh 1992). 6-Gingerol has been recently reported to protect from amyloid induced cytotoxicity and apoptosis by preventing intracellular ROS and nitrogen spiecies accumulation induced oxidative stress (Lee *et al.*, 2011).

Ant-inflammatory Effect of 6-Gingerol

Inflammation is an immune mediated complex process involving several mediators of inflammation like TNFα, interleukins and inflammatory cytokines. The currently available anti-inflammatory drugs are exerting their toxic effects like gastric ulcers, stomach pain and metabolic distress etc. 6-Gingerol present in significant amount in ginger have potent anti-inflammatory properties. It inhibits the NFκB activation which in turns inhibits the gene expression of inflammatory mediated cytokines. The strong anti-inflammatory activity exhibited by 6-gingerol is reflected in its therapeutic potential against diabetes,cancer and other life threatening diseases.

Effect of Gingerol on Prion disease

Prion diseases are neuronal degenerative disorders which are lethal in humans as well as in domestic animals. There occurs transformation of normal cellular prion protein (PrPc) into its mutated form known as scrapie prion protein (PrPsc) (Sajnani*et al.*, 2012). PrPscacts as infectious protein agent and accumulates in insoluble form and finally causes disruption of normal neuronal functions (Sakudo and Ikuta 2009). PrPsc after accumulating in neuronal cells leads to mitochondrial dysfunction which is the major mechanism of PrPsc involved in neurological disorder like Alzheimer's and Huntington's disease. 6-gingerol have been found to cause enhanced expression of Hypoxia-inducible factor-1α (HIF-1α) which in turn prevents prion induced neurotoxicity(Jeong*et al.*, 2012). It has been found recently that gingerol increases the HIF-1α protein levels (Jeong*et al.*, 2013). Besides its protection in prion disease it plays a key role in protection of other neurodegenerative disease (Dugasani*et al.*, 2010).

Hypolipidemic Effect of 6-Gingerol

Obesity has become a major challenge in the world and become an emerging problem to global public health due to changing life style and food habits. It is one of the fifth leading cause of mortalityin the world and plays a significant role in pathogenesis and development of type II diabetes. Dyslipidemia characterizing by decrease in High density lipoprotein, increase in total cholesterol, triglycerides and Low density lipoproteins is common finding in obesity (Despres, 1991). Ginger is having lipolytic effect and improves the lipid profile. The mechanism involved in its hypolipidemic effect is associated with its positive effects on insulin release, improving metabolism of carbohydrates and lipids (Li *et al.*, 2012). Ginger has been reported to stimulate the transformation of cholesterol into bile. It has also been reported that ginger inhibits the synthesis of cholesterol and attenuating the LDL receptor activity(Nammi *et al.*, 2009 and Ramudu *et al.*, 2011). 6-Gingerol the major component in ginger was found to significantly decrease total cholesterol, triglycerides, low density lipoproteins and fatty acids (Singh *et al.*, 2009). Okamoto *et al.* (2011) has found that 6-Gingerol prevents fat accumulation and increase in weight gain. 6-Gingerol counters the adipogenesis induced by rosigiltazone by reducing accumulation of oil droplet and size of droplet (Tzeng and Liu 2013).

Antimicrobial Effect of 6-Gingerol

Resistance and toxicity associated with allopathic antibiotics has challenged the researchers and opens new areas to find safe and effective antimicrobial agents which produce minimum toxicity. Ginger and its metabolites have been found to possess effective antimicrobial properties. Although 6-Gingerol was found less effective against some oral bacteria like *Prevotella intermedia, Porphyromonasgingivalis* and *Porphyromonasendodontalis* (Mahady *et al.*, 2003) but It was found quite effective against *H. Pylori* at MIC of 0.02 mg/ml (Zhang*et al.* 2013). Vibrio Cholera is one of the common pathogen known to cause chlorea induce diarrhea through its CT toxin. 6-Gingerol has been reported to bind strongly with CT toxin of Vibrio Cholera and prevents its binding with GM receptors of intestinal epithelial cells. (Saha *et al.*, 2013). Fungal amylase enzyme is inhibited by 6-Gingerol at the concentration of 0.1 mM (Tintu *et al.*, 2012).

6-Gingerol as Antidiabetic

Diabetes is growing as a pandemic metabolic disorder in all over world. Millions of people around the world are suffering from this panic metabolic disease. It has been recently estimated that 382 million of people are suffering from diabetes and 316 million are at high risk of developing diabetes. 80% of people affected with diabetes are living in developing countries. Trend of diabetes is changing towards younger generation and causing premature mortality in young people (Cho, 2013). Diabetes mellitus is a multiple factor associated disorder characterized by chronic hyperglycemia, oxidative stress,lipoprotein abnormalities and raised BMR. Obesity is found to be a lethal combo for developing type II diabetes. Although improving life style by regular exercise, better diet, have been found to decrease the risk of developing diabetes but due to difficulty in implementing them the battle with diabetes is being lost (IDF 2013). Insulin therapy and hypoglycemic drugs continue to represent the main agents of treatment but they are full of adverse effectsand yet not a single hypoglycemic drug has proven to be an ideal antidiabetic drug. This made us to explore the remedy that is having minimum side effects with potent antidiabetic activity. Plants are no more less in providing us effective and potential remedy for treatment of diabetes. Innumerable plants have been found to possess potent anti-daibetic activity (Omara *et al.*, 2010; Haung *et al.*, 2005). The currently used Metformin as a drug of choice for diabetes have its origin from plant natural products (Bailley and Day 2004). Hyperglycemia and hyperlipidemia are two major lethal combinations for development of diabetes mellitus and its lethal complications (Lender and sysko 2006). For optimum management of diabetes and its complications it is quite necessary to control both of these metabolic disturbances.

The potential of Ginger in reducing the diabetes and its complication are not known widely and yet remains mystery for number of people. Current pharmacological trials support the effectiveness and potential of ginger as hypolipdemic and hypoglycemic agent for the management of diabetes mellitus. The precise mechanism involved in its antidiabetic effect is yet to be identified. The chemical composition of ginger has been explored but which active constituent is responsible for effects in diabetes is being studied currently by researchers.

6-Gingeroldecreases Blood Glucose

Ginger has been found to improve the glycemic index. Recently it has been reported that oral administration of ginger in streptozotocin induced diabetic rats decreased blood glucose concentration by more than 50% (Ojewole, 2006; Saraswat *et al.*, 2010). 6-Gingerol was found to reduce blood glucose levels and improving glucose tolerance in diabetes (Singh *et al.*, 2009).

6-Gingerolaccelerates Glucose Uptake

The blood glucose concentration is physiologically maintained by insulin dependent and non-insulin dependent pathways (Youn and Zeirath 2006). Major portion of glucose uptake is insulin dependent and takes place through skeletal muscle cells which account almost 75% of total glucose uptake (Baron *et al.*, 1988). GLUT-4 is found in skeletal muscle cells (Perriott *et al.*, 2001) and remain in storage vesicles of intracellular compartment of cell. Insulin stimulation leads to the degradation of vesicles and translocation of GLUT-4 on plasma membrane of cell (Larance *et al.*, 2008). GLUT-4 transporter are mainly involved in glucose uptake in skeletal muscle cells (Kubo and Foley 1986; Perriott *et al.*, 2001). Due to imbalanced insulin signal transduction in type II diabetic patients glucose uptake does not occur in skeletal muscle cells (Krook *et al.*, 2000). However it remains unaffected in insulin independent cells e. g Brain cells (Musi et al 2001). It has been recently found that stimuli stimulating AMP-activated protein kinase (AMPK) can inducetranslocation of GLUT-4 by a pathway that is quite different from insulin signaling pathway. The agent which evoke AMPK pathway plays an important role as drug target. It has been found that 6-Gingerol present in significant amount in ginger showed dose dependent glucose uptake via GLUT-4 in skeletal L6 myotubes by AMPK pathway (Li *et al.*, 2012). 6-Gingerol has been found to increase dose and time dependent increase in phosphorylation of AMPK in L6 skeletal muscle cells. 6-Gingerol increases calcium ion (Ca^{+2}) signaling pathway by inducing AMPKα phosphorylation in skeletal muscle cells (Li *et al.*, 2013). AMPKα was found to be a dominant isoform mediating glucose uptake by 6-gingerol in L6 skeletal muscle cells. So the beauty of 6-Gingerol is that it causes effective glucose uptake without insulin signaling in skeletal muscle cells by evoking AMPK pathways.

6-Gingerol Modulates Proinflammatory Cytokines Involved in Daibetes

The pro-inflammatory cytokines (NFκB,TNF-α) play an important role in pathogenesis of diabetes. Reactive oxygen species (ROS) in combination with TNF-α leads to programmed cell death of beta cells of pancreatic islets besides TNF-α inhibits insulin transduction and has effect on glucose metabolism. NFκB activation by IL-1 in alloxan induced diabetes plays a key role in destruction of beta cells of pancreatic islets. It is a critical determinant in the progression of the disease (Park and Park 2001). NFκB is a redox sensitive transcription factor present in cytoplasm in inactivated form with inhibitory protein kappa B (I5B5). However stress induced stimuli leads to the phosphorylation of I5B5 and activation of NFκB which translocates into nucleus and activates genes encoding inflammatory cytokines (Li *et al.*, 2013). Inflammatory cytokines like TNF-α inturn inhibits insulin signal transduction. Ginger has been found to inhibit NFκB activated gene expression of inflammatory cytokines by suppression of NFκB activity through degradation of I5B5 kinase activity (Li *et al.*, 2013). 6-Gingerol in ginger is recently reported to have strong anti-inflammatory properties (Mcgrath *et al.*, 2009).

6-Gingerol Decreases Overcomes the Oxidative Stress in Diabetes

ROS plays a significant role in developing diabetes and the complications of diabetes. ROS induce oxidative stress and lipid peroxidation. Over production of ROS demotes antioxidant system. It is a well-established fact that reduced antioxidant system activates the pathway that generates proinflammatory cytokines (Roebuck, 1999). 6-Gingerol is being reported to have potent scavenging activity and acts as strong antioxidant(Lee *et al.* 2011).

6-Gingerol Decreases the Insulin Resistance in Daibetes

Insulin resistance is the main factor involved in type II diabetes. Inflammation of hepatic cells plays a central role in pathogenesis of several chronic diseases like type II diabetes, nonalcoholicfatty liver and atherosclerosis (Chaterjee, 2010). Recent studies have revealed that 6-gingerol has potent potential in protecting hepatic cells from interleukin induced inflammation and improving insulin resistance by inhibiting ROS activated NFκB inflammatory pathway. Insulin resistance is driven by hepatic inflammation throughNFκB activation. However 6-gingerol treatment have suppressed the inflammatory mediator cytokines by suppression of NFκB/COX pathways. The protection against hepatic inflammation which is mainly involved in progression of insulin resistance by 6-gingerol opens a novel ways for the treatment of type II diabetes (Basil, 2014).

6-Gingerol Exerts Protective Effect on Pancreas in Diabetes

Pancreas is a vital organ involved in metabolism of glucose through its endocrine (insulin) and exocrine (amylase) secretions. Insulin the main hormone responsible for glucose metabolism is secreted by pancreatic β cells. Deficiency of insulin secretion plays a significant role in progression of diabetes mellitus. It has been reported that 6-gingerol one of the active compound of ginger protects pancreatic β cells from degeneration through scavenging of free radicals (Aggarwal, 2010). Gingerol has been reported to have an insulin modulating effect in pancreatic β cells (Chakraborty *et al.*, 2012). The major enzymes invoved in carbohydrate maetabolismassociated hyperglycemia are amylases and glucosidases. It has been reported that ginger extract inhibited effectively these enzymes and this inhibitory action of ginger extract has been found to be associated with phenolic contents of Gingerol present in ginger(Chakraborty *et al.*, 2012).

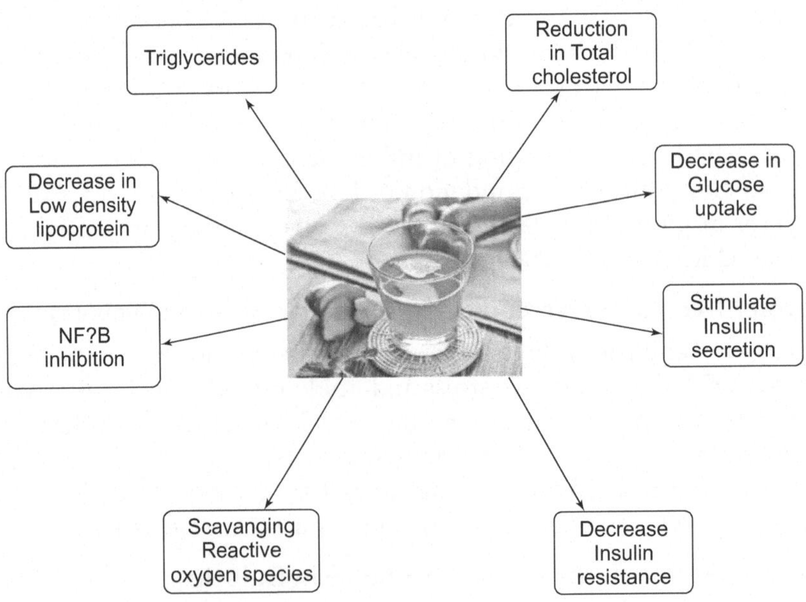

Summary of mechanism involved in antidiabetic effect of 6-Gingerol

Gingerol as Anticancer

Cancer is a lethal disease and causing tremendous mortality in allover the world. The transformation of normal dividing cell to uncontrolled cancerous cell is caused by so manyfactors including genetic,environmental and lifestyle changes. Providing the potent anticancer therapy with minimum side effect is need of hour. However the currently available anticancer drugs are having adverse side effects. Plants based compounds represent a valuable alternative anticancer therapy with minimum toxic effects. Since Tumor formation is result of inflammation and oxidativestress a compound possessing antioxidant and anti-inflammatory properties can strongly act as an anticancer agent(Rhode *et al.*, 2007; Sang *et al.*, 2009). Ginger and its phenolic component gingerol have potent anti-carcinogenic activity through inhibition of NFκB activation induced by several factors (Manju and Nalini, 2005). 6-Gingerol has been reported to inhibit the growth and metastasis of tumors by its anti-angiogenic activity (Kim *et al.*, 2005). Application of 6-gingerol tropically inhibited the expression of cycloxgenase-2(COX-2) along with suppression of binding of NFκB with its target genes in mouse skin (Kim *et al.*, 2004). 6-Gingerol have been reported to have potent anticancer effect in ovarian cancer through inhibition of NFκB mediated interleukin-8(IL-8). 6-Gingerol inhibited the proliferation of colon cancer in mice (Jeong*et al.*, 2009). 6-Gingerol have also been reported to have a strong anticancer properties against skin cancer (Nigam *et al.*, 2009), breast cancer Lee *et al.*, 2008); ovarian cancer(Rhode *et al.*, 2007). The anticancer activity of 6-Gingerol has been found to be associated with its srong activity in inhibiting extracellular signal-regulated kinases (ERK1/2/JNK/AP-1) pathway. 6-Gingerol has also been found to be effective against gastric cancers by inhibiting Tumor necrosis factor related inducing apoptosis legend (TRAIL) induced NFκB activation (Ishiguro *et al.*, 2007) etc.

Table 6.1: Chemopreventive Effect of 6-Gingerol in Different Types of Cancers

Cell line	Effect	Reference
Promyelocytic HL-60 (leukemia	Cytotoxic and suppression of proliferation is exerted by 6-Gingerol which in turn leads to cell death by apoptosis .	Lee and Surh 1998
Chronic myeloid K562 (leukemia)	Leads to Cytotoxic effect (IC50 = 10 IM)	Peng *et al.*, 2012
Breast, cervix and ovarian cancer MDA-MB-231 (human breast cancer	Decrease in cell adhesion has been reported. All gingerols have potential ability to inhibit the proliferation of fibroblast cells at the concentration of 500 IM	Lee *et al.*, 2008
HeLa cells (human cervical cancercells	DNA damage and increase in formation of TUNEL in tumor cells. Inhibition of expression of NFkb and down regulation in expression of Bcl2 genes in tumor cells. Modification of phosphatidyl serine residues	Chakraborty *et al.*,2012

SK-OV-3 (human ovarian cancercells)	Exerts Cytotoxic effect	Kim *et al.*, 2008
Colon cancerHT29 cells (human colon cancer cells)	Reduction in NFjB activity along with increase in transcriptional activity of PPARc activity. Finally causes apoptosis of cancer cells 100 lM	Tan *et al.*, 2013
COLO 205 (human colon cancer cells)	Growth of cancer cells is inhibited and mitochondria modulation leads to cell	Pan *et al.*, 2008
Lung cancer H-1299 (human lung cancer cell	6-Gingerol Inhibits the growth of cancer cells at the concentration of 150 lM	Sang *et al.*, 2009
Kidney cancer MDCK cells (dog renal tubular cells)	6-Gingerol leads to Stimulation of Ca^{2+} influx from the fextra cellular fluid and causes efflux ofthapsigargin-sensitive intracellular Ca2 present inside of cancer cells	Chen *et al.*, 2008
Liver cancer HepG2 (human liver carcinoma cells	Genotoxicity is induced by tremendous increase in Migration of DNA and DNA fragmentation at the concentration of 20-80 lM. Decrease in antioxidant enzymes and increase in	Yang *et al.*, 2010
Prostate cancerLNCaP (human prostateadenocarcinoma c	Modification of certain proteins involved in apoptosis pathway of prostate cancer cells	Shukla *et al.*, 2007
Mechanism involved in anticancer activity of 6-Gingerol.		

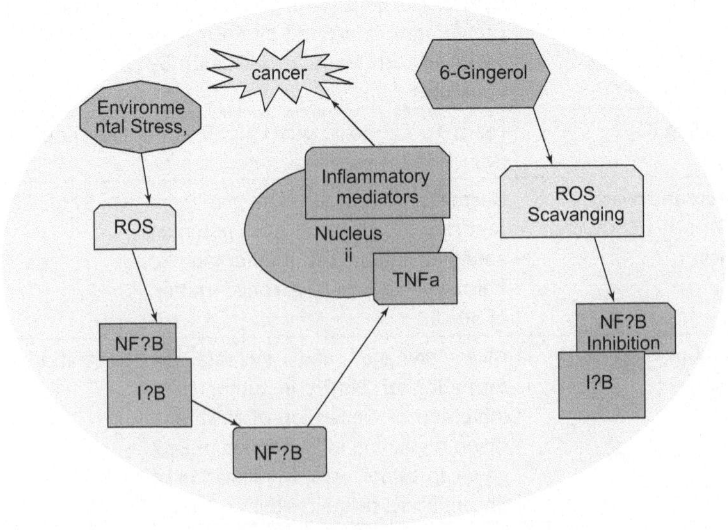

Hepatoprotective Effect of 6-Gingerol

Liver disorders continue to be a major challenge to global public health and makes a major contribution in the world mortality statistics. To combat the challenge of current liver disease in world is outmost importance. Hepatic injury is usually associated with disturbances in metabolic processes. Reactive oxygen species and nitrogen species plays a vital role in the progression of liver disorders like hepatitis, hepatic carcinoma (Nagata *et al.*, 2007) Based on previous reports the active compounds present in ginger has proven to play a significant role in prevention and treatment of liver disorders 6-Gingerol present in ginger recently have been reported to have hepatoprotective effect against acetaminophen induced liver toxicity by its strong antioxidant nature (Sabina *et al.*, 2011). It was observed that 6-gingerol neutralized the acetaminophen induced damage by facilitating effective consumption of reactive oxygen species (ROS) and increasing the activity of reduced glutathione (GSH).

CONCLUSION

Despite the availability of currently allopathic drugs for the treatment of various metabolic diseases yet they remain a major challenge for the global public healthbecause of their ineffectiveness, adverse side effects and heavy costs. Drug repositioning from natural plants have become need of hour. Natural compounds obtained from plants have proven to be quite effective with minimum side effects for the treatment of current challenging metabolic disease like cancer, diabetes and hepatotoxicity. Ginger is one of the natural medicinal plantcontaining numerous pharmacologically active compounds. 6-Gingerol is one of its major active compound that have full therapeutic potential by its strong antioxidant and anti-inflammatory activities. It has shown its full potential against the diabetes, cancer and hepatotoxicity by its potent antioxidant and anti-inflammatory nature. Besides it has proven to be an effective lipolytic agent. Further clinical trials in animals and humans are warranted to explore its proper and precise molecular target mechanism. Nevertheless 6-Gingerol is a novel compound with strong pharmacological and therapeutic properties and can act as a valuable remedy for diabetes, hepatotoxicity and cancer in future and protect the human health from ill effects of synthetic drugs.

REFERENCES

Aggarwal B. B. (2010). Targeting Inflammation-induced Obesity and Metabolic Diseases by Curcumin and Other Nutraceuticals. *Annu. Rev Nutr* 30: 173-199.

Ali BH, Blunden G, TaniraMO, Nemmar A. (2008). Some Phytochemical, Pharmacological and Toxicological Properties of Ginger (*ZingiberofficinaleRoscoe*): A Review of Recent Research. *Food Chem. Toxicol* 46 : 409-420.

White B . (2007). "Ginger: An Overview," *The American Family Physician* 75:1689–1691.

Bailley CJ, Day C. (2004). Metformin: Its Botanical Background. *Practical Diabetes International* 21: 115-117.

Basil D. Roufogalis. (2014) *Zingiberofficinale* (Ginger): A Future Outlook on Its Potential in Prevention and Treatment of Diabetes and Prediabetic States. *New Journal of Science* Article ID 674684

Brownlee M. (2005). The Pathobiology of Diabetic Complications: A Unifying Mechanism. *Diabetes* 54: 1615-1625.

Ceriello A, Mercuri F, Quagliaro L, *et al.* (2001). Detection of Nitrotyrosine in the Diabetic Plasma: Evidence of Oxidative Stress. *Diabetologia* 44: 834-838.

Chakraborty D, Mukherjee A, Sikdar S, et al . (2012). [6]-Gingerol Isolated from Ginger Attenuates Sodium Arsenite Induced Oxidative Stress and Plays a Corrective Role in Improving Insulin Signaling in mice. *Toxicol. Lett* 210: 34–43.

Chang WS, Chang YH, Lu FJ, *et al.* (1994). Inhibitory Effect of Phenolic on Xanthine Oxidase COX-2 Expression by Blocking the Activation of p38 MAP Kinase and NF-kappaB in Phorbolesterstimulated. *Anticancer Res* 14:501-506.

Chatterjee PK . (2010). Hepatic Inflammation and Insulin Resistance in Pre-diabetes m″^]′″ Further Evidence for the Beneficial Actions of PPAR-γ Agonists and a Role for SOCS-3 Modulation. *Br j Parmacol* 160:1889-1891

Chen CY, Chen CH, Kung CH, *et al.* (2008). [6]-gingerol Induces Ca^{2+} Mobilization in Madin–Darby Canine Kidney Cells. *J. Nat. Prod* 71: 137–140.

Cho NH, Baron AD, Brechtel G, *et al.* (1988). Rates and Tissue Sites of Non-insulin- and Insulin-Mediated Glucose Uptake in Humans. *The American Journal of Physiology—Endocrinology and Metabolism* 255: 769–774.

Dugasani S, Pichika MR, Nadarajah VD, *et al.* (2010). Comparative Antioxidant and Anti-Inflammatory Effects of [6]-gingerol, [8]-gingerol, [10]-gingerol and [6]-shogaol. *J Ethnopharmacolo* 127: 515-520.

Huang TH, Kota BP, Razmovski V, *et al.* (2005). Herbal or Natural Medicines as Modulators of Peroxisome Proliferator-Activated Receptors and Related Nuclear Receptors for Therapy of Metabolic Syndrome. *Journal of BasicandClinicalPharmacology and Toxicology* 96: 3–14.

IDF Diabetes Atlas, International Diabetes Federation, 6th edition, 2013

Jeong JK, Moon MH, Park YG, *et al.* (2013). Gingerol-Induced Hypoxia-inducible Factor 1 Alpha Inhibits Human Prion Peptide-mediated Neurotoxicity. *Phytother Res*27:1185–1192.

Jolad SD, Lantz RC, Solyom AM, et al (2004). Fresh Organically Grown Ginger (*Zingiberofficinale*) Composition and Effects on LPS-induced PGE2 Production. *Phytochem* 65 : 1937–1954

Kim JS, Lee SI, Park HW, *et al.* (2008). Cytotoxic Components from the Dried Rhizomes of Zingiberofficinale Roscoe. *Arch Pharm Res* 31: 415–418.

Kim SO, Chun KS, Kundu JK, *et al.* (2004). Inhibitory Effects of [6]-gingerol on PMA-induced COX-2 Expression and Activation of NFjB and p38 MAPK in Mouse Skin. *Biofactors* 21: 27–31.

Krook A, Björnholm M, Galuska D *et al.* (2000). Characterization of Signal Transduction and Glucose Transport in Skeletal Muscle from type 2 Diabetic Patients. *Diabetes* 49: 284– 292.

Kubo K, Foley JE. (1986). Rate-limiting Steps for Insulin Mediated Glucose Uptake into Perfused Rat Hindlimb. *TheAmericanJournal of Physiology—Endocrinology and Metabolism* 250: 100–102.

Larance M, Ramm G, James DE. (2008). The GLUT4 code. *Molecular Endocrinology* 22: 226–233.

Lee C, Park GH, Kim CY, *et al.* (2011). 6-Gingerol Attenuates β amyloid Induced Oxidative Cell Death via Fortifying Cellular Antioxidant Defence System. *Food Chem Toxicol* 49: 1261-1269.

Lee E, Surh YJ. (1998). Induction of Apoptosis in HL-60 Cells by Pungent Vanilloids, [6]-gingerol and [6]-paradol. *Cancer Lett* 134: 163–168.

Lee HS, Seo EY, Kang NE. (2008). [6]-Gingerol Inhibits Metastasis of MDA-MB-231 Human Breast Cancer Cells. *J. Nutr. Biochem*; 19: 313–319.

Lender D, Sysko SK. (2006). The Metabolic Syndrome and Cardiometabolic Risk: Scope of the Problem and Current Standard of Care. *Pharmacotherapy* 26:3-12.

Li XH, McGrath KCY, Tran VH, *et al.* (2013). Attenuation of Pro-Inflammatory Responses by [6]-S-gingerol via Inhibition of ROS/NF-kappa B/COX2 Activation in HuH7 Cells. *Evidence-Based Complementary and Alternative Medicine* Article ID 146142, 8 pages

Li Y, Tran VH, Koolaji N, *et al.* (2013). (S)-[6]-Gingerol Enhances Glucose Uptake in L6 Myotubes by Activation of AMPK in Response to [Ca2+]. *Journal of Pharmacy and Pharmaceutical Sciences* 16:304– 312.

Li Y, Tran VH, Duke CC, *et al.* (2012). Gingerols of *Zingiberofficinale* Enhance Glucose Uptake by Increasing Cell Surface GLUT4 Incultured L6 Myotubes, *Planta. Medica* 78 : 1549-1555.

Li Y, Tran VH, Duke CC, *et al.* (2012). Gingerols of Zingiberofficinale Enhance Glucose Uptake by Increasing Cell Surface GLUT4 in Cultured L6 Myotubes. *Planta Medica* 78: 1549–1555.

Mahady GB, Pendland SL, Yun GS, *et al.* (2003). Ginger (Zingiberofficinale Roscoe) and the Gingerols Inhibit the Growth of Cag A+ Strains of Helicobacter Pylori. *Anticancer Res* 2: 3699–3702.

ManjuV, Nalini N. (2005). Chemopreventive Efficacy of Ginger, A Naturally Occurring Anti-carcinogen during Mouse Skin. *Oncogene* 24: 2558–2567.

McGrath KCY, Li X H, Puranik R, *et al.* (2009). Role of 35-hydroxysteroid-Δ24 Reductase in Mediating Anti-inflammatory Effects of High-density Lipoproteins in Endothelial Cells. *Arteriosclerosis, Thrombosis and Vascular Biology* 29: 877–882.

Musi N, Fujii N, Hirshman MF, *et al.* (2001). AMP-activated protein kinase (AMPK) is activated in muscle of subjects with type 2 diabetes during exercise. Diabetes; 50: 921–927.

Nagata K, Suzuki H,. Sakaguchi S. (2007). Common pathogenic mechanism in development progression of liver injury caused by non-alcoholic or alcoholic steatohepatitis. *Journal of ToxicologicalSciences* 32: 453–468.

Nammi S, SreemantulaS Roufogalis BD. (2009). Protective Effects of Ethanolic Extract of *Zingiberofficinale* Rhizome on the Development of Metabolic Syndrome in High-fat Diet-Fed Rats. *Basic and Clini. Pharmacol. And Toxicol* 104 : 366–373.

Nicoll R, Henein MY. (2009). Ginger (*Zingiberofficinale Roscoe*): A Hot Remedy for Cardio-vascular Disease. *Int. J. Cardiol*131: 408-409.

Nigam N, George J, Srivastava S. (2009). Involvement of Mitochondrial Signaling Pathway in B[a]P Induced Mouse Skin Tumorigenesis. *Cancer ChemotherPharmacol* 65: 687– 696.

Ojewole JAO. (2006). Analgesic, Anti-inflammatory and Hypoglycaemic Effects of Ethanol Extract of *Zingiberofficinale* (*Roscoe*) rhizomes (*Zingiberaceae*) in Mice and Rats. *Phytother. Res* 20 : 764–772.

Okamoto M, Irii H, Tahara Y. (2011). Synthesis of a New [6]-gingerol Analogue and Its Protective Effect with Respect to the Development of Metabolic Syndrome in Mice Fed a High-fat Diet. *J. Med. Chem* 54: 6295–6304.

Omara EA, Kam A, Alqahtania A. *et al.* (2010). Herbal Medicines and Nutraceuticals for Diabetic Vascular Complications: Mechanisms of Action and Bioactive Phytochemicals. *Current Pharmaceutical Design* 16: 3776–3807.

Pan MH, Hsieh MC, Kuo JM. (2008). 6-Shogaol Induces Apoptosis in Human Colorectal Carcinoma Cells via ROS Production, Caspase Activation, and GADD 153 Expression. *Mol. Nutr. Food Res* 52: 527–537

Peng F, Tao Q, Wu X. (2001). Cytotoxic, Cytoprotective and Antioxidant Effectsof Isolated Phenolic Compounds from Fresh Ginger. *Fitoterapia* 83: 568–585

Perriott LM, Kono T, Whitesell RR, *et al.* (2012). Glucose Uptake and Metabolism by Cultured Human Skeletal Muscle Cells: Ratelimiting Steps. *The American Journal of Physiology: Endocrinologyand Metabolism* 28: 72–80.

Ramudu SK, Mllikarjuna K, Kesireddy SR. (2011). Efficacy of Ethanolic Extract of Ginger on Kidney Lipid Metabolic Profiles in Diabetic Rats. *Int. J. Diabet. Dev. Ctries* 31: 97-103.

Reddy AA, Lokesh BR. (1992). Studies on Spice Principles as Antioxidants in the Inhibition of Lipid Peroxidation of Rat Liver Microsomes. *Mol Cell Biochem* 111: 117-124.

Roebuck KA. (1999). Oxidant Stress Regulation of IL-8 and ICAM-1 Gene Expression: Differential Activation and Binding of the Transcription Factors AP-1 and NF-kappaB (Review). *InternationalJournal of Molecular Medicine* 4: 223–230.

Sabina EP, Pragasa SJ, Kumar S, et al. (2011). 6-Gingerol an Active Ingredient of Ginger Protects Against Acetaminophen Induced Hepatotoxicity in Mice, *Journal of Chinese integrative medicine* 9:1264-1271.

Sajnani G, Silva CJ, Ramos A, *et al.* (2012). PK-sensitive PrP is Infectious and Shares Basic Structural Features with PK-resistant PrP. *PLoSPathog*8:1002547.

Sakudo A, Ikuta K. (2009). Prion Protein Functions and Dysfunction in Prion Diseases. *Curr Med Chem* 16:380–389.

Sang S, Hong J, Wu H, *et al.* (2009). Increased Growth Inhibitory Effects on Human Cancer Cells and Anti-inflammatory Potency of Shogaols from Zingiberofficinale Relative to Gingerols. *J. Agric. Food Chem* 57: 10645–10650.

Saraswat M, Suryanarayana P, Yadagiri PR, *et al.* (2010). Anti-glycating Potential of *Zingiber Officinalis* and Delay of Diabetic Cataract in Rats. *Molecul. Visi*16 : 1525-1537.

Shengmin Sang, Jungil Hong, Hou Wu, *et al.* (2009). Increased Growth Inhibitory Effects on Human Cancer Cells and Anti-inflammatory Potency of Shogaols from *Zingiberofficinale* Relative to Gingerols. *J Agric Food Chem* 57: 10645– 10650.

Shukla Y, Prasad S, Tripathi C, *et al.* (2007). In vitro and In vivo Modulation of Testosterone Mediated Alterations in Apoptosis Related Proteins by [6]-gingerol. *Mol. Nutr. Food Res* 51: 1492–1502.

Shyur LF, Tsung JH, Chen JH, *et al.* (2005). Anti-oxidant Properties of Extracts from Medicinal Plants Popularly Used in Taiwan Oxidatative Stress Play a Siginificant Effect in the Pathogenesis of Various Types of Disease. *Int J ApplSciEng* 3: 195-202.

Singh AB, Akanksha N, Singh RM, *et al.* (2009). Antihyperglycaemic, Lipid Lowering and Anti-oxidant Properties of [6]-gingerol in db/db Mice. *Inter. J. of Medic. and Medic. Scie*1 : 536-544.

Surh YJ. (2003). Cancer Chemoprevention with Dietary Phytochemicals. *Nat Rev Cancer* 3: 768–80.

Tan BS, Kang O, Mai CW, *et al.* (2013). 6-Shogaol Inhibits Breast and Colon Cancer Cell Prolife Ration Through Activation of Peroxisomal Proliferator Activated Receptor c (PPARc*)*. *Cancer Lett* 336: 127–139.

Tintu I, Dileep KV, Remya C, *et al.* (2012). 6-Gingerolinhibits Fungal Alpha Amylase: Enzyme Kinetic and Molecular Modeling Studies. Starch-Staerke; 64:607–612.

Tjendraputra E, Tran VH, Liu-Brennan D. (2001). Effect of Ginger Constituents and Synthetic Analogues on Cyclooxygenase-2 Enzyme in Intact Cells. *Bioorganic Chemistry* 29:156–163.

Tzeng TF, Liu IM. (2013). 6-Gingerol Prevents Adipogenesis and the Accumulation of Cytoplasmic Lipid Droplets in 3T3-L1 cells. *Phytomedicine* 20:481–487.

Yang G, Zhong L, Jiang L. (2010). Genotoxic Effect of 6-gingerol on Human Hepatoma G2 Cells. *Chem. Biol. Interact* 185: 12–17.

Yun CL, Zierath JR. (2006). AMP-activated Protein Kinase Signaling in Metabolic Regulation. *Journal of Clinical Investigation* 116: 1776–1783.

Zhang YL, Zheng YM, Hu S. *et al.* (2013). Anti-Helicobacter Pylori Effect of 6-gingerol in vitro. *Modern Food Sci. Technol* 29: 1259–1261.

Nutraceuticals and Pharmaceuticals from Medicinal Plants
Edited by: Dr. Pawan Kumar 'Bharti'; Dr. M.M. Abid Ali Khan; Dr. Ashok K. Rathoure
ISBN: 978-93-86841-55-1
Edition: 2018
Published by: Discovery Publishing House Pvt. Ltd., New Delhi (India)

7

Allium Cepa : The Plant of Ethical Values

[1]PRASANN KUMAR

ABSTRACT

Onion (*Allium cepa* L.) is one of the most important commercial vegetable crop grown in the country. Onion contains some chemical compounds such as malic acid and sulphur bearing compounds in the volatile oil allyle propyl disulphide.

Keywords: Allium, Biology, Crop, Diffusion, Effect.

INTRODUCTION

The pungency in onion is due to allyle propyl disulphide. Onion protect against cancer, heart disease, heat shock, inner side wounded and also cause antifungal activities due to a phenolic factor i.e. catechol. Onions are very beneficial to women with scanty and painful menses. In case of sunstroke, use of onions relieves thirst and mitigates the effects of the sunstroke. Besides, onion has several medicinal uses described by various authors as remedy or cure for different ailments. China and India have first and second rank, respectively in total onion production in the world (based on FAO STAT in August 2010) (Table 7.1). Dhillon and Dev (1978) reported that the increasing level of sulphur on soybean significantly increased the crop sulphur uptake and the amount of sulphur derived from fertilizer and contents of protein-sulphur and sulphate-sulphur in plants but there was no significant effect on non protein organic sulphur content. The utilization of applied sulphur, however, was found to decrease when the dose was raised to 20 ppm sulphur. Ismunadji *et al*. (1987) reported that a sulphur deficiency appears to be widespread. It has been reported in red onion crops. The application of sulphur has a positive effect on the yield and quality of red onion. There is evidence that ammonium sulphate is superior to urea in increasing yields of the same crop. Jana and Kabir (1990) reported that seedling of onion was transplanted at an inter row spacing of 20 cm and an intra row spacing of 15 cm, sulphur powder was applied at 0, 30,

[1] Assistant Professor, Department of Agronomy, School of Agriculture, Lovely Professional University, Jalandhar, Punjab, 144411

40, or 50 kg ha^{-1}. Highest plant height, number of leaves, bulb diameter, root length, weight of 10 bulbs and yield were obtained with sulphur at 30 kg ha^{-1}. According to Saha and Singh (1992), nine soil test procedures for predicting S availability to ground nut grown under green house condition on 22 surface Inceptisols from Varanasi were evaluated for their relative suitability through soil test crop response correlation studies. Sulphur extracted by all the soil test procedures had significant correlation with relative yield and uptake of sulphur by the plant. In view of high degree of correlation of soil test values extracted by 0. 15% $CaCl_2$ solution with all the plant response parameters. This procedure has been considered to be the best amongst the procedure compared (Table 7.1).

Table 7.1: Onion Production of India in Different States is Given in Following Table

State	Area ('000 ha)	Production (in' 000 MT)	Yield(Ton/ha)
Andhra Pradesh	40. 40	628. 70	15. 56
Assam	8. 00	22. 10	2. 76
Bihar	54. 00	1,080. 00	20. 00
Chhattisgarh	11. 20	174. 20	15. 55
Delhi	1. 40	25. 00	17. 86
Gujarat	62. 00	1,514. 00	24. 42
Haryana	22. 20	383. 40	17. 27
Himachal Pradesh	2. 00	33. 9	16. 95
Jammu & Kashmir	2. 60	64. 80	24. 92
Jharkhand	14. 70	305. 50	20. 78
Karnataka	148. 30	2,379. 50	16. 05
Madhya Pradesh	58. 30	1,021. 50	17. 52
Maharashtra	414. 00	4,905. 00	11. 85
Orissa	33. 10	318. 10	9. 61
Pondicherry	0. 00	0. 20	0. 00
Punjab	8. 20	175. 40	21. 39
Rajasthan	48. 50	750. 00	15. 46
Sikkim	0. 30	1. 60	5. 33
Tamil Nadu	33. 80	338. 90	10. 03
Uttar Pradesh	23. 60	370. 90	15. 72
Uttaranchal	4. 20	45. 00	10. 71
West Bengal	21. 30	298. 00	13. 99
Total	1,012. 10	14,835. 70	14. 66

(**Source:** Directorate of Economics and Statistics, Krishi Bhawan, New Delhi (2010-2011)

Onion has high in food energy, intermediate in protein content and rich in calcium and riboflavin. Carbohydrates, protein, minerals and vitamins are the major constituents of onion. Small sized onions are more nutritive than large sized onions. The red and yellow colour of outer skin of the onion are due to presence of anthocyanin and quercetins, respectively. The nutritive value of onion has been given below (Per 100g of edible portion) (Table 7.2).

Table 7.2: Biochemcial Parameters of Onion

Sl. No.	Contents	Onion	
		Green	Bulb
1.	Moisture (g)	87. 6	86. 6
2.	Protein (g)	0. 9	1. 2
3.	Fat (g)	0. 2	0. 1
4.	Carbohydrate (g)	8. 9	11. 1
5.	Energy (K cal)	41. 0	50. 0
6.	Calcium (mg)	50. 0	47. 0
7.	Phosphorus (mg)	-	50. 0
8.	Iron (mg)	7. 5	0. 7
9.	Vitamin A (IU)	992	0
10.	Thiamin (mg)	0	0. 08
11.	Riboflavin (mg)	0. 01	0. 01
12.	Vitamin (mg)	17	11

(**Source:** Chaudhary *et al.*, 2009)

Role of Gypsum for S-Conatining Amino Acids in Onion

Sulphur is one of the essential elements for plant growth. Sulphur containing secondary compounds also provides resistance against pest and diseases (Bell, 1981). Onion is known for their affinity to sulphur because sulphur is a constituent of secondary compounds, i. e. allin, cycloallin and thiopropanol (Raina and Jaggi, 2008) therein. Sulphur import characteristic odors and flavors to onion and garlic. Sulphur is essential for the formation of proteins because of sulphur is found in cystine, cysteine and methionine, amino acids that make up plant proteins. It activates certain enzyme systems and is a component of some vitamins (vitamin A). Sulphur improves both yield and quality of crops (Patel and Patel, 1994). Studies have indicated that a deficiency of sulphur is increasing due to continuous use of S- free fertilizers and is more conspicuous in light textured soils low in organic matter (Sinha *et al.*, 1995). Calcium nutrition is often considered a yield limiting factor. Adequate supply of available calcium in the fruiting zone is extremely important to facilitate diffusion of calcium from the soil solution to developing bulbs. There are several separate sources of calcium and sulphur existed, but among them gypsum is found best due to its higher availability and greater solubility. Gypsum is considered as the cheapest and an excellent source of calcium (23%) and sulphur (18%). Gypsum application also improves the chemical properties of soil in terms of marginal decrease in pH, which on reaction to native calcium, release the calcium in soil solution. Patel *et al.* (1992) reported that the increasing level of nitrogen up to 75 kg ha^{-1} significantly increased the yield and attributing character, oil yield, nutrient content (N P S) and their uptake in mustard. Application of sulphur at 40 kg ha^{-1} significantly increased grain, straw, oil yield and uptake of sulphur, nitrogen and phosphorus by grain and straw (Figure 7.1).

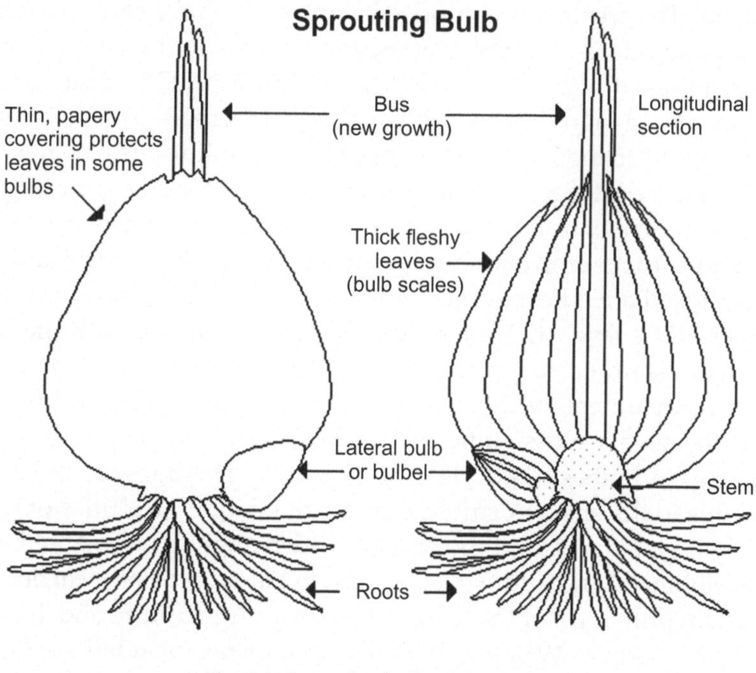

Fig. 7.1: Sprouting bulb of the Onion

(Source: Review of Litrature)

Jaggi (1994) reported that the 50 kg S ha^{-1} in a yield experiment on an Alfisol increased the seed yield, sulphur uptake and oil content of rye. Gypsum was the best source of sulphur. Sulphur application at an optimum rate (49.4 kg ha^{-1}) gave the highest benefit: cost ratio. According to Biswas *et al.* (1995), seed and straw yield of gobhi sarson (*Brassica napus* L.) var ISN-706 increased significantly due to nitrogen application in a green house experiment on sandy loam soil (Typic Ustochrept). Application of sulphur also enhanced the seed and straw yield. However, the effect was limited to the application at 50 kg sulphur ha^{-1} in the case of seed and 75 kg ha^{-1} in case of straw yield (seed 5.60 g pot^{-1}) N and S application also increased the uptake of N and S and oil yield significantly. Jaggi and Dixit (1995) found that sulphur application at a rate of 20 kg and 40 kg sulphur ha^{-1} increased cauliflower yield by 29 and 45%, respectively over control. Cauliflower yield also increased by Mo application. Singh and Pandey (1995) reported the effect of S and soil type on the yield of onions grown in pots. The soil was sandy to sandy clay loam in texture with available S in the range 5–22 ppm. Applied S had no significant effect on yield, but S uptake increased with increasing rate of S. Soil type significantly affected yield and S uptake. The highest S uptake was observed from a sandy loam soil amended by S at 40 ppm. Singh *et al.* (1995) reported the effect of doses and sources of sulphur on bulb yield and sulphur uptake by garlic on a Typic Ustipsament. The treatment comprised combination of 4 sources of sulphur (ammonium sulphate, gypsum, potassium sulphate and elemental sulphur) applied in 4 rates (0, 12.5, 25 and 50 Mg sulphur kg^{-1}). The mean bulb yield of garlic increased significantly with successive increase in level of sulphur application up to 25 mg kg^{-1}. Further increase in sulphur rates (50 mg sulphur kg^{-1} soil) decreased the garlic yield. The superiority of ammonium sulphate to the other sources may be attributed to its high solubility resulting in adequate sulphur supply to the crop and thus increase in bulb yield. Tripathi and Sharma (1995) conducted a field experiment with two sources of sulphur viz; gypsum and pyrites and 4 levels (20, 40, 60 and 80 kg S ha^{-1} along with the control). During the mustard crop, gypsum (16% S) and pyrites (22% S) were applied in respective treatments @ 20, 40, 60, and 80 kg S ha^{-1}. Sulphur application increased the seed yield significantly with increase in sulphur levels up to 40 kg ha^{-1} gave highest seed yield of 21 q ha^{-1}. The increase in seed yield might be due to the effect of sulphur in utilizing larger quantities of nutrients through their well developed root system which might have resulted in better plant development and ultimate yield. Dwivedi *et al.* (1996) carried a field experiment at pure form of the CSA University of Agriculture and Technology during *kharif* season of 1992 and 1993. The treatments included application of 37. 5 kg S ha^{-1} through elemental sulphur, pyrite and gypsum besides control (no sulphur). Sulphur application through various carriers increased the grain yield of black gram significantly. The uptake of some major nutrients (N, P, K and S) by black gram due to S applied were significantly higher than control. Singh and Singh (1996) reported that straw and pod yield oil content, oil yield and uptake of Ca and S by the ground nut crop increased significantly up to 300 kg ha^{-1} of gypsum application under limed as well as unlimited condition. The effect of applied gypsum on ground nut was higher in limed soil. Pod yield, straw yield and oil content also increased significantly. Islam *at al.* (1997)

conducted field experiments on a silt loam soil (Aeric Haplaquept) to study the effect of sulphur, zinc and boron application on autumn rice and their residual effects on following mustard crops. Autumn rice responded significantly to sulphur, zinc and boron applications. Application of any two nutrients together increased grain yield, but such increase was significant only when sulphur and zinc were combined. The highest grain yield 4.5 Mg ha^{-1} was found in sulphur + zinc and boron treatment with a record of 41.8% yield increase over control. While the application of sulphur, zinc and boron along brought 23.7, 21.7 and 14.6 percent yield increase, respectively. A large portion of the applied nutrient remained in the soil, which significantly increased the seed yield and nutrient uptake by the following mustard crop. The residual effect of sulphur, zinc and boron should be considered while applying fertilizers to crops. Meena and Singh (1998) reported that sulphur and zinc treatments significantly enhanced the dry weight of onion tops and bulbs. Higher levels of 30 mg S kg^{-1} caused an antagonistic effect. A sulphur dose of 20 mg S kg^{-1} on sulphur deficient soils and 10 mg S with 5 mg Zn kg^{-1} for low sulphur soils was appropriate for better onion yield. Total sulphur uptake by onion crop on all the three soils was enhanced significantly.

Role Of N, P, K Along with S on the Yeild Attributes of Onion

Dhillon *et al.* (1999) conducted a pot experiment to evaluate different indices of nitrogen, phosphorus, potassium and sulphur availability for gobhi sarson in Ustochrepts of Punjab. The result showed that amongst the various soil test methods employed organic carbon, Olsen P, 1*N* NH_4OAC-K and water soluble sulphur were significantly correlated with yield and uptake parameters. Critical levels of soil available N, P, K, and S under which the crops may respond to their application were 0.31% organic carbon, 11. 0 mg kg^{-1} of Olsen P, 56 mg kg^{-1} of 1*N*NH_4OAC-K and 10 mg kg^{-1} of soluble sulphur, respectively. Jaggi and Sharma (1999) conducted a pot experiment to study the sulphur response at three levels (0, 30 and 60 mg kg^{-1}) in raya (*Brassica juncea*) var. Varuna uses thirteen soils. With 30 and 60 mg kg^{-1} S application, a consistent significant increase in dry matter yield, sulphur uptake and a decrease in flowering period (advanced maturity) was noticed in all soils. An advancement in maturity by 2 to 4 and 4 to 11 days was recorded following S application @ 30 and 60 mg kg^{-1}, respectively. Nagaich *et al.* (1999)reported the effects of 4 rates of sulphur (0, 20, 40 and 60 kg ha^{-1}) on growth characters, yield attributes and quality of onion on a sandy loam soil in M. P. (India). Onion seed yield increased significantly upto 60 kg S ha^{-1}. Uptake of P, K and S also significantly increased at rates upto 60 kg S ha^{-1}. Prakash *et al.* (1999) reported that the sulphur availability of the soil with criticallimit of 10. 3 mg kg^{-1} soil, plant sulphur content was found to be positively correlated, critical concentration of S in cauliflower plants having sulphur concentration below the critical level of 5. 5 g kg^{-1} soil (Figure 7.2).

Fig. 7.2: Gypsum application on onion

(Source: Review of Literature)

Babhulkar *et al.* (2000) studied the individual and interactive effect of sulphur (0, 30, 45, 60 kg S ha^{-1}) and zinc (0, 15, 30, 45 kg Zn ha^{-1}) along with 50 kg each of N and P_2O_5 on safflower for yield, quality and nutrient uptake in a swell, shrink soil (Vertisol). Application of 45 kg sulphur ha^{-1} recorded significantly high, dry matter, seed yield and seed nutrient content. Increase in the level of sulphur and zinc significantly increased the oil and protein content in seed. The combined application of sulphur and zinc @ 45 and 15 kg ha^{-1}, respectively, significantly increased the straw and grain yield of safflower. Results of Misra (2003) showed that mustard crop responded significantly to the application of S and K. The seed and stover yields increased in linear order upto 40 kg S and 60 kg K_2O ha^{-1}. The highest seed yield (2035 kg ha^{-1}) at 40 kg S ha^{-1} was 27.59% higher in comparison to the yield at control. S showed a synergistic relationship with K. The uptake of N, K and S at maturity was significantly affected with treatments. The P uptake significantly increased upto 40 kg S ha^{-1} and thereafter decreased significantly. Percent utilization of added K and S was maximum when lowest levels of K and S were applied. Oil, protein, total S and amino acid contents increased significantly with the application of S and K. S and K also influenced remarkably the fatty acid composition oleic acid, linoleic acid content increased and erucic acid decreased showing improved quality of mustard oil. Jaggi (2004) observed significant positive effect of S application on dry-matter yield of onion 'Patna Red' *(Allium cepa* L.) bulbs and foliage over no S. Similar effects of S application were also reflected on N and S uptake by bulbs and foliage separately and also on their total (bulbs + foliage) uptake. Sulphur application upto 30 kg/ha significantly and positively influenced dry-matter yield of bulb and foliage, N and S content (%), and N:S ratio in bulbs and S uptake by bulbs, foliage and total (bulb + foliage) S uptake over S dose of 15 kg/ha. At 30 kg S dose, the increase in bulb yield was 105% over no S. Gypsum as S source proved significantly superior to S_{95}, as evident from its effects on S content and N:S ratio in onion bulbs; and N and S uptake by the onioncrop as a whole. Jaggi (2005 a) reported that sulphur application significantly reduced weight loss and rottening but increased sprouting during storage over no sulphur. Moisture loss in onion bulbs receiving sulphur @ 30 kg/ha was significantly less compared with the 15 kg/ha in the pooled data. Further, sulphur additions did not affect the moisture loss to a significant extent. Rottening (%) in onion consistently decreased with increasing S levels from 15 to 60 kg/ha in the pooled data although the differences were significant only at the S level of 60 kg/ha over 15 and 30 kg/ha. On the contrary sprouting increased with increasing levels of S upto 30 kg/ha. Further, S additions to 60 kg/ha brought down sprouting percentage to significant extent over the previous S level but not over the S dose of 15 kg/ha. Such effects were visible only during the first year. Gypsum proved to be superior sulphur source over S_{95} in reducing storage losses. Jaggi (2005 b) reported significant positive effect of S application on fresh and dry weight yields of onion; and plant height, leaves/plant and weight/10 bulbs over no-S. There was a significant positive response due to graded S doses upto 30 kg/ha on all these parameters. Further, S additions did not make any change. Gypsum proved superior S source to S_{95}. Duhan *et al.* (2006) reported that application of sulphur significantly increased the grain and straw yield of raya at all the level of sulphur application. Number of pods per plant and oil content in raya seed were increased with the increasing level of sulphur. The application of sulphur also increased the uptake of nitrogen, phosphorus, potassium and sulphur by raya. Available sulphur content in post harvest soil sample increased with the application of sulphur in raya. Jaggi *et al.* (2006) reported the superiority of gypsum in response both at linear and curvature level by 0.0721 and 0.00066 tonne/ha. This implies that not only the limiting (maximum yield) was higher but the response / kg gypsum was also more. Multifertilizer Response Model was used to work out the optimum dose of fertilizers. The results indicated optimum level of S_{95} to be 42.14 kg/ha as against 55.17 for gypsum. Jat *et al.* (2006) found that sulphur content in mustard growing soils of Jaipur district ranged from 101. 30 to 302.40 mg kg^{-1} with the mean value of 154.28. The mean value of organic sulphur, SO_4 – S and non SO_4 – S were 36.39, 14.52 and 102.12 mg kg^{-1}, respectively. All the forms of sulphur gave significant and positive correlation with organic carbon indicating sulphur as a integral part of soil organic matter. The step down multiple regression revealed that organic carbon had greater impact on different forms of sulphur followed by soil texture. Syed *et al.* (2006) reported that increasing levels of nitrogen and sulphur significantly increased the yield of sunflower. Maximum seed yield was recorded at 80 kg N and 60 kg S ha^{-1}. Stalk yield at harvest increased significantly with the increasing levels of N and S. The maximum stalk yield was recorded at 120 kg N and 60 kg S ha^{-1}. Jat and Mehra (2007) conducted field experiments for two years with mustard (*Brassica juncea,* L-Cern and

Coss) as a test crop on Hoplusteps with 5 doses of sulphur (0, 20, 40, 60, and 80.0 kg ha^{-1}) and zinc (0, 2.5, 5.0, 7.5 and 10. 0 kg Zn ha^{-1}). Seed and stover yield increased significantly up to 40 kg S and 5 kg Zn ha^{-1} application. Application of 60 kg S ha^{-1} and 2. 5 kg Zn ha^{-1} significantly increased the N, P, K and S content at 30, 60 and 90 DAS and at harvest in both year of experimentation. N, P, K and S uptake increased significantly upto 60 kg S and 50 kg Zn ha^{-1} application except nitrogen and potassium uptake in seed where significant increase was recorded only upto 40 kg sulphur ha^{-1}. According to Khan *et al*. (2007), a field experiment was initiated to study the effect of gypsum application on rice and subsequent wheat crop. The direct, residual and cumulative effects of gypsum were also noticed under rice-wheat system. The gypsum was applied as 0, 1 and 2 t ha^{-1} with the basal dose of N, P_2O_5, K_2O as 120, 90 and 60 kg ha^{-1} to both crops. The rice yield was significantly affected by gypsum application that ranged from 4807-5472 kg ha^{-1}. The highest rice yield was recorded by the application of 2.0 t gypsum application. The wheat grain yield ranged from 2598 to 4304 kg ha^{-1} with an increase of 13.8% over control. Similarly, all the yield components like number of panicles m^{-2}, panicle length, plant height and 1000 grain weight were also significantly affected by gypsum application. The wheat grain yield by 25. 25 and 65. 66% over check, respectively. The direct and residual application of 2 t gypsum ha^{-1} gave an increase of 46.80 and 15.05% over the check, respectively. The application of gypsum significantly affected the P and K that ranged from 4.50-7.50 and 4.70-9.32 mg kg^{-1} P while 70-110 and 78-112 kg^{-1} K in rice and wheat, respectively. Kulezycki (2007) reported that the application of low total sulphur sulphate content increased the yield of mustard, whereas the highest rate reduced the yield. The lowest rate of sulphate and elemental sulphur applied to medium soil. Which had a higher sulphur rate reduced the yield significantly. Sulphate and elemental sulphur increased the sulphur uptake by mustard. Sulphur application significantly increased the sulphur content of soil. Singh and Verma (2007) conducted a field experiment on mustard with different sources of sulphur (elemental sulphur, pyrite, gypsum, S.S.P and ammonium sulphate). They reported that the seed yield of mustard was highest with gypsum at 40 kg sulphur ha^{-1} followed by ammonium sulphate along with 80 kg nitrogen and 60 kg P_2O_5 ha^{-1}. The lowest yield was recorded with elemental sulphur. Tomar and Singh (2007) reported that the application of 30 kg S ha^{-1} significantly improved the yield attributes, seed and stover yield. Sulphur application increased oil content and oil yield of mustard. According to Jaggi and Raina (2008), significant positive effect of 30 g ha^{-1} of sulphur as manifested on yield and yield parameters of garlic were further carried over to following maize crop. Garlic bulb and foliage yield (6.3 and 0.8 ton ha^{-1}, respectively) obtained at 30 kg ha^{-1} of sulphur dose was significantly higher over without sulphur (3.7 and 0.5 ton ha^{-1}, respectively) as revealed from two years pooled data.

Similarly number of leaves per plant, weight of cloves/5 bulbs and weight/100 clove at the sulphate sulphur dose significantly increased over without sulphur from 10.5 to 11.9, 98. 3 to 141.2 g and from 159 to 217 g in a respective manner. Increase in grain yield of maize (residual effect) and in the economic yield of the whole cropping sequence (Bulb yield of garlic and grain yield of maize) ie. direct plus residual effect at 30 kg ha^{-1} of sulphur dose over without sulphur was from 28. 3 to 47.2 and from 71 to 116 q ha^{-1} in respective manner ie. with significant differences. Sulphur use efficiencies (kg yield kg^{-1} S) of these crops at 15, 30 and 45 kg ha^{-1} over no sulphur were 57, 43 and 32, 53, 63 and 6 and 160, 150 and 67 all in respective order. An optimum sulphur dose of 44.3 kg ha^{-1} produced increased bulb yield (over no sulphur). Karthikeyan and Shukla (2008) reported the effect of interaction between boron and sulphur on their uptake and quality parameters of mustard (*Brassica juncea*) and sunflower (*Helianthus annus* L.). The interaction effect between B and S significantly and synergistically influenced the dry matter and seed yields of both crops which were observed highest at 60 mg kg^{-1} of S in conjunction with 2 mg kg^{-1} of boron. The oil and protein contents of sunflower and mustard were significantly and synergistically improved by the application of both sulphur and boron. According to Raina and Jaggi (2008), field experiment conducted during 2003-06 to study the effects of 4 (0, 15, 30 and 45 kg/ha) S levels in the absence and presence of 25 tonnes farmyard manure/ha in onion (*Allium cepa* L.) – maize (*Zea mays* L.) system. The results show the positive effects of 30 kg S/ha on bulb yield over the previous levels of 0 and 15 kg/ha (direct effect). Addition of sulphur beyond 30 kg/ha brought the yield to the level of 0 and 15 kg/ha. Application of farmyard manure @ 25 tonnes/ha significantly increased bulb and foliage yield. Sulphur-farmyard manure interaction was positive at low and negative at higher levels of S. Highest yield was observed either in treatment combination of 25 tonnes farmyard manure/ha without S or 30 kg S/ha without farmyard manure. Plant height significantly increased only by farmyard manure (from 57. 4-59. 1cm) over without farmyard manure. In maize (residual effect) and also in onion-maize sequence as a whole (direct + residual effects) the same trend was visible except that the sulphur – farmyard manure interaction was significant only in the later. Sulphur addition beyond 30 kg/ha brought down the total economic yield and also the foliage yield of both the crops to the level of either 15 kg S/ha or even control. Sarangthem and Sarkar (2008) studied the response of rape seed to nitrogen and sulphur on a clayey soil. Treatments consisted of three levels of nitrogen (0, 40 and 60 kg ha^{-1}) and three levels of sulphur through gypsum (0, 20 and 40 kg ha^{-1}). Application of 60 kg N ha^{-1} produced the highest seed (1. 18 ton ha^{-1}) and straw (1. 69 ton ha^{-1}) yield of rape seed. Oil content in seed increased significantly with the application of nitrogen (60 kg ha^{-1}), sulphur (40 kg ha^{-1}). Total nitrogen uptake with rape seed progressively increased from 39. 6 to 72.

6 kg ha^{-1} with the increase in nitrogen levels. The uptake of sulphur increased with sulphur application upto 40 kg sulphur ha^{-1}, uptake of P and K by rape seed increased with graded levels. Jaggi and Sharma (2010) reported the response of onion (*Allium cepa*) var. Patana red at four sulphur levels (0, 15, 30 and 60 kg ha^{-1}) application through gypsum and S^{95}. The analysis was done to allocate the limited availability of sulphur for maximizing no profit over fertilizer cost. The result show that the dose of sulphur under its full availability is 43. 02 kg ha^{-1}. But under its scarce availability the maximum benefit would occur when it is applied upto 32. 11 kg ha^{-1} followed by even distribution of fertilizer ie. 20 kg ha^{-1}.

CONCLUSION

Onion has high in food energy, intermediate in protein content and rich in calcium and riboflavin. Carbohydrates, protein, minerals and vitamins are the major constituents of onion. Small sized onions are more nutritive than large sized onions. The pungency in onion is due to allyle propyl disulphide. Onion protect against cancer, heart disease, heat shock, inner side wounded and also cause antifungal activities due to a phenolic factor i. e. catechol. Onions are very beneficial to women with scanty and painful menses. In case of sunstroke, use of onions relieves thirst and mitigates the effects of the sunstroke.

REFERENCES

Babulkar, P. S., Kar, D., Badole, W. P. and Balpande, S. S. (2000) Effect of Sulphur and Zinc on Yield Quality and Nutrient Uptake by Safflower in Vertisol. *Journal of the Indian Society of Soil Science* **49**, 541-543.

Basumatari, Anjali, Das, K. N. and Borkotoki, Bikram (2010) Interrelationships of Sulphur with Soil Properties and Its Availability Index in Some Rape Seed-growing Inceptisols of Assam *Journal of the Indian Society of Soil Science* **58**, 394-402.

Bell, A. A. (1981) Biochemical Mechanism of Disease Resistance. *Annual Review of Plant Physiology* **32**, 21-81.

Biswas, D. R., Ali, S. A. and Khera, M. S. (1995) Response of Gobhi Sarson (*Brassica Napus L.)* var. I. S. N. -706 to Nitrogen and Sulphur. *Journal of the Indian Society of Soil Science* **43**, 220-223.

Chandel, S. R. S. (2004) A Hand Book of Agricultural Statistics. *Achal Prakashan Mandir,* Pandu Nagar, Kanpur.

Chaudhary, B. R., Manphool, Fageria, S. and Dhaka, R. S. (2009). A Textbook on Production Technology of Vegetables. *Kalyani Publishers*.

Chesnin, L. and Yien, C. H. (1951) Turbidimetric Determination of Available Sulphur in Soil. *Soil Science Society of America Proceeding* **15**, 149-151.

Chopra, S. L. and Kanwar, J. S. (2005) Analytical Agricultural Chemistry. *Kalyani Publishers,* New Delhi, pp. 22-225.

Dhillon, N. S. and Dev, G. (1978) Effect of Elemental Sulphur Application on the Soybean. *Journal of the Indian Society of Soil Science* **26**, 55-57.

Dhillon, N. S., Chhina, H. S., Sharma, K. N. and Baddesha, H. S. (1999) An Appraisal of Various Nutrient Availability Indices of N, P, K, and S for Gobhi Sorson (*Brassica napus* L.) in Ustochrepts of Punjab. *Journal of the Indian Society of Soil Science* **47**, 721-724.

Duhan, B. S., Grewal, K. S., Singh, B. and Satyavan, D. (2006) Effect of Sulphur on Yield and Nutrient Uptake by Two Cultivation of Raya. *Hariyana Journal of Agronomy* **22**, 161-163.

Dwivedi, K. N., Chandya, P. and Pandey, U. C. (1996) Relative Efficiency of Sulphur Carriers on Yield of Paddy and Nutrients Uptake by Black Gram. *Journal of the Indian Society of Soil Science* **44**, 790-791.

Islam, M. R., Riasal, T. M. and Jahiruddin, M. (1997) Direct and Residual Effects of S, Zn and B on Yield and Nutrient Uptake in a Rice-mustard Cropping System. *Journal of the Indian Society of Soil Science* **45**,126-129.

Ismunadji, M., Makarim, A. K. and Rushadi, A. (1987) Status Report on the Role of Sulphur as a Plant Nutrient in Indonesia. *Proceedings of Thesymposium on Fertilizer Sulphur Requirements and Sources in Developing Countries of Asia and the Pacific*, Bangkok, 26-30 January, **31**-37.

Jackson, M. L. (1973). Soil Chemical Analysis. Prentice Hall of India. Pvt. Ltd., New Delhi.

Jaggi, R. C. (1994) Response of Raya (*Brassica juncea*) to Sulphur Through Different Sources in an Acid Alfisol. *Journal of the Indian Society of Soil Science* **42**, 281-283.

Jaggi, R. C. (2004) Effect of Sulphur Levels and Sources on Composition and Yield of Onion (*Allium cepa*). *Indian Journal of Agricultural Sciences* **74**, 219-220.

Jaggi, R. C. (2005 a) Sulphur Levels and Sources Affecting Yield and Yield Attributes in Onion (*Allium cepa*). *Indian Journal of Agricultural Sciences* 7**5**, 154-160.

Jaggi, R. C. (2005 b) Sulphur as Production and Protection Agent in Onion (*Allium cepa*). *Indian Journal of Agricultural Sciences* **75**, 805-808.

Jaggi, R. C. and Dixit, S. P. (1995) Response of Cauliflower to Sulphur and Molydenum in Vegetable Growing Area of Palm Valley. *Journal of the Indian Society of Soil Science* **43**, 229-231.

Jaggi, R. C. and Raina, S. K. (2005) Nutrient Content in Garlic (*Allium sativum*) as Indices of Yield and Yield Attributes. *Agropedology* **15**, 107-109.

Jaggi, R. C. and Raina, S. K. (2008) Direct, Residual and Direct + Residual Effect of Sulphur in Garlic (*Allium sativum*) - Maize (*Zea mays*) Cropping Sequence. *Journal of the Environmental Biology* **29**, 85-88.

Jaggi, R. C. and Sharma, R. K. (1999) Sulphur Response Pattern on Flowering, Dry Matter, Yield and Sulphur Utilization in Raya (*Brassica juncea*) var. Varuna in Soils of District Kangra. *Journal of the Indian Society of Soil Science* **47**, 513-518.

Jaggi, R. C. and Sharma, R. K. (2010) Sulphur Management in Onion (*Allium cepa*) Cultivation in Hills of Himanchal Pradesh. *Journal of the Environmental Biology* **31**, 391-393.

Jaggi, R. C., Sharma, R. K. and Gupta, Sonika (2006) Comparative Response of Onion (*Allium cepa*) to Two Sources of Sulphur. *Indian Journal of Agricultural Sciences* **76**, 145-147.

Jana, B. K. and Kabir, J. (1990) Effect of Sulphur on Growth and Yield of Onion C. V. Nasik Red. *Crop Research* **3**, 241-243.

Jat, J. R. and Mehra, R. K. (2007) Effect of Sulphur and Zinc on Yield, Micronutrient Content and Uptake by Mustard Haplustepts. *Journal of the Indian Society of Soil Science* **55**, 190-195.

Jat, J. R. and Yadav, B. L. (2006) Different forms of Sulphur and these Relationship with Properties of Entisols under Mustard Cultivation. *Journal of the Indian Society of Soil Science* **54**, 208-212.

Karthikeyan, K. and Shukla, L. M. (2008) Effect of Boron-sulphur Interaction on their Uptake and Quality Parameters of Mustard (*B. juncea* L.) and Sunflower (*Helianthus annus* L.). *Journal of the Indian Society of Soil Science* **56,** 225.

Khan, R. U., Gurmani, A. R., Khan, M. S. and Gurmani, A. H. (2007) Effect of Variable Rates of Gypsum Application on Wheat Yield Under Rice-wheat System. *Pakistan Journal of Biological Science* **1:10,** 3865-9.

Kulezycki, G. (2007) The Influence of Sulphate and Elemental Sulphur Fertilization on Yield, Chemical Composition of Plants and Chemical Soil Properties Czartory Skich, Poland. *Polish Society of Agronomy* **24,** 140-149.

Losak, T. and Wishiowska-Kieliam, B. (2006) Fertilization of Garlic (*Allium sativum*) with Nitrogen and Sulphur. Annales Universitates Mariae Curie Skodowska Section E. *Agricultura* **61,** 45-50.

Majumdar, B., Venkatish, Kumar, Kailash and Ram, Pati (2003) Response of Garlic (*Allium sativum*) to Phosphorus and Sulphur Application in Acid Alfisol of Meghalay. *Journal of Spices and Aromatic Crops* **12,** 183-186.

Meena, O. S. and Singh D. (1998) Effect of Sulphur and Zinc Application of Onion Yield and Sulphur and Zinc Uptake in Three Soil Orders. *Journal of the Indian Society of Soil Science* **46,** 636-640

Mishra, S. K. (2003) Effect of Sulphur and Potassium on Yield, Nutrient Uptake and Quality Characteristics of Mustard (*Brassica Juncea*) in Udic Haplusteps of Kanpur. *Journal of the Indian Society of Soil Science* **51,** 544-548.

Nagaich, H. N., Trivedi, S. K. and Lekgi, R. (1999) Effect of Sulphur and Potassium Fertilization in Onion (*Allium cepa* L.). *Horticultural Journal* **12,** 25-31.

Nagaich, H. N., Trivedi, S. K. and Lekgi, R. (2003) Effect of Sulphur and Potash on Growth Yield and Quality of Garlic (*Allium sativum*). *Scientific Horticulture* **8,** 143-147.

Narseen, S., Imamul-Haq, S. M. and Hossain, M. A. (2003) Sulphur Effects on Growth and Yield of Onion. *Asian Journal of Plant Sciences* **2,** 897-902.

Oliveira, S. A. de, Cavariani, C., Silva, E. C. da, Soratto, R. P. and Crusciol, C. A. da C. (2009) Residual Effects of the Liming and Gypsum on the Seeds Productivity on and Quality of Common Bean Under no Tillage. *Journal – Cultura Agronomica* **18,** 29-43.

Patel, L. R., Patel, N. R. and Patel, R. H. (1992) Effect of Nitrogen, Phosphorus and Sulphur on Seed Yield and Quality of Mustard. *Journal of Oil Seeds Research* **9,** 333-334.

Patel, P. C. and Patel, J. R. (1994) Effect of Phosphorus and Sulphur on Forage Yield and Nutrient Uptake by Lucerne. *Journal of the Indian Society of Soil Science* **41,** 154-156.

Prakash, O. M., Singh, Vinay and Dev, P. (1999) Critical Level of Sulphur for Cauliflower in Alluvial Soil. *Journal of the Indian Society of Soil Science* **47,** 808-809.

Rao, R. S., Reddy, T. B. and Reddy, G. H. S. (1986) Direct and Residual Effect of Gypsum and Zinc on Irrigated Ground Nut. *Indian Journal of Agronomy* **29,** 244-248.

Saha, S. C. and Singh, B. (1992) An Appraisal of Some Soil Test Procedures for Predicting Sulphur Availability to Ground Nut in Inceptisols of Varanasi. *Journal of the Indian Society of Soil Science* **40,** 786-791.

Sarangthem, Indira, Sarkar, A. K. (2008) Response of Rape Seed to Nitrogen and Sulphur. *Journal of the Indian Society of Soil Science* **56,** 222.

Singh, D. and Pandey, R. N. (1995) Effect of Applied Sulphur on Dry Matter Yield and Sulphur Uptake by Onion in Different Soil Series of Delhi. *Annals of Agricultural Research* **16,** 348-350.

Singh, D. and Verma, B. S. (2007) Effect of Different Sources of Sulphur on the Yield of Indian Mustard (*Brassica Juncea* L.) in Pearl Millet-Mustard Cropping System. *Annals of Biology* **23**, 17-18.

Singh, Fateh, Singh, Vinay and Singh, Rajvir (1995) Effect of Different Doses and Sources of Sulphur on Yield and Uptake of Sulphur by Garlic. *Journal of the Indian Society of Soil Science* **43**, 130-131.

Singh, Jagpal, Singh, Sandeep and Singh, Vinay (2010) Soil Potassium Fractions and Response of Cauliflower and Onion to Potassium. *Journal of the Indian Society of Soil Science* **58**, 384-387.

Singh, Surendra and Singh, K. P. (1996) Effect of Gypsum on Yield Oil Content and Uptake of Ca and S by Ground Nut on an Acid Alfisol of Ranchi. *Journal of the Indian Society of Soil Science* **44**, 695.

Sinha, R. B., Sakal, R. and Kumar, S. (1995) Sulphur and Phosphorus Nutrition of Winter Maize in Calcareous Soil. *Journal of the Indian Society of Soil Science* **43**, 413-418

Sistani, K. R. and Morrill, L. G. (1992) Foliar Application of Phosphorus and Residual Effect of Gypsum on Peanuts. *Journal of Environmental Science and Health* **27**, 317-327.

Subbiah, B. V. and Asija, G. L. (1956) A Rapid Procedure for Estimation of the Available Nitrogen in Soil. *Current Science* **25**, 259-260.

Syed, T. H., Ganai, M. R., Tahir, A. and Mir, A. H. (2006) Effect of Nitrogen and Sulphur Fertilization on Yield and Nutrient Uptake by Sunflower. *Journal of the Indian Society of Soil Science* **54,** 375-376.

Tandon, H. L. S. (1998) Nutrients in Soils, Plants, Waters, Fertilizers and Manures. In Methods of Analysis of Soils, Plants, Waters, Fertilizers FDCO, New Delhi P, 1-12.

Tomar, S. K. and Singh, K. (2007) Response of Indian Mustard (*Brassica juncea)* to Nitrogen and Sulphur Fertilization Under Rainfed Condition of Diara Land. *International Journal of Agricultural Science* **3**, 5-9.

Tripathi, P. N. and Sharma, N. L. (1995) Effect of Gypsum and Pyrites on Yield and Quality of Mustard in Salt Affected Soils of Western Uttar Pradesh. *Journal of the Indian Society of Soil Science* **43**, 209-291.

Walkley, A. and Black, I. A. (1934) Estimation of Soil Organic Carbon by the Chromic Acid Titration Method. *Soil Science* **37**, 29.

Wani, M. A. and Chatto, M. A. (2005) Effect of Sources and Doses of Sulphur on the Performance of Garlic (*Allium sativum*). *Horticultural Journal* **18,** 114-116.

Nutraceuticals and Pharmaceuticals from Medicinal Plants
Edited by: Dr. Pawan Kumar 'Bharti'; Dr. M.M. Abid Ali Khan; Dr. Ashok K. Rathoure
ISBN: 978-93-86841-55-1
Edition: 2018
Published by: Discovery Publishing House Pvt. Ltd., New Delhi (India)

8 Fruit and Vegetable Wastes – A Source of Antimicrobial, Antioxidant and Phyto-chemicals

[1]Neeta Singh

Fruits and vegetables are considered as an important part of a good diet. Besides their delicious taste and flavor, they are known to reduce risk of several chronic diseases. Fruits and vegetables contain significant amounts of phytoconstituents which are negatively associated with the morbidity and mortality from cerebrovascular, cardiovascular and certain types of cancers. Foods are generally consumed for their nutritive value and bioactive compounds. Fruits and vegetables wastes and their by-products are formed in great amounts during industrial processing and hence represent a serious problem, as they exert harmful impact on environment. So they need to be managed or they can be utilized. Vegetables are cooked in Indian kitchens as curries and are eaten along with bread or chapatis and fruits are eaten as such. Different components having activities like antimicrobial, antioxidant, anti proliferative, anti-inflammatory, etc. have been isolated from different peels. Growing knowledge about antioxidants, that their presence in everyday foods promotes health, combined with the assumption that a number of common synthetic preservatives may have hazardous effects has led to multiple investigations in the field of natural antioxidants (Parashar, *et al* 2014). The growing, processing and preparation of food result in the production of varying degree of waste material. The waste material may be in the form of leaf/straw, waste during harvesting, processing industry waste and after processing waste (Joshi and Devraj, 2008). The waste obtained from fruit processing industry is extremely diverse due to the use of wide variety of fruits and vegetables, the broad range of processes and the multiplicity of the product (William, 2005). Vegetables and some fruits yield between 25% and 30% of non-edible products (Ajila *et al.,* 2010). The full utilization of horticultural produce is a requirement and a demand that needs to be met by countries wishing to implement low-waste technology in their agribusiness (Kroyer, 1995). Depending on plant species, variety and tissue, high levels of health protecting antioxidants, such as vitamin

[1] Assistant Professor, ASPEE College of Home Science and Nutrition, SDAU, SK Nagar Sardarkrushinagar-385506, Di: Banaskantha, (Gujarat) India

C and E, phenolic compounds including phenyl-propanoids and flavonoids, and or carotenoids such as lycopene can be found. The waste materials such as peels, seeds and stones produced by the fruit and vegetable processing can be successfully used as a source of phytochemicals and antioxidants. The entire tissue of fruits and vegetables is rich in bioactive compounds, such as phenolic compounds, carotenoids, vitamins and in most cases, the wasted by products can present similar or even higher contents of antioxidant and antimicrobial compounds than the final produce can (Ayala-Zavala *et al.*, 2010). The new aspects concerning the use of these wastes as byproducts for further exploitation on the production of food additives or supplements with high nutritional value have gained increasing interest because these are high value products and their recovery may be economically attractive. The by-products represent an important source of sugars, minerals, organic acid, dietary fibre and phenolics which have a wide range of action which includes antitumoral, antiviral, antibacterial, cardio protective and antimutagenic activities (Jasna *et al.*, 2009). Because of increasing threat of infectious diseases, the need of the hour is to find natural agents with novel mechanism of action. Natural products provide unlimited opportunities for new drug leads because of the unmatched availability of chemical diversity. Fruit and vegetable peels are thrown into the environment as agro waste which can be utilized as a source of antimicrobics. Utilization of by-products is, however, limited due to the poor understanding of their nutritional and economic value (Schroeder, 1999).

The extent of total losses in these commodities is approximately estimated as 20-30% of the total production, amounting to a loss of ₹ 30,000 crores per annum. Sliced apples produced 10.91% of pulp and seed (core) by-products and 89.09% of the final products. Peeled mandarins produced 16.05% of peels and 83.95% of final products. Diced papayas produced 6.51% of seeds, 8.47% of peels, 32.06% of unusable pulp (due to the lack of shape uniformity in a cube), and 52.96% of final products. Pineapples produced 9.12% of core, 13.48% of peels, 14.49% of pulp, 14.87% of top, and 48.04% of finished products. Mangoes produced 13.5% of seeds, 11% of peels, 17.94% unusable pulp, and 57.56% of final products. It is emphasized that considerable amounts of fruit material are the by-products of the minimal processing, and the possibility of creating alternative processes to give added value to this wasted material must be considered (Ayala-Zavala *et al.*, 2010). While according to FAO (2003), the total waste generated from fruits was estimated as 3.36 million tonnes (MT) out of the total production of 16.8 MT and particularly for banana it was 6.4 MT. India is producing 3 million tonnes of citrus fruits like mandarins, lime, lemon, and sweet orange. Citrus wastes are rich source of oil, pectin and variety of by-products. The failure or inability to salvage and reuse such materials economically results in the unnecessary waste and depletion of natural resources (Bhalerao *et al.*, 1989). The extent of the waste produced and available from processing industries of some of the important fruits and vegetables is given in Table 8.1 and 8.2.

Table 8.1: Quantities of Various Fruit and Vegetable Processing Wastes

Commodity Percent weight basis	Commodity Percent weight basis
Apple	12-47
Apricot	8-25
Grape fruit	3-58
Orange	3
Peach	11-40
Pear	12-46
Asparagus	3. 2- 30
Bean, green	5-20
Beet	7-4
Broccoli	20
Cabbage	5-25
Carrot	18-52
Cauliflower	8
Peas	6-79
Potatoes	5
Spinach	10-40
Sweet potato 15	15
Tomato	5-25

Source: Gera IB and Kramer, 1969

Table 8.2: Fruits and Vegetable Processing Wastes Available in India

Vegetable	Nature of waste	Production (content) (tones)	Approx. waste (%)	Potential quantities of waste (tones)
Mango	Peel, stones	6987. 7	45	3144. 4
Banana	Peel	2378. 0	35	832. 3
Citrus	Peel, rag and seed	1211. 9	50	6-06. 0
Pineapple	Skin, core	75. 7	33	24. 7
Grapes	Stem, skin and seeds	565	20	—
Guavas	Peel and core and seeds	565	10	—
Peas	Shell	107. 7	40	68. 3
Onion	Outer leaves	1102. 0	—	—
Apple	Peel, pomace and seeds	1376. 0	—	412. 0

Source: Gupta and Joshi, 2000

Chemical composition: The amount of pollution load and characteristics of the waste depend on the food being processed. Chemical composition of the wastes from fruits and vegetables show that it is a rich source of various nutrients. Some of these fruit and vegetable wastes are a rich source of vital constituents like carbohydrates, proteins, fats, minerals, fibres etc. The association between the diet rich in fruits and vegetables and a decreased risk of cardiovascular diseases and certain forms of cancer is supported by considerable epidemiological evidence (Ness and Powles, 1997; Riboli and Norat, 2003). Different studies have shown that free radicals present in the human organs cause oxidative damage to various molecules, such as lipids, proteins and nucleic acids, and are thus involved in the initiation phase of the degenerative diseases. Phenolic and other phytochemical antioxidants found in fruits and vegetables are capable of neutralizing free radicals and may play a major role in the prevention of certain diseases (Kaur and Kapoor, 2001). Numerous studies have provided evidence for decreased risk of some chronic diseases e.g., some types of cancer, cardiovascular and neurodegenerative disorders with increased dietary intake of vegetables, fruits, teas, spices and other plant-based foods and supplements. The most abundant by-products of minimal processing of fresh-cut fruit and vegetable are peel and seed and those are reported to contain high amounts of phenolic compounds with antioxidant and antimicrobial properties (Shrikhande, 2000; Muthuswamy *et al.*, 2008; Tuchila *et al.*, 2000).

Phytochemicals: Plants synthesize a diverse array of secondary metabolites (phytochemicals) known to be involved in plant defence against microbial and fungal pathogens and insect pests, and in the last few decades several classes of phytochemicals have been shown to help reduce the risk of various diseases e.g. cancer and coronary heart disease. Nowadays, there is a growing interest in finding phytochemicals as an alternative to synthetic substances, which are commonly used in the food, pharmaceutical and cosmetic industry. Epidemiological studies have pointed out that the consumption of fruits and vegetables imparts health benefits, e.g. reduced risk of coronary heart disease and stroke, as well as certain types of cancer. Apart from dietary fibre, these health benefits are mainly attributed to organic micronutrients such as carotenoids, poly-phenols, tocopherols, vitamin C and others. Flavonoids from fruits and vegetables probably reduce risks of diseases associated with oxidative stress, including cancer. Apples contain significant amounts of flavonoids with antioxidative potential. The products and byproducts obtained during the minimal processing of the fruits were analyzed for the phytochemical content and antioxidant status. It was found that the total phenolics and flavonoid contents were higher in the byproducts as compared to the final products, being more pronounced in mango seeds and peels. These compounds could be responsible for free radical inhibition activity. Several studies have shown that the content of phytochemical compounds is higher in peel and seeds with respect to the edible tissue. Gorinstein *et al.,* (2001) found that the total phenolic compounds in the peels of lemons, oranges, and grapefruits were 15% higher than that of the pulp of these fruits. Peels from apples, peaches, pears as well as yellow and white flesh nectarines were found to contain twice the amount of total phenolic compounds as that contained in fruit pulp (Gorinstein *et al.,* 2001). While the edible pulp of bananas (Musa paradisiaca) contains 232 mg/100 g of dry weight phenolic compounds, this amount is about 25% of that present in the peel (Someya *et al.,* 2002). Similarly, other studies have reported that pomegranate peels contain 249.4 mg/g of phenolic compounds as compared to only 24.4 mg/g phenolic compounds found in the pulp of pomegranates. Apple peels were found to contain up to 3300 mg/100 g of dry weight of phenolic compounds (Wolfe and Liu 2003). Grape seeds and skins, the byproducts of grape juice and white wine production, are also sources of several phenolic compounds, particularly mono, oligo, and polymeric proanthocyanidins (Shrikhande, 2000). It has been reported that the total phenolic compounds of seeds of several fruits, such as mangos, longans, avocados, and jackfruits, were higher than that of the edible product, and that the byproducts could be a valuable source of phytochemicals (Soong and Barlow, 2004). The peels and seeds of tomatoes are richer sources of phenolic compounds than the pulp of the tomatoes are. The phenolic compounds of 12 genotypes of tomatoes have been studied, and, in general, lower levels were found in the flesh, ranging from 9.2 to 27.0 mg/100 g, as compared to 10.4 to 40.0 mg/100 g in the peels (George *et al.,* 2004). A similar observation was reported, and the total phenolic compounds (expressed as milligram of gallic acid equivalents per 100 g) of the skin, seeds, and pulp of tomatoes were found to be 29.1, 22.0, and 12. 7 mg/100 g, respectively (Toor and Savage, 2005). It was also found that the peel byproduct of tomato cultivars (Excell, Tradiro, and Flavorine) had significantly higher levels of total phenolic compounds, total flavonoids, lycopene, ascorbic acid, and antioxidant activity as compared with the pulp and seeds (Toor and Savage, 2005).

Natural antioxidants: Vegetables and some fruits yield between 25% and 30% of non-edible products (Ajila *et al.,* 2010). The failure or inability to salvage and reuse such materials economically results in the unnecessary waste and depletion of natural resources (Bhalerao *et al.,* 1989). The entire tissue of fruits and vegetables are rich in bio-active compounds, such as phenolic compounds, carotenoids, flavonoids, anthocyanins, vitamins and in most cases the waste by-products can present similar or even higher contents of antioxidant and antimicrobial compounds (Ayala-Zavala *et al.,* 2004).

The waste materials such as peels, seeds and stones produced from the fruit and vegetable processing unit can be successfully used as a source of phytochemicals and antioxidants. Higher amount of phenolic compounds and ascorbic acids has been reported in the peel than in pulp (Goulas and Manganaris, 2012) and in green form than in ripe (Fatemeh *et al.*, 2012) for most of the fruits. The majority of fruit peels exhibited 2 to 27 fold higher antioxidant activity than the fruit pulp (Guo *et al.*, 2003). Edible pulp of bananas (*Musa paradisiaca*) contains 232 mg/100g of dry weight phenolic compounds, this amount isabout 25% of that present in the peel (Someya *et al.*, 2002). Residues from star fruit (*Averrhoa carambola* L.) grape pomace (*Citrus paradise* M.) citrus fruits peel (Xu *et al.*, 2008), byproducts from pomegranate (*Punica granatum* L.) (Singh *etal.*, 2002) and banana peel (*Musa acuminata* Colla AAA) have been evaluated as inexpensive sources of antioxidants. The dry crude extracts of agro-industrial wastes such as peels of *Aloe vera, Cucumis sativus, Citrus paradisi,Citrus aurantium, Punica granatum* and leaves of *Oliveeuropaea* were evaluated for their antimicrobial and antifungal activities by Lutfullah *et al.* (2014). These were tested against the pathogenic bacterias like *Bacillus cereus, Xanthomonas sp., Clostridium sp., Staphylococcus aureus, Salmonella heidelberg, Salmonella typhi, Klebsiella pneumoniae* and *Escherichia coli.* All the extracts inhibited the growth of bacterias like *E. coli* and *S. aureus and fungal pathogens like A. niger* and *P. digitatum.*

Antimicrobials: The antimicrobial constituents are present in all parts of the plant viz. bark, stalks, leaves, fruits, roots, flowers, pods, seeds, stems, latex, hull and fruit rind. The antimicrobial activities of a variety of naturally occurring phenolic compounds from different plant sources have been studied in detail (Burt, 2004). Recent research has revealed that the fruit peels and seeds, such as grape seeds and peels, pomegranate peel and mango seed kernel (Kabuki *et al.*, 2007) may potentially possess antimicrobial property. Various fruits (peel, flesh or seed) have been used in traditional medicine for stomach ache, sore eyes, fever, etc. Papaya has been shown to contain sulphydroxyl protease which can inhibit virals or microbial infection (Rajashekhara *et al.*, 1990).

These compounds play an important role in fruits' protection against pathogenic agents, penetrating the cell membrane of microorganisms, causing lysis. Phenolic compounds from spices such as gingeron, zingerone, and capsaicin have been found to inhibit the germination of bacterial spores (Burt 2004). Polyphenols contained in green tea (*Camellia sinensis*) combat against *Vibrio cholerae* O1, *Streptococcus mutans* and *Shigella* (Si *et al.*, 2006). The fruit and vegetable peel extracts showed better antifungal activity than antibacterial activity; Gram-negative bacteria were more susceptible than Gram-positive bacteria The most susceptible organism was fungi and Gram-negative *K. pneumoniae. M. indica* showed maximum and best antimicrobial activity. The antimicrobial activity of an ethanol extract from mango seed kernels against food-borne pathogenic bacteria has also been reported. The mango extract was more effective against Gram-positive than Gram-negative bacteria, with a few exceptions (Kabuki *et al.*, 2007). In addition, flavonoids have been reported to enhance the antibacterial, antiviral, or anticancer activities of compounds such as naringenin, acycloguanosine and tamoxifen (Bracke *et al.*, 1999). The mixture of phytochemical constituents in plant extracts can be an advantage due to the synergistic effect that the constituents may have (Bakkali *et al.*, 2008).

Citric, succinic, malic, acetic, and tartaric acids are commonly found in fruits and fresh-cut byproducts. They have been traditionally used in the food industry as preservative agents, attributing their antimicrobial efficacy to the pH changes of the treated media. In general, bacteria grow at a pH close to 6.5 to 7.5, but tolerate a pH range from 4 to 9. Yeasts are more tolerant to low pH values than bacteria are, whereas molds can grow in the widest pH range. One effective way of limiting microbial growth is increasing the acidity of a particular food by adding an acidic substance (Massilia *et al.*, 2009). Acids attack cell walls, cell membranes, metabolic enzymes, protein synthesis systems, and the genetic material of microorganisms (Tripathi and Dubey, 2004).

Ethanol extract of cinnamon bark (1% w/v) reduced the aerobic growth of bacteria inoculated fresh-cut apples significantly during storage at 6 °C up to 12 d. Catechin, chlorogenic acid, and phloridzin, 3 phenolic compounds that are abundant in apple processing byproducts, exhibited varying degree of inhibitory action toward the growth of tested food pathogenic and spoilage bacteria, fungi, and yeasts (Muthuswamy and Rupasinghe, 2007). However, it is important to note that these phenolics (except 25 mm phloridzin) did not inhibit the probiotic bacterium Lac. rhamnosus suggesting no or minimal threat to the beneficial colon microflora, if the phenolics are used as food additives at the desirable concentrations. Also these authors suggest that the major phenolic compounds of apple byproducts could find use as food additives, however, the regulatory aspects of the use of plant extracts as fresh-cut fruit additives must be contemplated.

Essential oils from citrus offer the potential for all natural antimicrobials for use in improving the safety of organic or all natural foods (Joshi *et al.*, 2011). Subba *et al.*, (1967) determined that orange and lemon oil had in vitro antibacterial effects on Salmonella and other food-borne microorganisms. However, Fisher and Phillips (2006), on the other hand, found that Gram positive bacteria were more sensitive than Gram-negative in vitro. Seven citrus essential oils were screened by disc diffusion assay for their antibacterial activity against 11 serotypes/strains of Salmonella (Bryan *et al.*, (2008). The 3 most active oils were selected to determine the minimal inhibitory concentration (MIC) against the some Salmonella. Orange terpenes (C4), singles-folded d-limonene (C5), and orange essence terpenes (C6) all exhibited inhibitory activity against the *Salmonella spp*. On the disc diffusion assay orange terpens and d-limonene both had MICs of 1%. The most active compound, terpenes from orange essence, produced MIC that ranged from 0.125% to 0.5% against the 11 *salmonella* tested.

Mohamed *et al.*, 1994 evaluated antimicrobial activity of extracts of ripe, unripe and leaves of guava (*Psidium guajava*); ripe, unripe and leaves of starfruit (*Averrhoa carambola*); ripe and unripe banana (*Musa sapientum* variety *Montel*); ripe and unripe papaya (*Carica papaya*); passionfruit (*Passiflora edulis F. Flavicarpa*) peel; two varieties of Lansium domesticum peel (*langsat and duku*); rambutan (*Nephelium lappaceum*) peel and rambai (*Baccaurea motleyana*) against Gram positive bacteria, Gram negative bacteria, yeast and fungi (*Staphylococcus aureus, Bacillus subtilis, Bacillus cereus, Lactobacillus bulgaricus; E. coli, Proteus vulgaricus, Pseudomonas aeruginosa, Salmonelli typhi; Saccharomyces cerevisiae, Candida lypolytica; Rhizopus spp., Aspergillus niger, and Chlamydomucor spp*) by using both the filter paper disc diffusion and tube dilution assays. Extracts from ripe starfruit, guava leaves and rambai peel showed strong activity against all the bacteria tested, in most cases with activity stronger than 50 μg streptomycin. Passionfruit peel, ripe and unripe guava showed activity against all the bacteria tested except *E. coli*. Rambutan peel too showed activity against all the bacteria tested except towards *Pseudomonas aeruginosa*. Most of the fruit wastes showed some activity towards bacteria but poor activity against yeast or fungi. Extracts from bananas, papayas, passion fruit peel, *Lansium domesticum* peels and rambutan peels showed activity against *Candida lypolytica while* extracts from guava showed strong activity against *Saccharomyces cerevisiae*. Other than guava, ripe starfruit, rambai peel and rambutan peel showed potential for use against bacteria.

Table 8.3: Antimicrobial Activity of Some Plant Peels Against Some Microorganisms Causing Infectious Diseases

Plant name	Extract	Microorganisms
Citrus grandis (Rutaceae)	Hexane, ethyl acetate, butanol, methanol, benzene: acetone	*Bacillus subtilis, Bacillus cereus, Staphylococcus aureus, Escherichia, coli, Salmonella enteritidis*
Citrus reticulata Blanco (Rutaceae)	Oil	*Alternaria alternata, Rhizoctonia solani, Curvularia lunata, Fusarium oxysporum, Helminthosporium oryzae*
Vitis vinifera (Vitaceae)	80% ethanol	*Staphylococcus aureus, Bacillus cereus Escherichia coli, Salmonella infantis, Campylobactercoli*
Citrus reticulate Blanco (Rutaceae)	Flavonoid extract	*Escherichia coli, Staphylococcus aureus, Staphylococcus epidermidis, Enterococcus faecalis, Salmonella typhimurium, Enterobacter cloacae*

Citrus acida Roxb. (Rutaceae)	Oil	*Bacillus subtilis, Bacillus cereus, Staphylococcus aureus, Escherichia coli, Enterobacter aerogenes, Salmonella typhimurium, Aspergillus ficuum, Aspergillus niger, Aspergillus fumigatus, Aspergillus flavus, Fusarium saloni, Fusarium oxysporum, Pencillium digitatum, Candida utilis*
Ficus carica L. (Moraceae)	Aqueous	*Bacillus cereus, Staphylococcus epidermidis, Staphylococcus aureus, Escherichia coli,Pseudomonas fluorescens*
Citrus bergamia Risso (Rutaceae)	Ethanolic fraction	*Escherichia coli, Pseudomonas putida, Salmonella enterica, Listeria innocua, Bacillus subtilis, Staphylococcus aureus, Lactobacillus lactis, Sacharomyces cerevisiae*
Nephelium lappaceum L. (Sapindaceae)	Ether, methanol, aqueous	Escherichia coli, Klebsiella pneumoniae, Pseudomonas aeruginosa, Salmonella typhi, Vibrio cholerae, Enterococcus faecalis, Staphylococcus aureus, Staphylococcus epidermidis
Musa sapientum (Musaceae)	Chloroform, ethyl acetate, aqueous	*Staphylococcus aureus, Bacillus subtilis, Bacillus cereus, Salmonella enteritidis, Escherichia coli*

Source: Joshi, *et al.* (*2012)*

REFERENCES

Ajila CM, Aalami M, Leelavathi K and Rao UJSP. 2010. Mango Peel Powder: A Potential Source of Antioxidant and Dietary Fiber in Macaroni Preparations. *Innov Food Sci Emerg.* 11:219–224.

Ayala-Zavala JF, Rosas-Dominquez C, Vega-Vega V and GonzalezAguilar GA. 2010. Antioxidant Enrichment and Antimicrobial Protection of Fresh-Cut Fruits Using their Own By-products: Looking for Integral Exploitation. J Food Sci.; 75: R175–R181.

Bakkali F, Averbeck S, Averbeck D and Waomar M. 2008. Biological Effects of Essential Oils—A Review. Food Chem Toxicol. 46(2):446–475. [PubMed]

Bhalerao SD, Mulsmuky GV, Anthanthakishna SM and Potty VH. (1989). Effluent Management in Food Industry. *Ind Food Pack,* 43 (2): 5.

Bracke, Depypere HT, Boterberg T, Van Marck VL, Vennekens KM, Vanluchene E, Nuytinck M, Serreyn R and Mareel MM. 1999. Influence of Tangeretin on Tamoxifen's Therapeutic Benefit in Mammary Cancer. J Natl Cancer Inst. 91:354–359. [PubMed]

Bryan CA, Crandall PG, Chalova VI and Ricke SC. 2008. Orange Essential Oils Antimicrobial Activities Against *Salmonella spp. J Food Sci.,* 73: 264–267.

Burt S. 2004. Essential Oils: Their Antibacterial Properties and Potential Applications in Foods—A Review. Int J Food Microbiol. 94:223– 53. [PubMed]. Bryan CA, Crandall PG, Chalova VI and Ricke SC. 2008. Orange Essential Oils Antimicrobial Activities Against Salmonella spp. J Food Sci., 73: 264–267.

Gera IB and Kramer A. 1969. The Utilization of Food Industries Waste *In*. Advances in Food Research, Chichester CO, Mark EM and Stewart GF (Eds), Academic Press, New York, London, pp. 28.

George B, Kaur C, Khurdiya DS, Kapoor HC. 2004. Antioxidants in Tomato (*Lycopersium esculentum*) as a Function of Genotype. *Food Chem*. **84**:45–51.

Gorinstein, Martin-Belloso O, Park YS, Haruenkit R, Lojek A, Ciz M, Caspi A, Libman I and Trakhtenberg S. 2001. Comparison of Some Biochemical Characteristics of Different Citrus Fruits. *Food Chem*. **74**:309.

Goulas, V. and Manganaris, G. A. (2012). Exploring the Phytochemical Content and the Antioxidant Potential of Citrus Fruits Grown in Cyprus. Food Chem. 131: 39 – 47.

Gupta K and Joshi VK. 2000. Fermentative Utilization of Waste from Food Processing Industry In : Postharvest Technology of Fruits and Vegetables : Handling Processing Fermentation and Waste Mangement,Vol. 2 Verma L R and Joshi VK (Eds). Indus Pub Co, New Delhi.

Fisher K and Phillips CA. 2006. The Effect of Lemon, Orange and Bergamot Essential Oils and their Components on the Survival of *Campylobacter Jejuni, Escherichia coli* 0157:H7, *Listeria monocytogenes, Bacillus cerecis and Staphylococcus aureus* in vitro and in Food Systems. *J. Appl. Microbiol*. 101:1232-1240.

Jasna S D, Brunet C, and Æetkoviæ G. 2009. By-products of Fruits Processing as a Source of Phytochemicals. Chemical Industry and Chemical Engineering Quarterly. 15:191-202.

Joshi VK *et. al*. 2012. Bicolours: Chemistry, Production, Safety and Market Potential. In. Food Biotechnology Principles and Practices. ed. JoshiVK, Singh RS. pp. 641:658.

Joshi VK and Devrajan A. 2008. Ethanol Recovery from Solid State Fermentated Apple Pomace and Evaluation of Physico-chemical Characteristics of Residue. *Nat Prod Rad* 7: 127-132.

Kabuki T, Nakajima H, Arai M, Ueda S, Kuwabara Y, Dosako S. 2007. Characterization of Novel Antimicrobial Compounds from Mango (Mangifera indica L.) Kernel Seeds. Food Chem. 71:61–6.

Kaur C and Kapoor HC. 2001. Antioxidants in Fruits and Vegetables – the Millennium's Health. *Int J Food Sci. and Technol*. 36:703-725.

Kroyer GT. 1995. Impact of Food Processing on the Environment—An Overview. Lebensm Wiss Technol. 28:547–52.

Lutfullah, G., Tila, H., Hussain, A. and Ali Khan, A. (2014). Evaluation of Plants Extracts for Proximate Chemical Composition, Antimicrobial and Antifungal Activities. American-Eurasian J. Agric. Environ. Sci. 14 : 964-970.

Ness AR and Powles JW. 1997. Fruit and Vegetables and Cardiovascular Disease. *Int J Epidemiol*. 26:1-13.

Massilia RM, Mosqueda-Melgar J, Soliva-Fortuny R and Martin-Belloso O. 2009. Control of Pathogenic and Spoilage Microorganisms in Fresh-cut Fruits and Fruit Juices by Traditional and Alternative Natural Antimicrobials. *Compr Rev Food Sci Food Saf*. 8:157–180.

Muthuswamy S and Rupasinghe HPV. 2007. Fruit Phenolics as Natural Antimicrobial Agents: Selective Antimicrobial Activity of Catechin, Chlorogenic Acid and Phloridzin. *J Food Agric Environ*. 5(3- 4):81–5.

Parashar, S., Sharma, H., Garg,M. Antimicrobial and Antioxidant Activities of Fruits and Vegetable Peels: A Review. *Journal of Pharmacognosy and Phytochemistry*. 2014; 3 (1): 160-164.

Rajashekhara E, Tippannavar CM, Sreenivasa MN, and Sharma JS. 1990. Inhibition Activity of Papain on Facultative Pathogens. *Zentralblatt Fuer Microbiologie.* 145:455-456.

Riboli E. and Norat T. 2003. Epidemiologic Evidence of the Protective Effect of Fruit and Vegetables on Cancer Risk. American Clinical Nutrition. 78: 559–569.

Schroeder JW. 1999. By-products and Regionally Available Alternative Feedstuffs for Dairy Cattle. North Dakota State University. NDSU Extension Service. http:// www. ext. nodak. Edu/ext pubs/ansci/dairy/as/180 w. html.

Shrikhande AJ. 2000. Wine by Products with Health Benefits. Food Res Int. 33:469–474.

Si WD, Gong J, Tsao R, Kalab M, Yang R and Yin YL. 2006. Bioassayguided Purification and Identification of Antimicrobial Components in Chinese Green Tea Extract. *J Chromatogr.* **1125**:204–210.

Someya S, Yoshiki Y and Okubo K. 2002. Antioxidant Compounds from Bananas (*Musa cavendish*). *Food Chem.* **79**:351–354.

Soong YY, Barlow PJ. 2004. Antioxidant Activity and Phenolic Content of Selected Fruit Seeds. *Food Chem.* **88**:411–7.

Subba MS, Soumithri TC and Rao RS. 1967. Antimicrobial Action of Citrus Oils. *J food Sci.* **32**:225-227.

Toor RK, Savage GP. 2005. Antioxidant Activity in Different Fractions of Tomatoes. Food Res Int. 38:487–494.

Tripathi P, Dubey NK. 2004. Exploitation of Natural Products as An Alternative Strategy to Control Postharvest Fungal Rotting of Fruit and Vegetables. *Postharvest Biol Technol.* 32:235–240.

Tuchila C, Jianu I, Rujescu CI, Butur M, Ahmadi-Khoie M and Negrea I. 2008. Evaluation of the Antimicrobial Activity of Some Plant Extracts Used as Food Additives. J Food Agric Environ. 6:68–70.

William PT. 2005. Water Treatment and Disposal. John Wally (eds.) Greet Britain pp. 9.

Wolfe KL, Liu RH. 2003. Apple Peels as a Value-added Food Ingredient. *J Agric Food Chem.* **51**:1676–83.

Xu, G. H., Chen, J. C., Liu, D. H., Zhang, Y. H., Jiang, P. and Ye, X. Q. (2008). Minerals, Phenolic Compounds and Antioxidant Capacity of Citrus Peel Extract by Hot Water. J. Food Sci. 73: C11–C18.

Nutraceuticals and Pharmaceuticals from Medicinal Plants
Edited by: Dr. Pawan Kumar 'Bharti'; Dr. M.M. Abid Ali Khan; Dr. Ashok K. Rathoure
ISBN: 978-93-86841-55-1
Edition: 2018
Published by: Discovery Publishing House Pvt. Ltd., New Delhi (India)

9

Taxonomical and Ethnobotanical Study of Wild Edible Plants of Nainital District in Uttarakhand, India

[1]Lalit M. Tewari, [1]Brij M. Upreti, [1]Neetu Bohra, [1]Neha Chopra, [1]Naveen Chandra Pandey, [1]Mamta Bharti and [2]Ashish Tewari

INTRODUCTION

The loss of traditional knowledge has been recognized as one of the major factors that have negative effects on the conservation of biological diversity. Thus, it is becoming urgent to document and revitalize traditional knowledge of WEPs to assess the existing threats in the study areas and to preserve genetic and cultural diversity. There is limited literature on diversity, distribution, taxonomy, phenology and uses of WEPs of India. It is essential therefore to identify, evaluate, improve, propagate and cultivate these under-utilized species for its sustainable use which can broaden our choice of food and enrich the livelihoods of rural poor.

Over harvesting of mature fruit from parent-tree influenced the regeneration of the species. If this unsustainable harvesting by local people continues, the capacity of the species to maintain its wild population is significantly reduced. Therefore, management and conservation strategies that incorporate this factor are required. There are few studies and documents available on diversity, population and regeneration status of WEPs plants. The traditional knowledge on the use as plants is well documented (Maheshwari, 2000)., however, the knowledge on the use of WEPs as food is very much limited (Jain, 1964; Durby, 1997; Uniyal *et al.*, 2002). Large sections of population of Kumaun living in villages and remote forests depend on WEPs.

WEPs play an important role in ensuring food security and improve the nutrition in the diets of many people in developing countries (Lulekal *et al.*, 2011; Ghorbani *et al.*, 2012). They are potential sources of species for domestication and provide valuable genetic traits for developing new crops through breeding and selection (Ford-Lloyd *et al.*, 2011).

The traditional knowledge on the use as plants is well documented; however, there is a lacuna in accurate documentation of the folk knowledge on

---

[1] Deprtment of Botany, D. S. B. Campus Kumaun University Nainital
[2] Department of Forestry and Environmental Science, D. S. B. Campus Kumaun University Nainital

WEPs. It is of outmost importance to document the folk knowledge on WEPs before this knowledge disappears. An inadequate understanding concerning taxonomy, biology and local knowledge of these plants has contributed to suboptimal utilization of these valuable resources. It is essential therefore to identify and evaluate these plants which can broaden our choice of food and enrich the livelihoods of rural poor. The tradition of using wild palatable plants is still alive in the rural populations of Lesser Himalayas, but is vanishing. Consequently, the recording, preserving, and infusing of this traditional knowledge to upcoming generations is pressing and vital.

Still many more wild species are believed to be edible and undocumented yet. More recently, some ethnobotanical studies have undertaken in some parts of the country. However, the majority of these studies have the dealt with medicinal species and little emphasis has been paid to WEPs. This study has therefore sought to document indigenous knowledge related to uses of wild edible plant species and to assess the existing threats to WEPs in the study areas. Current over harvesting of mature fruit from parent-tree influenced the regeneration of this species. If this unsustainable harvesting by local people continues, the capacity of the species to maintain its wild population is significantly reduced. Therefore, management and conservation strategies that incorporate this factor are required. Conservation and management of WEPs and fruits will help to enhance and maintain the regional biodiversity with minimal adverse impact on the biodiversity.

Although, the Himalaya sustains a great diversity of valuable natural resources, the local people may have preferences over the use and importance of both crops and wild edibles. The information on such plants may help in adding variety to the monotonous diet so that requirements of minerals and vitamins etc. are easily met and help in publicizing the hitherto less known resources of wild fruits to many naturalists, visitors, tourists, mountaineers, researchers and local population etc. (Pangtey, 1980; Naithani, 1984 &1985). Many ethnobotanical surveys have been conducted by different workers (Abbasi *et al.*, 2012; Hazarat *et al.*, 2011; Abbasi *et al.*, 2010; 2010; Abbasi *et al.*, 2009; Bohra *et al.*,2017 & Hussain *et al.*, 2008) in different areas of Central Himalayas but to our knowledge no systematic investigation on ethno-botany of WEPs of Nainital district of Uttarakhand of central Himalayas, has been made. In this context, the present study will serve as a useful reference with particular emphasis on traditional uses of wild edible fruits and vegetables as there is dramatic loss of traditional knowledge regarding WEPs. The rapidity with which environmental damage, loss of floristic and cultural diversity occurs today, a necessicity is felt for the recording and documentation of traditional knowledge about the uses of edible plants which is widely disappearing. Therefore, there is an urgent necessity to document traditional knowledge.

Methodology

Study Area

This study was done for sub-tropical forest of Nainital district (Fig. 9.1 and Photoplate 1). Wild edible plants were collected from Ramnagar, Betalghat, Bhowali, Shyamkhet, Bhowali gaon and Ramgarh (Photoplate 1).

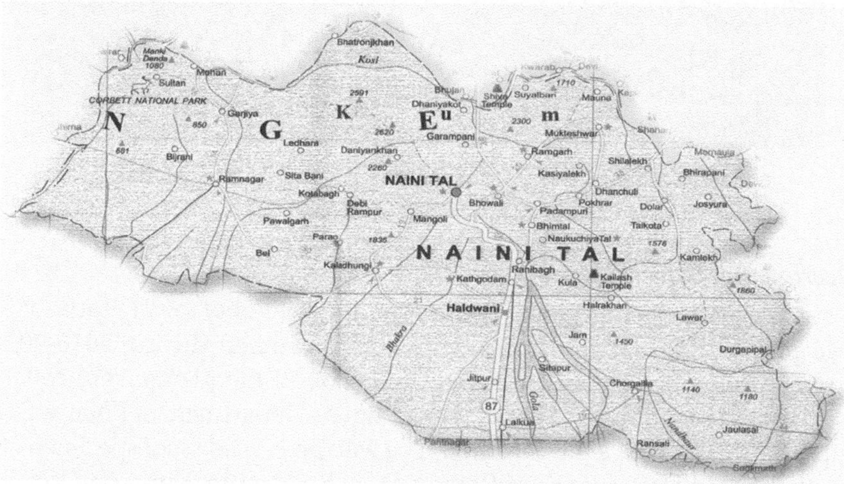

Fig. 9.1: Map of Nainital District (http://www. uttaranchal. org. uk)

Ramnagar

Betal ghatt

Bhowali

Shyamkhet

Bhowali Gaon **Ramgarh**

Photoplate 1: Photographos of sites

Collection and Identification of Plants

The study is based on ecology, taxonomy and ethnobotanical study of wild edible plants. Regular field surveys were conducted during 2016-2017 to document the wild edible plants. Specimens of all the plants were collected, preserved and identified by Prof. Y. P. S. Pangtey, Department of Botany, D. S. B. Campus, Kumaun University, Nainital. The well preserved plant specimens were deposited in the Department of Botany, D. S. B. Campus Kumaun University Nainital. Photographs of some important specimen have been taken for further details (Photoplate 2). The collection of wild edible plants was recorded with the help of local/rural peoples and the information regarding local names, edible part, mode of use and ethnobotanical importance of wild edible was gathered. The information was collected by the observation and semi structured interview method with people of different genders and age groups.

RESULTS

Identification and taxonomic description of all wild edible plants distributed in the study areas with their relevant names and habitat distribution.

The identification of wild edible plants was done by taxonomist Prof. Y. P. S. Pangtey. An analysis of wild edible plants of Nainital district indicated the presence of 48 genera and 59 species of wild edibles belonging to 33 families (Photoplate 2). Twenty three families were represented by one genus and one species each, 5 families by one genus and 2 species each and one family by one genus and three species and 6 families by 2 genera and 2 species each. Family Caesalpinaceae, Rosaceae and Rutaceae were dominated by 10.2% species followed by Moraceae (6.8%), Anacardiaceae, Euphorbiaceae (5.1% each), Combretaceae, Dioscoreaceae, Tiliaceae (3.1% each) and rest of the families are represented by 1.7% species each. Besides, correct botanical name with original citation, respective family, followed by local name, if any, in italics, together with a brief description, flowering and fruiting period and abundance along with their range of distribution in Nainital district are given under each species. This has been done to facilitate their proper identification in the field and plants are arranged in alphabetical order. The maximum dominance was exhibited by trees (33), followed by shrubs (14), herbs (9) and climbers (3).

1. ***Aegle marmelos*** (L.) Correa, Trans. Linn. Soc. Lond. 5: 222 (1800)

   Aegle marmelos is small deciduous tree, with sharp, straight, axillary spines. Leaves are trifoliate, ovate-lanceolate, crenate, membranous. Flowers are greenish-white, in short lateral panicles. Fruits are large, globose, grey or yellowish.

   Flowering: February-March and

   Fruiting: uiting: May-August.

   Habitat: Common in dry miscellaneous forests.

2. ***Asparagus racemosus:*** Willd., Sp. P1. 2: 152. 1799; Hooks. f. in F1. Brit. India 6: 316. 1892; Babu, Herb. F1. D. Dun 517. 1977.

   Asparagus racemosus is a scrambling undershrubs. Stems are terete branched, with sharp, straight spines. Cladoded in tufts of 11-16, terete, acute, glabrous. Flowers are white in racemes of 3-5 cm long. Bracts are ovate, acuminate. Tepals are nearly equal, white, oblanceolate-oblong. Three stigmasare present. Fruits are ovoid.

   Habitat: Common in scrub forests.

3. ***Bauhinia purpurea*** Linn., Sp. Pl., 375. 1753; Duthie, Cat. Pl. Kumaon, 52. 1906; Fl. Brit. India, 2:284; Osmaston, For. Fl. Kumaon, 191. 1927.

   Bauhinia purpurea is a tree. Leaves are about half way deeply cleft more long than breadth. Flowers are rose coloured in few fowered terminal panicles. Fruit are linear, flat and seeds 12-15, sub-orbicular.

   Flowering: September-November;

   Frts: January-March.

   Habitat: Frequently found open forest, road side, slopes.

4. ***Bauhinia vahlii*** Wt. & Arn (Wt. & Arn.) Benth. Pl. Jungh. 263, 1853; de Wit, Reinwardtia 3 (4): 478, 1956; *Bauhinia vahlii* Wt. & Arn., Prodr. 297, 1834; Kanjilal, For. Flora 211.

   It is a profuse evergreen climber, with thick, cable-like branches. The leaves are upto 45 cm across, about as broad as long, deeply cordate, lobes obtuse, dark green. Flowers in dense, terminal long-peduncled corymbs or corymbose racemes. Petals are white and fruit pod, flat, woody.

   Habitat: Common in forested area and in field margins.

5. ***Bauhinia variegate*:** Linn., Sp. Pl. 375. 1753. Baker in Hook. f., Fl. Brit. Ind. 2: 284. 1878; Parker l. c. 180; Ali l. c. 243.

It is a medium sized tree with dark brown nearly smooth bark. Leaves are petiolate, lobes obtuse, the base is deeply heart shaped, nerved, pubescent beneath when young. Inflorescence is few flowered pubescent raceme. Pedicel is short or absent, bracteole minute; hypanthium slender. Ovary is hairy, stipe 10-17 mm long; style long, stigma capitate. Pods is hard, flat, dehiscent 10-15 seeded; stipe glabrous.

Flowering: Feb-May **& Fruiting:** Mar-Jul

6. ***Berberis aristata*** DC. Syst. Nat. 2: 8. 1821; Hook. f. Fl. Brit. Ind. 1 : 110. 1872.

   It is a large, deciduous shrubs. Leaves are obovate or elliptic, entire or spinous toothed, prominently veined. Flowers are bright yellow, arranged in drooping racemes. Fruits are ovoid to oblong-ovoid, blue-black.

   Flowering: April-June & **Fruiting:** June-July.

   Habitat: Common in forested areas and often forming gregarious patches.

7. ***Berberis asiatica*** Roxb. ex DC. Syst. Nat. 2: 13. 1821; Hook. f. Fl. Brit. 1: 119. 1972.

   It is an evergreen shrubs. Leaves are oblong, elliptic or broadly obovate-elliptic, entire or distantly spinose. Flowers are yellow, racemose or fascicled. Fruits are oblong-ellipsoid, ovoid, blue-black.

   Flowering: March-April & **Fruiting:** May-June.

   Habitat: Common in open banj-oak and chir-pine forests.

8. ***Bischofia javanica*** Blume, Bijdr. :1168 (1827)

   It is a deciduous tree. Leaves are trifoliate; leaflets elliptic-oblong to obovate, crenate, glabrous. Flowers are greenish-yellow, in much branched axillary or terminal peduncled racemes. Fruits are globose, fleshy and yellowish-brown.

   Flowering: March-May & **Fruiting:** December-January.

   Habitat: Frequent in moist-shaded ravines and swamps.

9. ***Boerhavia diffusa*** R. Brown; B. repens var. diffusa (Linnaeus) Heimerl ex J. D. Hooker.

   This is a perennial herb. Stems are trailing, to 200 cm; stems glabrous or sparsely pubescent. Roots are thick, fleshy. Inflorescences are terminal, capitate-cymose panicles; peduncle slender, sparsely pubescent. Pedicel is short to almost absent. Bracts small, lanceolate, pubescent. Perianth limb is bright purple or purple-red, Anthocarp is clavate, with viscid glands and sparse pubescence and apex rounded.

   Flowering: & Fruiting: spring-autumn.

   Habitat: Open places near sea, dry and warm river valleys.

10. ***Bombax ceiba*** Linn., Sp. Pl., 511., 1753. *B. malabaricum*DC., Prodr., 1: 479. 477. 1824; Duthie, Cat. Pl. Kumaon,24. 1906; Osmaston, For. Fl. Kumaon, 54. 1927.

    It is a tree. Leaflets are lanceolate, acuminate, entire, glabrous. Flowers are scarlet in clusters. Capsule are 5-valved.

    Flowering: Feburary-March; **Fruiting:** April-May.

    Habitat: Occasionally found near road side.

11. ***Bridelia retusa*** (L.) Spreng., Syst. Veg, ed. 16, 3:48(1829)

    It is a deciduous trees. Leaves are elliptic-oblong, entire or slightly crenulate, bright green, glabrous above and finely tomentose beneath. Flowers are greenish-yellow and in axillary clusters. Fruits are globose, greenish-purple.

    Flowering: April-July & **Fruiting:** January-February.

    Habitat: Occasional in sal forests in the subhimalayan tracts.

12. ***Buchanania lanzan*** Spreng., J. Bot. 2:234(1801).

    It is a subdeciduous tree. Leaves are oblong or elliptic-oblong, entire, coriaceous, glabrescent above and pubescent beneath. Flowers are greenish-white in terminal or axillary, densely rusty-haired panicles. Fruits re globose, ovoid-oblong and black.

    Flowering: March-April & **Fruiting:** May-June.

    Habitat: Common in sal and miscellaneous forests.

13. ***Cannabis sativa*** L., Sp. Pl. 1027. 1753; Hook. f. in Fl. Brit. India 5: 487. 1888; Babu, Herb. Fl. D. Dun 474. 1977. C indica Lam., Encycl. 1: 695. 1783.

    It is an annual-perennial, erect, aromatic herb or undershrub. Leaves are palmately or partite. Male flowers in lax terminal panicled-cyme, oblong, obtuse and ciliate. Female flowers are solitary or clustered, axillary and sessile. Perianth segment-1, leaflike, glandular-viscid, enclosing the ovary. Achenes greyish-brown, smooth, ovoid, enclosed with persistent perianth. Seeds are globose or ovoid and smooth.

    Flowering: May-Aug. & **Fruiting:** Aug.-Oct.

    Habitat: Common; road sides, waste places.

14. ***Callicarpa macrophylla*** Vahl, Symb. Bot. 3: 13, t. 53 (1794)

    It is an evergreen or subdeciduous shrub. Leaves are elliptic-oblong or ovate-lanceolate, closely crenate, tomentose when young, glabrescent when mature and densely woolly beneath. Flowers are pink inaxillary and dichotomous cymes. Fruits are white and succulent.

    Flowering: June-August & **Fruiting:** December-February.

    Habitat: Common in miscellaneous forests.

15. ***Carissa opaca*** Stapf ex Haines, Indian For. 47:378. (1921)

    It is an evergren, bushy-diffused shrubs with straight or forked spines. Leaves are elliptic or ovate to sub-orbicular, glabrate or pubescent beneath. Flowers are white, fragrant, in few-flowered corymbose cymes. Fruits are subglobose or elliptic and purplish black when ripe.

    Flowering: April-June & **Fruiting:** January-March.

    Habitat: Occasional in open exposed places, grassy slopes.

16. ***Cassia fistula*** Linn., Sp. Pl. 377. 1753. Baker in Hook. f., Fl. Brit. Ind. 2: 261. 1878.

    It is a tree. Bark in young tree is smooth and ash coloured becoming rough and dark brown in old. Stipules are deltoid and acute. Leaves are compound, smooth above and hairy below. Flowers are arranged in drooping racemes, each raceme. Pedicel are slender, slightly hairy or quite smooth. Bracts are ovate, acute and hairy. Ovary is slender, thinly appressed, hairy, style sturdy and stigma punctiform. Pods are terete, glabrous, indehiscent, black glossy brown and 40-100 seeded.

    Flowering & Fruiting: March-July.

    Habitat: Common in deciduous forests.

17. ***Cassia tora*** Linn., Sp. Pl. 376. 1753. Cooke, Flowering Bomb. Pres. 1: 447. 1903.

    It is an erect, usually annual, often profusely branched herb or under-shrub. Leaves are mostly obovate, glabrous, base oblique, cuneate to rounded and apex delicately acute. Racemes are short, peduncle hairy and axillary solitary. Pods are glabrescent, subtetragonous, often curved, indehiscent. Seeds are 20-30 rhomboidal, glossy and dark.

    Flowering & Fruiting: November-December.

    Habitat: Occasionally found in area.

18. ***Castanea sativa*** Mill., Gard. Dic. Abr. ed. 4:278 (1754).

    It is a deciduous tree. Leaves are crowded towards the ends, elliptic-lanceolate, irregularly and sharply serrate, teeth bristle-tipped, glabrous above, pale pubescent beneath. Flowers are yellowish; male flowers catkins erect; female catkins 1-3 together; fruits with 3-nuts, smooth, shining, brown.

    Flowering: March-April & **Fruiting:** August-September.

    Habitat: Occasional in temperate region.

19. ***Chenopodium album*** L. Sp. Pl. ed. 1, 1 : 219. 1753 ; Hook. f. Flowering Brit. Ind. 5 : 3. 1886.

    It is an erect herb. Leaves are stalked, ovate or lanceolate; upper ones entire variable, mealy beneath. seeds are smooth.

Habitat: Common along wayside or roadside, waste places, field margins and agriculture fields.

20. ***Cinnamomum tamala*** (Buch. -Ham.) Nees and Eberm. Handb. Med. Pharm. Bot. 2: 426. 1831; Hook. f. Flowering Brit. Ind. 5: 128. 1886; Collett, Flowering Siml. 431. 1902; Kanjilal, For. Flowering Chakrata 397. 1928. Laurus tamala Buch. –Ham. In J. Linn. Soc. 13: 555. 1822.

    It is a moderate-sized tree, with dark-brown wrinkled bark. Leaves are both alternate and opposite, ovate oblong, acute or acuminate and 3 nerved. Panicles are scarcely exceeding the leaves. Perianths are segments unequal, silky-pubescent. Stamens are 9. Drupes are ovoid.

    Habitat: Occurs sporadically in damp ravines.

21. ***Cordia dichotoma*** Forst. f., Prodr. :18 (1786)

    Cordia dichotoma is a deciduous tree. Leaves are broadly ovate or obovate oblong or suborbicular and sinuate-dentate. Flowers are white in terminal or axillary and pedunculate cymes. Fruits are yellowish or orange, globose or ovoid, apiculate.

    Flowering: March-April & **Fruiting:** May-July.

    Habitat: Common in moist-shaded places.

22. ***Costus speciosus*** (J. König) Smith, Trans. Linn. Soc. London, Bot. 1: 249. 1791. *Banksea speciosa* J. König in Retzius, Observ. Bot. 3: 75. 1783

    It is a herb. Stems base slightly woody, apex branched and spirally twisted when old. Leaf blade is oblong or lanceolate, abaxially densely sericeous, apex acuminate or caudate-acuminate. Inflorescences are terminal, ellipsoid or ovoid, leathery, pubescent, apex sharply pointed; bracteoles pale red. Seeds are black and glossy.

    Flowering: Jul-Sep & **Fruiting:** Sep-Nov.

    Habitat: Forest margins, moist places in valleys, roadsides.

23. ***Dioscorea belophylla*** (Prain) Voigt, Haines, For. Flowering Chota Nagpur. 530. 1910. Prain and Burkill in Ann. Roy. Bot. Gard. Calcutta, 14 (2): 348. 1938; Parker, l. c. 515.

    It is a glabrous climber, turning to the right. Leaves are simple and the flowers are individually inconspicuous, greenish - yellow, with six petals. Spike inflorescence; perianth – segments ovate; fruit capsule.

    Habitat: Common in forest.

24. ***Dioscorea deltoidea*** Wall. ex Kunth, Enum. 5:340. 1850. Collett, l. c. 518; Parker, l. c. 515.

    Tubers are ligneous, irregular. Stems are glabrous and twining clockwise. Leaves are alternate, simple, ovate or subdeltoid-ovate, often cordate, the basal lobes rounded or sometimes dilated outwards, acuminate, glabrous above, pubescent on the nerves beneath. The petiole is slender.

Male spikes are solitary, axillary, simple or sometimes branched, slender, lax,. flowers in small distant clusters; stamens 6, antheriferous. Female spikes are solitary, slender, few-flowered. Capsule obovate or obcordate. Seeds are winged unequally all round.

Flowering: May-Jun. & **Fruiting :** Jun—Sep.

Habitat: Very common throughout the Himalayas.

25. ***Duchesnea indica*** *(Anderws)* Focke in Engler, Pflanzen. 3,3:339 (1888).

    It is prostrate, creeping, perennial herb. Leaves are mostly radical, trifoliate leaflets ovate-oblong, silky-pubescent and toothed in upper half. Flowers are yellow, solitary or a few in axillary or terminal cymes. Fruits are red.

    Flowering: March-July & **Fruiting:** October-April.

    Habitat: Common in moist-shaded places throughout the hills.

26. ***Diplazium esculentum*** (Retz.) Sw., Schrad. J. Bot. 1801(2): 312. 1803; Tardieu & C. Chr., Flowering Indo-China 7(2): 269. 1940; Tagawa & K. Iwats., SouthE. Asian Stud. 3(3): 88. 1965.

    Rhizome is erect. scales are dark brown and black-margined. Laminae are variable in size, bipinnate, or pinnate when young or small; larger pinnules subsessile or shortly stalked, subcordate or auricled at base, narrowing towards acuminate apex. 1 Lobes are rounded at apex and serrate.

    Habitat: Mostly found along water courses and riverside.

27. ***Elaeagnus parvifolia*** Wall. ex Royle, Ill. Bot. Him. :323, t. 81,f. 1(1836).

    It is a deciduous thorny shrub. Leaves are elliptic-oblong, coriaceous, sparsely pubescent above, clothed with bright silvery scales beneath. Flowers are silvery-white, arranged in axillary clusters on short arrested branches. Fruits are ovoid.

    Flowering: March-April & **Fruiting:** June-September.

    Habitat: Occasional in open scrub forest.

28. ***Ficus auriculata*** Lour. Flowering Cochinch. 666. 1790. F. roxburghii Wall. Ex Miq. In. Ann. Mus. Bot. Lugd. Bat. 3: 296. 1867; Hook. f. Flowering Brit. Ind. 5 : 534. 1888.

    It is a small, evergreen or subdeciduous, spreading tree. Leaves are boadly orbicular elliptic or oblong, subcoriaceous, glabrous above and pubescent beneath. Figs clusters on short, thick leafless branches, pink or reddish with pale tubercular spots when ripe.

    Flowering: March-April & **Fruiting:** June-July.

    Habitat: Mostly found in forest, rocky slopes, exposed places and field margins

29. ***Ficus palmata*** Forssk. Flowering Aegypt – Arab. 179. 1775; Hook. f. Flowering Brit. Ind. 5 : 530. 1888.

    It is a small deciduous or subdeciduous tree. Leaves are orbicular or broadly ovate, entire, sometimes palmately lobed, dentate or serrate, scabrid above and tomentose beneath. Figs are usually solitary, axillary, solitary or in pairs, subglobose or pyriform, dark purple or pink when ripe.

    Flowering: May-June & **Fruiting:** June-August.

    Habitat: Common in open places particularly along the banks of streams and rivers.

30. ***Ficus racemosa*** L., Sp. Pl. :1060(1753).

    Ficus racemosa is a deciduous tree. Leaves are elliptic-lanceolate or ovate, entire, glabrous. Figs are usually on warty short leafless branches or main stem, globose or pyriform and orange-red when ripe.

    Flowering: March-April & **Fruiting:** June-August.

    Habitat: Common in open moist-shaded places, way-sides and crop field borders.

31. ***Flacourtia indica*** (Burm. f.) Merrill, Interpr. Rumph. Herb. Amb. :377 (1917)

    It is a subdeciduous shrub or small tree, often with branched thorns. Leaves are ovate, broadly elliptic, orbicular, toothed or crenate, glabrous. Flowers are yellowish-green, unisexual, in few-flowered leafless racemes. Fruits are ellipsoid to subglobose, dark purple.

    Flowering: February-March & **Fruiting:** April-June.

    Habitat: Common in scrub jungles and chir-pine forests.

32. ***Fragaria vesca*** Linnaeus, Sp. Pl. 1: 494. 1753. *Fragaria chinensis* Losinskaja; *F. concolor* Kitagawa.

    It is a perennial herb. Stems together with petioles spread pilose, rarely glabrescent. Leaves are rarely pinnate. Leaflets are sessile or central one shortly petiolulate, abaxially greenish, adaxially green, obovate, elliptic or broadly ovate. Inflorescence is corymbiform, subulate or petiolate, leafletlike bract. Aggregate fruit ripening red, ovoid. Achenes are ovoid and not prominently rugose.

    Flowering: Apr–Jun & **Fruiting:** Jun–Sep.

    Habitat: Forests, mountain slopes.

33. ***Glycosmis pentaphylla*** Correa in Ann. Mus. Par. 6:386. 1805. Hook. f., l. c. 499; Cooke, l. c. 192; Talbot, l. c. 191; Parker, l. c. 65.

    It is a small glabrous tree or shrub. Leaves are 3-5-foliolate; leaflets glandular-punctate, sessile, elliptic to ovate-lanceolate or obovate, entire to crenate, undulate; acute to obtuse. Panicles bracteate; peduncles and pedicels pubescent. Berry white or pink, globose.

Flowering: Jul-Oct&**Fruiting:**:Jan-Mar.

Habitat: Throughout Himalaya.

34. ***Grewia optiva*** J. R. Drumm. ex Burret, Notizbl. Bot. Gart. Berlin-Dhlem. 9:692 (1926)

    Small, medium-sized, deciduous trees. Leaves ovate-lanceolate, serrate, stellately hairy on both surfaces. Flowers are white or pale yellow, in axillary or leaf-opposed cymes. Fruits are blue-black when ripe and glabrous, 2-4 lobed.

    Flowering: April-June & **Fruiting:** August-November.

    Habitat: Very commonly throughout the area.

35. ***Grewia sapida*** Roxb. ex DC., Prodr. 1:512. 1824. Roxb., Flowering Ind. 2:590.1832; Hook. f., Flowering Brit. Ind. 1:387.1874; For. Flowering 41.1874; Brandis, Ind. Trees 98.1906; Parker, For. Flowering Punj. ed. 3.52.1956.

    It is a small shrub, perennating by woody underground stem. Young shoots are stellate pubescent. Leaves are stout, hairy petiole; lamina subglabrous or sub scabrous above, ovate or obovate to suborbicular. Flowers are yellow; pedicels divergent, as long as petiole; bracts small. Torus are glabrescent. Drupe subglobose, somewhat faintly 4-lobed and fleshy.

    Flowering & Fruiting: April-May.

    Habitat: Occasionally found in pine forest.

36. ***Indigofera heterantha*** Wall. Ex Brandis For. Flowering 135.1874. I. gerardiana Wall. Ex Baker var. hetarantha Hook. F. Flowering Brit. Ind, 2: 100.1876.

    It is a silvery-pubescent shrubs. Leaflets are 7 – 35; bracts minute; flowers pale - red or purple; pods cylindric pubescent.

    Habitat: Common in forest and exposed areas.

37. ***Morus alba*** L., Sp. Pl. : 986 (1753)

    This is a small deciduous trees or large shrubs. Leaves are ovate, acute, dentate or lobed, glabrous above. Flowers in short ovoid spikes, male and female flowers on different branches. Fruiting spikes are white or red-purple.

    Flowering & Fruiting: February-June.

    Habitat: Common in the outer hill ranges.

38. ***Murraya koenigii*** (Linnaeus) Sprengel, Syst. Veg. 2: 315.1817. *Bergera koenigii* Linnaeus, Mant. Pl. 2: 555, 563. 1771; *Chalcas koenigii* (Linnaeus) Kurz.

Shrubs or trees. Leaves are foliolate; leaflet blades ovate, base obtuse to rounded and oblique, margin entire or crenulate. Inflorescences are terminal, paniculate, many flowered. Flowers are ellipsoid in bud. Fruit are bluish black, ovoid to oblong, 2-seeded. Seed coat is membranous.

Flowering: Mar-Apr & **Fruiting:** Jul-Aug.

Habitat: Moist forests.

39. ***Myrica esculenta*** Buch.-Ham. ex D. Don, Prodr. Flowering Nep. 56.1825; Naithani, Flowering Chamoli 2: 593.1985. M. nagi auct. non Thumb., Nov. Acta Soc. Upsal. 4: 37.1783; Hook. f. in Flowering Brit. India 5: 597. 1888.

These are evergreen trees, bark brownish-grey, rough and vertically wrinkled. Leaves are alternate, crowded at the end of branches, oblanceolate, entire, acute, glossy above, glaucous dotted below. Flowers are minute, 1-sexual; male flowers pale-brown reddish catkins, in branched axillary clusters. Female flowers in erect axillary spikes. Fruits are sessile, to 1 cm long, ovoid or ellipsoid, succulent, dark red or purplish when ripe, with rough stone.

Flowering: Aug.-Oct. **& Fruiting:** Apr.-Jun.

Habitat: Abundant in Oak-Rhododendron forests, usually in shady localities.

40. ***Oroxylum indicum*** (L.) Kurz, Forest Flowering Burma 2: 237.1877. *Bignonia indica* Linnaeus, Sp. Pl. 2: 625.1753; B. pentandra Loureiro; *Calosanthes indica* (Linnaeus) Blume.

This is a tree, with gray-rown bark. Leaves are large, opposite, pinnately compound, leaflets elliptic-ovate, entire, subacuminate, base oblique; flowers purple-red, opening at night, in terminal, hardened in fruit; capsule woody, flattened and brown.

Habitat: Found in low altitude open forests, roadsides, slopes.

41. ***Phyllanthus emblica*** L., Sp. Pl. 982.1753; Hook. f. in Flowering Brit. India 5: 289.1887; Naithani, Flowering Chamoli 2: 572.1985. *Emblica officinalis* Gaertner, Fruct. Sem. 2: 122. T. 108.1791.

This is a deciduous tree. Leaves are subsessile, linear-oblong, entire, glabrous, obtuse, arranged distichously on deciduous branches appearing like pinnate leaves. Flowers are minute, greenish- yellow in axillary clusters; both male and female flowers on the same branch, solitary. Fruits are subglobose, 3-valved, yellow and smooth.

Flowering: March-May & **Fruiting:** Sep-Nov.

Habitat: Common in miscellaneous forest.

42. ***Pyracantha crenulata*** (D. Don) M. Roemer, Fam. Nat. Reg. Syn. 3: 220. 1847; Babu, herb. Flowering D. Dun 181.1977; Naithani, Flowering

Chamoli 1: 202.1984. *Mespilus crenulata* D. Don, Prodr. Flowering Nep. 238.1825. *Crataegus crenulata* Roxb., Flowering Inica 2.2: 509.1832; Hook. f. in Flowering Brit. India 2: 384.1878.

It is an evergreen, spinescent, undershrubs or shrubs, to 5 m high; spines straight and stout; bark ashy grey. Leaves are crowded at the ends or short lateral branches, shortly petioled, narrowly oblong or oblong-lanceolate, apex obtuse, shining green above and glaucous beneath. Flowers are white and terminal corymbs. Fruits of 4-5 pyrenes, orange-red, orbicular to ovoid, shining, from the enlarged hypanthium.

Flowering: Mar. -May & **Fruiting:** Jun.-Oct.

Habiat: Abundant; exposed sloped, forest edges, bank of streams and other miscellaneous localities.

43. ***Pyrus pashia*** Buch. – Ham ex D. Don Prodr. Flowering Nep. 236.1825; Hook. F. Flowering Brit. Ind. 2: 374.1878.

It is a deciduous tree. Leaves are simple, long- pointed, toothed, hairless and shining with an ovate to ovate-lanceolate. Flowers are white fragrant and fruits are brown turning black rough.

Habiat: Common in forest and in field margins.

44. ***Rhododendron arboreum*** Sm., Exot. Bot. 1: 9.t.6.1804; Cl. in Hook. f. Flowering Brit. Ind. 4: 465.1882; Collett, Flowering Siml 294.1902; Kanjilal, For. FloweringChakrata 287.1982.

Evergreen trees; bark pinkish-brown, rough; young twigs white or brown pubescent. Leaves are oblong-lanceolate, entire, dark-green, glabrous above and white or rusty-brown tomentose beneath. Flowers are many, deep red or pink, crowded in large, globose, terminal, compact corymbs. Ovary 6-10 celled, ferruginous woolly. Capsules are cylindric; seeds many and ellipsoid.

Flowering: Mar.-May. & **Fruiting::** Apr.-Nov.

Habitat: Common; Oak forests.

45. ***Rubus ellipticus*** Smith in Rees Cyclop.30:n.16 1819; Hook. F. Flowering Ind. 2:336.1878.

Rubus ellipticus is an evergreen, arched or straggling shrubs with short and conical prickles. Leaves are trifoliate; leaflets elliptic-obovate or ovate, green, glabrescent above, hoary-tomentose or bristly. Flowers are white in dense axillary fascicles or short terminal panicles. Fruits are yellow or golden yellow.

Flowering: March-April & **Fruiting:** May-June.

Habitat: Abundant throughout the hills in open slopes and scrub forests.

46. ***Rubus niveus*** Thunb. Dessert. De Rub. 9, t.1.f.3; 1813; Kanjilal, For. Flowering Chakrata 217.1928. R. lasiocarpus Sm. in Rees. Cyclop. 30:

no. 6.1819; Hook. f., Flowering Brit. Ind. 2: 339.1878; Collett, Flowering Siml. 161.1902.

These are large, rambling, prickly shrubs. Leaves are pinnately foliate; leaflets ovate-lanceolte, upper surface green, glabrous, lower surface white-tomentose. Flowers are pink or pinkish-white in axillary or terminal peduncled corymbs. Fruits are globose, hairy-tomentose.

Flowering: March-June & **Fruiting:** June-July.

Habitat: Common in moist-shaded oak forests and open scrub jungles.

47. ***Rumex hastatus*** D. Don, Prodr. Flowering Nep. 74.1825; Hook. f. in Brit. India 5: 60.1886; Babu, Herb. Flowering D. Dun 447.1977; Naithanr, Flowering Chamoli 2: 547.1985.

Perennial, erect or scandent, glabrous herbs or undershrubs. Stem is pale-grey and much branched. Leaves are narrlowly triangular or hastate, fleshy, glaucous; upper ones sometimes linear. Flowers are polygamous, greenish-white, arranged in lax. inner fruiting whorls orbicular, entire, pinkish. Nuts are 3-gonous, narrowly winged, net veined.

Flowering: Feb.-Jun. & **Fruiting:** Jun.-Oct.

48. ***Semecarpus anacardium*** L. f., Suppl. Pl. :182 (1781).

Semecarpus anacardium is a deciduous tree. Leaves are crowded at the ends of branches, ovate-oblong, entire, coriaceous, more or less hispidly pubescent and pale beneath. Flowers are greenish yellow, polygamous or unisexual in fascicles, arranged on large and terminal panicles. Fruits are obliquely ovoid, compressed, black when ripe.

Flowering: June-September & **Fruiting:** February-March.

Habitat: Very common in sal forests throughout the subhimalayan tracts and outer hills.

49. ***Solanum nigrum*** L., Sp. Pl. 186. 1753; Cl. in Hook. f., Flowering Brit. Ind. 4: 229. 1883; Collett, Flowering Siml. 341. 1902; Babu, Herb. Flowering Dehra Dun 340. 1977.

It is an erect or rambling, glabrous, annual-perennial herb. Leaves are ovate, ovate-lanceolate, entire or toothed. Flowers are white or with dark blue center, nodding in subumbellate, extra-axillary peduncled cymes. Fruits are globose, bright red, orange or black when mature.

Flowering & Fruiting: Almost throughout the year.

Habitat: Common in waste places, crop fields, way-sides and road-sides.

50. ***Spondias pinnata*** (Linnaeus f.) Kurz, Prelim. Rep. Forest Pegu. App. A, 44; App. B, 42. 1875. *Mangifera pinnata* Linnaeus f., Suppl. Pl. 156. 1782.

It is a deciduous tree. Branchlets are yellowish brown and glabrous. Petiole and rachis are glabrous. Leaf blade is imparipinnately compound with opposite leaflets. Inflorescence is paniculate, terminal. Flower sessile or subsessile, white, glabrous. Drupe ellipsoid to elliptic-ovoid, yellowish orange at maturity, mature fruit usually with 2 or 3 seeds.

Flowering: Apr-Jun & **Fruiting:** Aug-Sep. **Habitat:** Lowland and hill forests.

51. ***Syzygium cumini*** (L.) Skeels, U. S. Dept. Agric. Industr. Bull. 248:25 (1912).

    Large, evergreen, glabrous trees. Leaves are lanceolate, elliptic-oblong or broadly ovate-elliptic, entire. Flowers are greenish-white in 3-flowered trichotomous cymes, fragrant. Fruits are oblong or ovoid-oblong and dark purple.

    Flowering: March-May & **Fruiting:** June-July.

    Habitat: Very common in the sub Himalayan ranges in most forest types.

52. ***Tamarindus indica*** L., Sp. Pl. :34 (1753).

    It is a medium-sized, evergreen tree. Leaves are pinnate; leaflets 10-12 pairs, oblong-lanceolate, obtuse, entire, glabrous. Flowers are yellowish-orange in terminal racemes. Fruits are oblong, usually falcate and subcompressed.

    Flowering & Fruiting: January-December.

    Habitat: Occasionally found along road-sides and waste places.

53. ***Terminalia bellirica*** (Gaertn.) Roxb., Flowering Corom. 2:54, t.198 (1805).

    Large, deciduous trees. Leaves are crowded towards the ends of the branches, elliptic or elliptic-obovate, coriaceous, entire. Flowers are ale greenish-yellow, in solitary or extra-axillary spikes. Fruits are obovoid, grey-velvety.

    Flowering: April-June & **Fruiting:** June-July.

    Habitat: Common throughout the subHimalayan tracts and outer hills.

54. ***Terminalia chebula*** Retz., Obs. Bot. 5:31 (1789).

    It is a small or medium-sized deciduous tree. Leaves are oblong-ovate or elliptic-ovate, glabrous when mature. Flowers are pale on terminal, pubescent, panicled spikes. Fruits are obovoid, yellowish-green, smooth and glabrous.

    Flowering: April-June & **Fruiting:** January-March.

    Habitat: Common in sal and dry miscellaneous forest.

55. ***Trema orientalis*** (L.) Blume, Mus. Bot. 2:62 (1856).

    Shrubs or small evergreen trees. Leaves are obliquely ovate or ovate-lanceolate, crenate-serrate, more or less scabrid above, silky pubescent beneath. Flowers are small in axillary cymes, cymes lax, spreading, pubescent. Fruits are ovoid, glabrous and black when ripe.

    Flowering: March-April & **Fruiting:** May-June., **Habitat:** Rather rare in open dry slopes.

56. ***Urtica parviflora*** Roxburgh, Flowering Ind., ed. 1832.3: 581.1832.

Herbs perennial, monoecious. Rhizomes are long stoloniferous. Stems are slender, simple or few branched; stems, petioles, and both surfaces of leaf blade sparsely hirtellous and armed with stinging hairs. Inflorescences are unisexual; male inflorescences in distal axils, spicate; female ones in proximal axils, subspicate, slender. Male flowers are sessile or short pedicellate; perianth lobes connate. Female flowers are perianth lobes connate at base, unequal, dorsal-ventral lobes suborbicular, sparsely setulose and lateral lobes broadly obovate. Achene is yellowish green, broadly ellipsoid-ovoid, smooth and invested by persistent perianth lobes.

Flowering: May-Jun, & **Fruiting:** Jul-Aug.

Habitat: Partly shady, moist places of evergreen forests, along streams, roadsides.

57. ***Zanthoxylum armatum***DC., Prodr. 1:727.1824; Hartly, J. Arnold Arb. 47:211.1996; Naithani, Flowering Chamoli 1:113.1984. Z. alatum Roxb., Flowering Indica 2.3:768.1832; Hook. f. in Flowering Brit. India 1:493. 1875; Duthie, Flowering U. Gang. Pl. 1:134.1903.

Subdeciduous, aromatic shrubs or small trees, armed with shout; bark pale-brown, rough, corky; branches prickly. Leaves are alternate, imparipinnate; leaflets, toothed; leafstalk narrowly winged. Flowers are small, 1-2 sexual or polygamous, pale-yellow, pubescent panicles; Fruit 1-3, small, pale-red, globose or reniform, aromatic and tubercled.

Flowering: Mar.-May & **Fruiting:** Jul.-Oct., **Habitat:** Common; open exposed localities, edges of crop fields.

58. ***Ziziphus mauritiana*** Lam., Encycl. 3:319 (1789).

Subdeciduous, spinous trees or shrubs. Leaves are variable, elliptic-oblong, serrulate, base subcordate, dark green, glabrous above and pale tomentose beneath. Flowers are greenish-yellow, in short axillary, subsessile cymes. Fruits are globose, yellow or reddish, fleshy.

Flowering: June-August & **Fruiting:** December-February, **Habitat:** Common throughout the subhimalayan.

59. ***Ziziphus xylopyra*** (Retz.) Willd., Sp. pl. 1(2):1104. 1798 (Syn: *Rhamnus xylopyrus* Retz.).

It is a small tree. Bark is thin, brownish-grey, branchlets tomentos and sparsely armed. Leaves are simple, alternate, stipulate; tomentose, slender; base rounded; apex obtuse, apiculate, margin serrulate, glabrous above, tomentose. Flowers are bisexual, in axillary cymes, greenish-yellow, pubescent; ovary 3-celled, ovules solitary. Fruit is a drupe, globose, woolly containing 3 seeds.

Flowering & Fruiting: May-June, **Habitat:** Dry and moist deciduous forests

Aegle marmelos **(L.) Correa**

Murraya koenigii **(L.) Spr.**

Phyllanthus emblica **L.**

Zizypus mauritiana **Lamk**

Zizyphus xylopyrus **(Retz) Willd**

Zanthoxylum armatum **DC.**

Pyracantha crenulata **(D. Don) M. Reom.**

Terminalia chebula **Retz.**

Solanum nigrum **L.**

Fragaria vesca **L.**

Rubus ellipticus **Sm.**

Berberis asiatica **Roxb.**

Ficus auriculata **Lour.**

Rumex hastatus **D. Don**

Aspargus curillus **Buch. -Ham**

Pyrus pashia Buch-Ham. **ex D. Don**

Rubus panculatus **Sm**

Rhododendron arboreum **Sm.**

Myrica esculenta **Buch. -Ham. ex D. Don**

Castanea sativa **Mill.**

Bauhina variegata **L.**

Glycosmis pentaphylla **(Retz.) DC**

Cannabis sativa **L.**

Ficus palmata Forsk.

***Cassia fistula* L.**

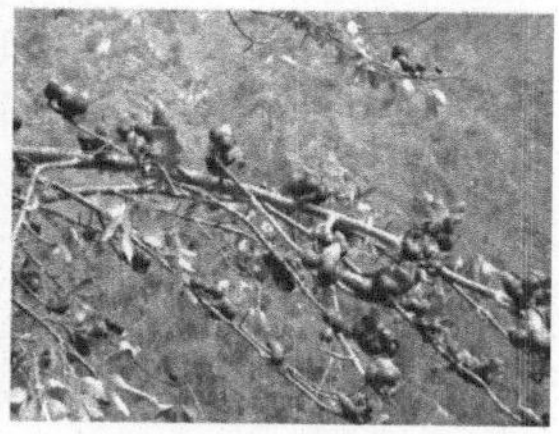
Bombax ceiba L.

***Chenopodium album* L.**

Photoplate 2: Photographs of some of the collected wild edibles

Ethnobotanical Studies of WEPs

The present work documented 59 plant species belonging to 33 families under 48 genera that are being traditionally used in the area. A list of plant species along with their local names, plant parts used and ethnobotanical uses was documented (Table 9.1). The herbal remedies are commonly effective against cuts and wounds, fever, joints pain, headache, constipation, diarrhea, eye disorders, skin ailments, cough and cold, antidote for poisonous insects, stomach disorders, urinary troubles, liver complaints, digestive problems, jaundice, asthma, bronchitis, inflammations and anemia, piles, mental disorder, abdominal pain, and bone fracture, paralysis, epilepsy, impotency, general weakness etc.

Table 9.1: List of Wild Edible Plants

Species	Family	Habit	Local Name	Part Used*	Ethnobotanical use
Aegle marmelos (L.) Correa	Rutaceae	T	Bel	St. Br, Rt, Fr	The pulp of the ripe fruit is nutritious and is relished by all people. Medicinal (Typhoid, bronchitis, consti-pation, diabetes, diarrhea and dysentery, piles).
Asparagus racemosus Willd.	Asparagaceae	Sh	Kariu	Rt	The tuberous roots are pickled, young shoots eaten as vegetable. Medicinal (Anthelmintic, aphrodisiac, rheumatism, bleeding from nose,cough, dysentery, gastric complaints, gonorrhea, headache, menstrual complaints).
Bauhina variegata L.	Caesalpinaceae	T	Kachnar	Br, Rt	Tender shoots and leaves are cooked as vegetable. Medicinal (Ulcer, skin diseases, scrofula, dyspepsia and snake bite).

Bauhinia purpurea L.	Caesalpinaceae	T	Khair-wal	Sd, Bd	Flower buds are made into a curry and are also pickled. Ripe seeds are edible.
Bauhinia vahlii Wight & Arn.	Caesalpinaceae	Cl	Malu	Sd, Lf	Seeds are eaten raw or after roasting.
Berberis aristata Roxb.	Berbaridaceae	T	Kilmora	Fr	Ripened fruits edible. Medicinal (Rat and snake bite, boil, eye complaints, anticancer, blood pressure, malaria, piles, diabetes).
Berberis asiatica Roxb.	Berbaridaceae	Sh	Kilmora	Rt, Lf, Br, Fr	Ripened fruits edible. Medicinal (Conjunctivitis, jaundice and diabetes).
Bischoffia javanica Blume	Euphorbiaceae	T	Kanji	Fr	Fruits edible.
Boerhaavia diffusa L.	Nyctaginaceae	H	Punarnava	Lf, Rt	Young leaves are cooked as vegetable. Medicinal (Asthma, stomach ache, edema, anemia, jaundice, and in snake bite).
Bombax ceiba L.	Bombacaceae	T	Semal	Gm, Fl, Fr	Flower and fruits are cooked as vegetable. Medicinal (Diarrhea, dysentery and women diseases. Flower and fruits used in snake bite).
Bridelia retusa (L.) Spereng.	Euphorbiaceae	T	Khaja	Fr, Bk	Ripened fruit is sweetish and the flesh is eaten. Rheumatic pain.
Buchanania lanzan Spreng.	Anacardiaceae	T	Chironji	Gm	The flesh of the ripe fruit is very palatable and is largely eaten. Diarrhea.
Callicarpa macrophylla Vahl.	Verbenaceae	Sh	Daya	Fr, Lf	Fruits edible. Medicinal (Rheumatic pain).
Cannabis sativa L.	Cannabinaceae	Sh	Bhang	Fr	Medicinal (Anthelmintic, appetite, bronchitis, cuts, dyspepsia, gonorrhea, narcotic, piles, skin disorders, cold cough, epilepsy, laxative, stimulant, paralysis of tongue, sleep piles, sores).
Carissa opaca Stapf ex Haines	Apocynaceae	Sh	Karonda	Fr	Ripened fruit is much eaten; it has an acidulous sweet taste.
Cassia fistula L.	Caesalpinaceae	T	Amaltas	Fr	Young leaves and flower buds are edible. Medicinal (Rheumatic pain and snake bite).

Cassia tora L.	Caesalpinaceae	H	Banar	Sd	Young leaves and pods are eaten as a vegetable. Seeds are also eaten and can be used as a substitute for coffee.
Castanea sativa Mill.	Fagaceae	T	Chestnut	Fl, Fr	Fruits edible. Medicinal (diarrhea, fevers).
Chenopo-dium album L.	Chenopodiaceae	H	Bathuwa	Lf, St	The green plant is popularly consumed as vegetable after cooking. Medicinal (Skin diseases, urine complaints)
Cinna-momum tamala (Buch. -Ham.)	Lauraceae	T	Tejpat	Lf	Used as spices
Cordia dichotoma Forst. f.	Ehretiaceae	T	Lashora	Fr, St, Br	Ripe fruit is eaten fresh or stewed, unripe green fruits are eaten as a vegetable or pickled. Medicinal (Urinary disorder, dyspepsia, fever).
Costus speciosus(Koeng ex Retz.)	Zingiberaceae	H	Kewa	Rh	Rhizome is used as vegetable. For this purpose they are grinded to make paste and cooked as vegetable. Medicinal (Snake bite).
Dioscorea belophylla Voigt ex Prain & Burk.	Dioscoreaceae	Cl	Tarur	Tb	Tubers edible.
Dioscorea deltoidea Wall. ex Kunth	Dioscoreaceae	Cl	Gethi	Tb, Lf	Medicinal (Dysentery, fever, skin diseases).
Diplazium esculentum (Retz.) Sw.	Dryopteridaceae	H	Lingura	Young frond	Young fronds edible
Duchesnea indica (Andrews)Focke in Engler.	Rosaceae	H	Bhikafal	Fr	Fruits edible.
Elaeagnus parvifolia Wall. Royle	Elaeagnaceae	Sh	Gewai	Fr, Fl	Fruits edible. Cuts, ulcer, wound, Astringent, diarrhea, pulmonary infections
Ficus auriculata Lour.	Moraceae	T	Timil	Fr	Fruits edible, unripe fruits made into vegetable. Skin diseases, urine complaints

Ficus palmata Forsk.	Moraceae	T	Bedu	Fr	Fruits edible. Medicinal (Dysentery, indigestion, laxative, Digestive disorders, cough, constipation, diabetes, dysentery, stomachache, boils)
Ficus racemosa L.	Moraceae	T	Gular	Fr, Lf, Rt	Fruits edible, Ripe fruits are eaten fresh; unripe green fruits are eaten cooked. Medicinal (Dysentery, diabetes, piles and diarrhea).
Flacourtia indica (Burm. f.) Merr.	Flacourtiaceae	T	Kangu	Fr, Gm	Fruits edible. Medicinal (Jaundice, cholera).
Fragaria vesca L.	Rosaceae	Sh	Bhi Kafal	Fr, Lf	Medicinal (Gastric disorder, ulcer, diabetes cuts and wounds).
Glycosmis pentaphylla (Retz.) DC	Rutaceae	Sh	Ban Nimbu	Fr, Lf, Rt	Ripened fruits edible. Medicinal (Fever).
Grewia optiva Buch–Ham. ex D. Don.	Tiliaceae	T	Bhimal	Fr, Br, Lf	Fruits edible.
Grewia sapida Roxb. ex DC	Tiliaceae	T	Phalsinya	Fr, Br, Lf	Fruits edible.
Indigofera heterantha Wallich ex Brandis	Fabaceae	Sh	Sakina	Fl, Lf	Flowers used as vegetable, leaf juice taken in Medicinal (diarrhea, dysentery and cough).
Morus alba L.	Moraceae	T	Kimu	Fr	Ripened fruits edible. Medicinal (Fever, diarrhea, nervous disorders).
Murraya koenigii (L.) Spr.	Rutaceae	Sh	Karipatta	Lf, Fr	Leaves possess medicinal value used in curry by local people.
Myrica esculenta Buch. -Ham. ex D. Don	Myricaceae	T	Kafal	Fr, Wd,Br	Fruits edible. Medicinal (Asthma, cholera, cough, fever, indigestion, malaria, rheumatism).
Oroxylum indicum (L.) Vent.	Bignoniaceae	T	Tantia	Fl, Sd	Flowers edible. Seeds are also eaten parched.
Phyllanthus emblica L.	Euphorbiaceae	T	Amala	Fr, Lf	Fruits are eaten raw and used for making pickles and preserves. Medicinal (Anemia, diarrhea, dysentery, dyspepsia, hemorrhage, inflammation of eyes, jaundice, liver disorders).

Pyracantha crenulata (D. Don) M. Reom.	Rosaceae	T	Ghingaru	Fr, Lf	Ripened fruits edible. Medicinal (Ear diseases, constipation.)
Pyrus pashia Buch-Ham. ex D. Don	Rosaceae	T	Jangli Mehal	Lf	Ripened fruits edible. Medicinal (Cuts, wounds, fungal infections).
Rhododendron arboreum Sm.	Ericaceae	T	Burans	Fr, Lf	Medicinal (Dysentery, fever, headache, rheumatism, wounds, nose bleeding).
Rubus ellipticus Sm.	Rosaceae	Sh	Hisalu	Fr	Ripened fruits edible. (Dysentery, malaria, stomachache, worms)
Rubus niveus Thunb.	Rosaceae	Sh	Kala Hisalu	Fr, Lf	Ripened fruits edible. Medicinal (Fever, stomach-ache.)
Rumax hastatus D. Don	Polygonaceae	H	Bhilmora	Lf, St	Leaves are used for their sour taste and Chatni is also prepared from the leaves. Medicinal (Astringent, stomachic, carminative, dysentery).
Semecarpus anacardium L. f.	Anacardiaceae	T	Bhilwa	Fr	Fruits edible. Medicinal (Dyspepsia, piles, leprosy).
Solanum nigrum L.	Solanaceae	H	Makoi	WP	Ripe fruits are eaten raw by the local people, the extract of plant is used in liver, piles and dysentery. Medicinal (Fever, diarrohea, eye diseases, liver disorder).
Spondias pinnata (L. f.) Kurz.	Anacardiaceae	T	Amra	Fr, Fl, Sd	Fruits edible, also made into pickle. The aromatic flower buds make an agreeable curry. Seed is also eaten and is very tasty.
Syzygium cumini (L.) Skeel.	Myrtaceae	T	Jamun	Fr, Br, Lf	Ripened fruits edible and are often served with a little salt. They are good in tarts and puddings. Medicinal (Diarrhea, dysentery, diabetes).
Tamarindus indica L.	Caesalpinaceae	T	Imali	Fr	Fruit edible and are also used for making chutneys. Medicinal (Boils, inflammatory swelling, pain and bilious vomiting).

Terminalia bellirica (Gaertn.) Roxb.	Combretaceae	T	Bahera	Fr	Seed kernel is locally eaten raw, it tastes like a filbert. Medicinal (Diarrhea, dropsy, dyspepsia, eye troubles, headache, fever, leprosy and piles.)
Terminalia chebula Retz.	Combretaceae	T	Harar	Fr	Seed kernel is eaten. Medicinal (Cronical ulcer, cough and wounds).
Trema orientalis (L.)	Ulmacea	T	Jiwanti	Fr	Fruits edible.
Urtica parviflora Roxb.	Urticaceae	H	Bichhu	Lf	Young leaves or twigs are cooked as vegetable. Medicine (Bone fracture, Swelling).
Zanthoxylum armatum DC.	Rutaceae	T	Timur	Fr	Fruits are eaten and stems used as toothbrush. Medidicinal (Cough, cholera, fever, eczema, itching, leucoderma, piles, rheumatism, tonic, tooth complaints).
Zizyphus mauritiana Lamk.	Rutaceae	Sh	Ber	Fr	Fruits edible, Medicinal (Blood purifiyer, fever, wounds and ulce)r.
Zizyphus xylopyrus (Retz.) Willd.	*Rutaceae*	*Sh*	*Khatberi*	*Fr*	*Fruits edible, Dysentry.*

***Note:** St. - Stem,Br. - Berry, Rt - Root, Fr - Fruit, Lf. - Leaf, Fl. - Flower, Sd. - Seed, Wp. - Whole plant, Wd. - Wood, Gm. - Gums, Tb. - Tuber, Bk. - Bark Bd. - Bud, Sh - Shrub, T - Tree, H -Herb.

CONCLUSION

Fifty nine wild edible plant species have been collected along with their ethnomedicinal importance. The present study aimed to investigate the indigenous knowledge with the identification, documentation, ethnobotanical exploration, plant diversity and regeneration status of Wild Edible Plants (WEPs) consumed by the people of Nainital district of the Central Himalaya. An inadequate understanding concerning taxonomy, biology and local knowledge of these plants has contributed to suboptimal utilization of these valuable resources. The neighbouring villages were visited and surveyed for identification of wild edible plant species. The local people were interviewed to explore more information about the plant parts used and ethnobotanical uses by indigenous people. A total of 59 species belonging to 48 genera and 33 families was recorded. Plant species commonly used by local inhabitants for food, medicine and in other fields of their lives. A list of plant species along with their family, habit, local names, plant parts used and mode of application was documented. It was reported that the fruit is the mostly used plant part (40) followed by leaves (21), flowers (6), berries (8), roots (7) stems (4), whole plant (1) and tuber (2). These plant species are utilized by local people against various ailments such as cuts and wounds, fever, joints pain, constipation, diarrhoea, eye disorders, skin problems, cough and cold, jaundice, asthma, bronchitis etc. The present study indicated the conservation value of the area and the documentation will give an understanding of the diversity, pattern of population and regeneration of the tree species which may help in forest management and conservation of the species.

REFERENCES

Anonymous, 1994. Ethnobotany in Indi—A Status Report (Ministry of Environment and Forests, Govt. of India).

Arora, R. K. and P. Anjula, 1996. Wild Edible Plants of India: Diversity Conservation and Use. ICAR New Delhi, India.

Asfaw, Z., 1997. Indigenous African Food Crops and Useful Plants: Survey of Indigenous Food Crops, their Preparations and Home Gardens. The United Nations University Institute for Natural Resources in Africa. ICIPE Science Press, Nairobi, Kenya, p. 65.

Abbasi A. M., Khan, M. A., Ahmad M., Zafar, M., Khan, H., Muhammad, N., Sultana, S., 2009. Medicinal Plants Used for the Treatment of Jaundice and Hepatitis Based on Socio-Economic Documentation. Afric J. Biotech 8:1643–1650.

Abbasi, A. M., Khan, M. A., Ahmad, M., Zafar, M., Jahan, S., Sultana, S., 2010. Ethnopharmacological Application of Medicinal Plants to Cure Skin Diseases and in Folk Cosmetics Among the Tribal Communities of North-West Frontier Province, Pakistan. J Ethnopharmacol. 128:322– 335.

Abbasi, A. M., Khan, M. A., Ahmad, M., Zafar, M., 2012: Medicinal Plant Biodiversity of Lesser Himalayas-Pakistan. New York: Springer. 1–212.

Curtis, J. T., 1959. The Vegetation of Wisconsin. An Ordination of Plantcommunities,University Wisconsin Press, Madison Wisconsin.

Durby, W. J., Gatiounglic, P., Grivetti, L. E.,1997. Food-The Gift of Orissis (Academic Press, London).

Ford-Lloyd, B. V., Schmidt, M., Armstrong, S. J., Barazani, O., Engels, J., Ge, S., Hadas, R., Hammer, K., Kell, S. P., Kang, D., Khoshbakht, K., Li, Y., Long, C. L., Lu, B. R., Ma, K. P., Nguyen, V. T., Qiu, L. J., Wei, W., Zhang ZW, Maxted N. Crop Wild Relatives-Undervalued, Underutilized and Under Threat? BioScience. 2011. 9:559–565. doi: 10. 1525/bio. 2011. 61. 7. 10. [CrossRef]

Fentahun, M. T., Hager, H., 2009. Exploiting Locally Available Resources for Food and Nutritional Security Enhancement: Wild Fruits Diversity, Potential and State of Exploitation in the Amhara Region of Ethiopia. J. Food. 1(2):207-219.

Gaur, R. D., 1977. Wild Edible Fruits of Garhwal hills. The Himalaya 1: 66-70.

Gaur, R. D., 1999. Flora of the District Garhwal, North West Himalaya (with Ethnobotanical Notes), Trans Media, Srinagar (Garhwal).

Gupta, R. K., 1968. Flora Nainitalensis, Navyug Publication, New Delhi. Ghorbani A, Langenberger G, Sauerborn J. A Comparison of the Wild Food Plant Use Knowledge of Ethnic Minorities in Naban River Watershed National Nature Reserve, Yunnan, SW China. J Ethnobiol Ethnomed. 2012; 9:17. doi: 10. 1186/1746-4269-8-17. [PMC Freearticle] [PubMed] [Cross Ref]

Hooker, J. D.,(1875 –2006). Flora of British India. Vols. I – VI. L. Reeve and Company Ltd. The East House Book, Ashford, Kent, UK.

Hazrat, A., Nisar, M., Shah, J., Ahmad, S., 2011. Ethnobotanical Study of Some Elite Plants Belonging to Dir, Kohistan Valley, Khyber Pukhtunkhwa, Pakistan. Pak J Bot., 43(2):787–795.

Hussain, K., Shahzad, A., Hussnain, S. Z., 2008. An Ethnobotanical Survey of Important Wild Medicinal Plants of Hattar District Haripur, Pakistan. Ethnobot Leaflets. 12:29–35.

Jain, S. K., 1989. Methods and Approaches in Ethnobotany. Society of Ethnobotany, Lucknow, India.

Jain, S. K., 1964. Wild Food Plants of the Tribals of Bastar (M. P), Proc Nat Inst Sci India, 30(B), 56.

Jain, S. K., 1990. Contribution to Ethnobotany of India, Scientific Publishers, Jodhpur, India.

Lulekal, E., Asfaw, Z., Kelbessa, E., Van Damme, P., 2011. Wild Edible Plants in Ethiopia: A Review on their Potential to Combat Food Insecurity. Africa Focus. 9:71–121.

Martin, G. J., 1995. Ethnobotany-A Methods Manual, Chapman and Hall, London.

Maheshwari, J. K., 2000. Ethnobotany and Medicinal Plants of Indian Subcontinent, (Scientific publisher Jodhpur), 672.

Negi, K. S., Gaur, R. D., 1991. A Contribution to the Edible Wild Fruits of Uttar Pradesh Hills. Bull. Bot. Surv. India 33: 233-266.

Negi, K. S., Gaur, R. D., 1994. Principal Wild Food Plants of Western Himalaya, Uttar Pradesh, India. Higher Pl. Indian Subcont. 3:1-147.

Neetu Bohra, Lalit M. Tewari and Ashish Tewari 2017. Ethnobotany of Wild Edible Plants Traditionally Used by the Local People in the Ramnagar Region from Nainital District, Uttarakhand, India. Biolife. 5(1), pp 12-19. doi:10. 17812/blj. 2017. 5103 Osmaston, A. E., 1927. A Forest Flora for Kumaun. International Book Distributors, Dehradun, pp. 605.

Pangtey, Y. P. S., 1980. Some Wild Edible Fruit Plants of Kumaun Hills in Science and Rural Development in Mountains, Singh J.S. et al., (Eds.), Gyanodaya Publication Nainital.

Shannon, C. E., Wiener, 1963. The Mathematical Theory of Communications. Univ. Illinois, Urbana, pp. 117.

Simpson, E. H., 1949. Measurement of Diversity. Nature, 163-688.

Sundriyal, R. C., E. Sharma., 1996, Anthropogenic Pressure on Tree Structure and Biomass in the Temperate Forest of Mamlay 'Ilatershed in Sikkim, Forest Ecology and Management 81:113-134.

Uniyal, K. S., Awasti, A., Rawat, G. S., 2002. Traditional Ethnobotanical Uses of Plants in Bhagirathi Valley (Western Himalaya), Indian J Traditional Knowledge, 1(1), 7.

Index